PRAISE FOR *RESPECTABLE*

"I know of no other work that addresses contemporary respectability politics through the lens of higher education with such breadth: from the mundane schoolyard rituals that one might see at a prep school, to the question of how to 'deal with' gender-nonconforming students, to what to do about the problem of rape, to the question of how to promote our successful Black men and reinvigorate 'the brand.' This is a novel and necessary read."

—Laurence Ralph, author of *The Torture Letters:*
  Reckoning with Police Violence

"With incisive breadth and analytical rigor, Saida Grundy unveils the motivations, mechanisms, and institutional processes that Morehouse College puts in play in order to maintain its brand by reproducing its go-to product: 'The Morehouse Man.'"

—Karida L. Brown, coauthor of *The Sociology of W. E. B. Du Bois:*
  Racialized Modernity and the Global Color Line

The publisher and the University of California Press Foundation gratefully acknowledge the generous support of the Atkinson Family Foundation Imprint in Higher Education.

Respectable

POLITICS AND PARADOX
IN MAKING THE MOREHOUSE MAN

Saida Grundy

UNIVERSITY OF CALIFORNIA PRESS

University of California Press
Oakland, California

© 2022 by Saida Grundy

Library of Congress Cataloging-in-Publication Data
  Names: Grundy, Saida, 1982– author.
  Title: Respectable : politics and paradox in making the Morehouse
Man / Saida Grundy.
  Description: Oakland, California : University of California Press,
[2022] | Includes bibliographical references and index.
  Identifiers: LCCN 2021042978 (print) | LCCN 2021042979 (ebook)
| ISBN 9780520340381 (cloth) | ISBN 9780520340398 (paperback) |
ISBN 9780520974517 (epub)
  Subjects: LCSH: Morehouse College (Atlanta, Ga.) | African
American men—Social aspects. | Masculinity—Social aspects. |
African American universities and colleges—History.
  Classification: LCC LC2851.M72 G78 2022 (print) | LCC
LC2851.M72 (ebook) | DDC 378.1/982996073—dc23/eng/20211006
  LC record available at https://lccn.loc.gov/2021042978
  LC ebook record available at https://lccn.loc.gov/2021042979

31 30 29 28 27 26 25 24 23 22
10 9 8 7 6 5 4 3 2 1

I grew up craning my neck up and to the side at my father's massive bookshelves to read their vertical spines. The titles and names of every work that did anything to advance the truth of our people were precisely aligned like a thousand monuments to a thousand thinkers.

I've been waiting my whole life just to get on your shelf.

This book is for Ann and Chester Grundy, who gave me *everything...*

And to Gibran and Garvey Meadows, to whom I will pay the debt forward...

And to my ancestors, and to my descendants.

After we are dust, what is written shall remain to say that we were here.

Our path is the straight one.

Contents

Preface   *ix*

Introduction   *1*

1   The Masculine Arc of Uplift   *40*

2   Branding the Man   *87*

3   Of Our Sexual Strivings   *135*

4   Who among You Will Lead?   *186*

Conclusion: The Journey Back   *239*

Acknowledgments   *271*
Appendix A: Respondent Demographics   *279*
Appendix B: Participant Screening Questionnaire   *283*
Appendix C: Informed Consent Contract   *285*
Notes   *291*
Index   *331*

Preface

The best men I know went to Morehouse and the worst men I know went to Morehouse. This conflict is chief of all the paradoxes you will read in these pages. It is a feeling akin to how the great James Baldwin described his relationship to America—that he loved this country and therefore reserved the right to be fiercely critical of it. Black people know the America that America does not want to know, and I love the Morehouse College that Morehouse College does not love. All the queerness and working classness that slurs together like a southwest Atlanta accent are the parts of Blackness that are too easily clipped off the brochure image advertised by their version of Morehouse manhood. My life has been made better by my lifelong bonds with the best of Black men, most of them Morehouse graduates. L'Heureux Lewis-McCoy, Lumas Helaire, Chuck Curtis, Justin Miller, Kwabena Haffar, Dwayne Wright, Geoffrey Bennett, Faraji Whalen-Robinson, Thomas Oden, David Calloway, Jarrod Loadholt (and Bakari Sellers), Et'Chane Williams-Towers, Christian Nwachukwu, Colin Hosten, Benjamin Cory Jones, Clark Jones, Darrel Hudson, Robert Kilpatrick, Michael Sterling, Joseph Carlos, Levar Smith, Matthew Platt, Christopher Eaglin, Ian Labitue, Joseph Edelin, Ariel Weekes, Jason Torrey, Lonzy Robertson, Jon-Sesrie Goff, Jason Vann Hamer, Roderick Waldon, Lewis Miles, Kyle

Yeldell, Christian Grant-Fields have been consistent friends to me, along with dozens more I will inevitably remember after the fact of having written this.

Weeks before my dissertation defense, as I was spending nearly every minute with thoughts and audio recordings of my respondents in my head, I saw a recurring name flooding my social media feeds as my laptop lay open. It was Myron Gerard Burney, the undisputed social captain of the class of 1998, who was mentioned repeatedly in the college memories of my respondents. He had a big, warm, country personality with an accent to match. His nickname was "B-Doe" based on when he introduced himself to a group of young women his freshman year and said in his Carolina drawl, "My name is Myron, you can call me B [for Burney], though." He was my sister's friend and someone she insisted I know for this project. Late one evening in the summer of 2014, while working on dissertation data that featured him, I saw his name fluttering my social media feeds. He had been killed in a tractor trailer accident. I wailed at my desk as though he were my relative and sobbed my way home.

Timothy Cunningham was one of my closest classmates, and throughout graduate school while he was at Harvard and I was at the University of Michigan we spent hours on the phone catching up on our maturing friend group. In our doctoral programs we had the lifestyle of old southern women, and a typical weekend "What you up to?" call might be answered with "Sitting here soaking these beans" or bragging about the latest accomplishment of his younger sister. Tim was exceedingly smart, and we met when he was managing editor of the *Maroon Tiger* and I was a senior columnist. He was a consistent friend, and maybe I wasn't, because when he went missing in February 2018, I hadn't talked to him in months and had no insights into his whereabouts or state of mind. He was a senior officer at the Center for Disease Control so the story got plenty of media traction.

Weeks turned into months, and I knew what the outcome would be, but it didn't soften the blow when my sister called to tell me that his body was discovered in the Chattahoochee River. I was in my Boston University office, and my scream sent my colleagues running in. It wasn't just grief, it was guilt. He felt alone. I wasn't there for him. I'm talking to him even now.

There is no shortage of charming young men at Morehouse but Henry Stewart is another dimension because he is so genuinely kind and exceedingly well-mannered. Trying to reduce him to a paragraph is a challenge—he was exceptionally bright with a massive social intelligence and exceeding professionalism, particularly in the world of Capitol Hill politics. Always tailored and always in great physical shape, he thrived on connecting people to resources, opportunities, and each other. Henry is a lot of people's favorite person, and in his class of 1999, my sister's class, he was something of a crown prince, and reunions gathered wherever he was present. It wasn't homecoming if Henry wasn't there. When anyone in that Spelman-Morehouse cohort thinks of the best of Morehouse, they are likely thinking of Henry Allen Stewart. It's still unclear what happened. He called in to work on March 16, 2021, after having tested positive for COVID-19, and then never awoke out of his sleep. His service back home at the Maryland church his father pastored had mourners wrapped around the parking lot, and thousands more streaming virtually online.

Knowing that men who were my friends and my research participants gave a piece of themselves to me, to our community, and to this work isn't a gift I take lightly. I hope my gratitude and affection for them shows through in this work. It is my respect for them that requires me to frame their experiences in a larger sociological context with great care to representing them accurately, even when our reflection of ourselves isn't one we like. I wanted to be the one to tell this story because this community is my home, and these men are important to me. Black men contain multitudes, and like all of us they grow, change, and reconsider their former selves. With this story I hope my gift back to my friends is a catalyst for rethinking their experience from another view.

Introduction

Gregory Love told the jurors that he had only been looking for his roommate but had forgotten his glasses in his dorm room. In November 2002, the promising pianist and glee club vocalist was a sophomore at Morehouse College, the nation's only historically Black[1] college for men. In the shower room of his dormitory, Love peered over a stall to find a fellow sophomore, nineteen-year-old Aaron Price, who immediately took the intrusion as a sexual advance. Price was enraged and began shouting antigay epithets as he stormed back to his room to retrieve a baseball bat. Minutes later, Love lay clinging to life on the cold ceramic floor tiles as his blood ran toward the drain. His skull had been fractured.[2]

Price, the son of a prominent Chicago pastor, received two ten-year sentences for aggravated assault (to be served concurrently).[3] In the trial, which concluded in June 2003, Love insisted that he was not gay, thus sparing his classmate an additional five years in mandatory sentencing under Georgia's newly enacted antihate crime law—the first time the state had attempted to prosecute such a crime. Most Morehouse students and staff defended the perpetrator. Justifications for Price's violence swiftly smacked of a gay panic defense—the controversial criminal defense strategy in which mostly male perpetrators of (even lethal) violence against mostly gay men and trans women often claim temporary insanity, self-defense, or provocation due to unwanted same-sex sexual advances.[4] Responses from administrators attended not to the safety of queer students, but to the loud outcries of a largely homophobic student body. The college's president assembled a task force that issued a lengthy campus survey with questions that included, "How far should Morehouse go to separate heterosexuals and homosexuals in the residence halls?" and "To what degree does Morehouse's tradition of producing strong men affect your views about homosexuality?"[5] The survey normalized antigay institutional practices as a response to antigay violence, while elsewhere public relations and media-related efforts from administrators sought to sweep the issue under the rug.[6] While issuing the perfunctory public statements about civility, safety, and zero tolerance, they never addressed the central issues of homophobia, sexuality, masculine violence, the rights of an undeniably significant population of queer Morehouse students in a city that, by the 2000s, was largely considered to be a destination school within networks of gay and same-sex-loving Black men.[7] This incident, the subsequent outcry, and the aftermath of institutional response blew a mask off the face of Morehouse College that it had held tight for so long. How could an institution so preoccupied with refuting stereotypes of violent Black manhood and presenting a face of Black male respectability to the world be stoking the flames of homophobic violence against Black men within its own walls?

When the controversy over this brutal attack erupted, I was a twenty-year-old junior at the adjacent all-women's Spelman College and the senior columnist for the *Maroon Tiger*, Morehouse's official student newspaper. The incident shook me, but the responses incensed me. The dearest friends I met in school were integral to my coming of age then as they remain cherished friends now. When you are part of the family of Historically Black Colleges and Universities

(HBCU) there is both a relief and a reassurance that comes from knowing that as classmates we had each other's backs as we poised to face the cold blows of white supremacy beyond this incubator of Blackness that forged our adulthood. It didn't sit right with me that there were students among us who felt on guard from sexual and homophobic violence within Black institutions while the rest of us experienced this place as an oasis and a retreat from being constantly on guard from white violence. How was it that these eloquent thinking men who could exhaustively articulate their racial subjugation could not bring themselves to understand how they were in similar positions of power to do to queer Black people what white supremacy did to all of us?

In that moment, a powerful set of questions about Black masculinity was born within me that I pursued for the next fifteen years, and this book is the culmination of that inquiry. Beyond merely provoking my curiosity, this troubling incident combined with other doubts and misgivings to engender a state of dissatisfaction with Morehouse, despite its stellar reputation within Black communities. I began addressing these questions through the lens of feminist theory in my undergraduate senior thesis. In graduate school, I became a sociologist in order to comprehend the full scope of what was at play for the Black men on that campus. This book, at its core, is a story of how the worst things Black men can do—like Price's assault on Love—can happen within an institution so invested in promoting "the best" of Black men. Moreover, I hope that this book pushes us to consider that these rigidly institutionalized forms of Black male respectability and success are what lead to such acts of gendered violence and their toleration by the college's leadership.

Over nearly two decades, I have witnessed a series of events that turn on issues of gender and sexuality among Black men and women thrust Morehouse into the national spotlight. A 2010 *Vibe* magazine exposé documented a subculture of transgender and gender-queer

"Mean Girls of Morehouse" who were systemically targeted by the college's dress code policy.[8] A shocking January 2016 *Buzzfeed* investigation revealed the systemic cover-up and continuous mishandling of rape allegations against Morehouse students.[9] More recently, *The Root* published a damning account of in-fighting in the nearly all-male upper administration and the board of trustees titled "The War at Morehouse."[10] In both 2017 and 2019 the *New York Times* reported on Title IX investigations that were triggered by the gross mishandlings of several reports of rape and sexual harassment by students, some of which accused a student services staff member of sexual misconduct.[11] By September 2019 a headline in the *Chronicle of Higher Education* announced that the college had a "culture of hypermasculinity" in which exaggerated masculine behaviors that included sexual harassment, gender violence, and male aggression among students and some employees were largely enabled by the college's overwhelmingly male leadership.[12] This pattern of occurrences has led me to believe that there is something deeply disconcerting about the ways Morehouse serves as a model for many of the largely held beliefs and presumptions about how Black men should be groomed to be racial representatives to the white mainstream. In promoting the belief that certain types of Black men best represent the race, rarely do many of us stop to consider the problematic "side effects" that result from a pursuit of such a narrowly constructed prototype of highly visible Black manhood. Men at this institution are a critical site for examining how such side effects occur when gender and sexuality become inextricably linked with class ideologies in pursuit of that racial ideal.

In a scholarly journey that has expanded my worldview far beyond what I could have ever imagined as a twenty-year-old, I have come to see Morehouse and its tribulations as situated within a much broader social and historical narrative. The glaring problems at the institution all have a social context that is both wider and more nuanced than what has been captured by contemporary accounts. The headlines of today arise from issues that were decades in the making, at a time when the rise of mass incarceration and race and class warfare against Black life in American cities gave birth to a campaign of urgently talking about young Black men as a national problem. Across party lines, white interest groups and prominent Black leaders and elected officials repeated a rhetoric of Black male criminality (albeit to differing degrees and with different aims)[13] and spoke of the emergence of violent Black male adolescent and young adult "super-predators" (I unpack this racist propaganda in the following chapter). The passage and enforcement of the 1994 crime bill coincided with demographic shifts in higher education and white-collar employment, so that, for the first time, a cohort of young Black men were coming of age in a generation where Black women outnumbered Black men in college and within the professional-managerial Black middle class that was rapidly expanding. As college-aged Black men could no longer count on outpacing Black women educationally and professionally, that shift was branded as their failure. These young men—the very cohort who were my college classmates and, later, participants in my research—were bombarded with moralistic messages about "endangered" Black manhood and panic over a "Black male crisis" just as they were inching toward success.[14] A dramatic shift has occurred since earlier Jim Crow generations of African Americans who viewed state violence and white supremacy as relentlessly bludgeoning the dignity of persecuted Black men. This was the first generation of Black men who came of age under a belief that they had contributed to degrading and annihilating themselves and thus were partly responsible for being the problem within the race's problems.

We have had thirty years to autopsy the 1994 crime bill and to experience the long dark night of mass incarceration that packaged Black male crisis within it. In those decades, many academic and public discourses have finally come to dismiss the cultural and behavioral explanations of Black male underachievement and deviance that were widely popular in the late twentieth century. A few, in the Bill Cosby "Pound Cake" speech[15] manner, may still believe that a well-tailored suit and a two-parent household can change the outcome of being targeted by police racial profiling, but in the present-day discourse these views are more likely to be met with backlash, critiques of victim blaming, and thorough explanations of the systemic undergirding that is both concealed by and belies these cultural prescriptions. When it comes specifically to the advancement of young Black men and boys, however, many of us both within and beyond African American communities paradoxically can understand the fallacy of cultural prescriptions and yet still cling to a received faith in these cultural and behavioral elixirs. We applaud the viral videos of where Black male grammar-schoolers spend school hours being taught how to tie a necktie and are largely uncritical of the belief that Black boys need rigid dress codes, gender segregated schooling, and stricter disciplinary environments to succeed academically (even as no evidence exists to argue that boys learn differently from girls, nor that Black boys fare better in single-sex schools).[16]

The promise of schools, mentorship programs, camps, churches, and outreach services that button up Black young men and boys are still presented as the cultural antidote to Black men and boys gone astray. The vestiges of neoliberal rhetoric about the "personal responsibility" of Black communities may have fallen out of favor when describing such issues as poverty or drug abuse, but those beliefs did not entirely disappear. Neoliberalism is still widely accepted in both Black and white liberal politics so long as it is folded within a narrative in which Black boys and their sagging pants are held responsible for bettering their own condition. This "no excuses" approach to Black male success allowed educators and community leaders to forego the hard job of assessing multiple forms of Black male intelligence and replace that assessment with a lazier presumption that the promise of Black young men and boys can be best measured by good behavior. Moreover, as Black male youth are still seen as having more problems and challenges than other gender and age demographics of African Americans, the exigencies of "improving" Black men and boys have bolstered a moral validation that these unproven cultural prescriptions are antiracist and thus prima facie beneficial for African Americans.

Throughout my graduate training, as I read and critiqued the canon of sociological works on Black men, I learned that my own discipline could not resist the allure of locating ethnographies of Black male experiences within the street life of the urban poor. The bulk of sociological writing on Black men has an almost axiomatic relationship to studies of crime, incarceration, academic underachievement, limited social resources, and widespread social marginalization. When the social sciences were primarily asking why Black men operated so differently from their non-Black counterparts in mainstream society, the answer for many of these researchers was found in masculinity—where either Black men were falling victim to the inadequacies of their own manhood or their masculinity was under siege by structural racism. In these works, Black men's widespread social marginalization was all too often explained, at least in part, as an outcome of Black men's historical and cultural resistance to normative gender models and white male dominance in middle-class culture.[17] These studies not only commonly assumed that taking on white heteronormative masculine roles would be best for Black men and their families, but in their myopic focus on Black men who were "failing" masculinity they also overlooked an equally important fact: that these normative masculine gender roles (often associated with breadwinning, patriarchal family structures, and male dominance in Black communities) were also pushed onto Black men who were *not* socially marginalized, but who, rather, were navigating their lives to exist and thrive within conventional cultural expectations for mainstream middle-class men. These gendered prescriptions of Black male respectability were sold as cultural vehicles of upward mobility and race betterment for African Americans as a group. Throughout Black men's history in this country, social and political campaigns were conducted as reactive parallel responses to the challenges facing Black men's putative leadership in Black communities. Black manhood has not simply evolved alongside the history of African American racialization in this country, it is repeatedly and strategically positioned to frame a narrative about the race's most pressing problems and immediate solutions. In this, I see sociology as having missed two opportunities to better understand Black men and their racialized masculinities. First, sociologists have missed a critical opportunity to tell not only a more complete and multidimensional story about how Black men think about and deploy masculinity as they navigate their social worlds but also to capture how and why these ways of thinking are deployed within the institutions with which they have the most contact. Second, the field has sorely missed the mark in revealing how Black masculinity is not only about how these men come to be raced and gendered in their social worlds but also that ideologies and expectations of Black manhood—due to the priority and disproportionate attention it receives within Black political discourses—have consistently determined how racialization is experienced and delimited for African Americans overall.

We are currently in a heightened moment of *reactive respectability* politics. This notion of respectability—which historian Evelyn Higginbotham described as a marginalized group's belief that adhering to mainstream standards of appearance, behavior, and cultural expression will buffer them against discrimination and social injustice[18]—has always been staked on ideologies and performances of sexuality and gender. In that way, all Black respectability politics respond to pernicious stereotypes about our behavior. *Reactive* respectability, however, is a political project that is organized and institutionalized into social and political campaigns that respond to a particular historical moment in which prominent Black leadership, clergy, and public figures launch a moralistic discourse in response to a social, political, or economic panic.

My approach to this book was particularly informed by the work of historian Michelle Mitchell, whose book, *Righteous Propagation*, captures an earlier moment of reactive respectability when both Black and white abolitionists conducted sexual morality campaigns among the formerly enslaved and socially prescribed strictly Victorian sexual mores in order to secure and sacralize marital and parental ties during Reconstruction. The following chapter unpacks how sex and gender ideologies were socially promulgated in the years following emancipation to prove the moral aptitude, and therefore worthiness, of Black citizenship—particularly for recently enfranchised Black men. Morehouse is but one of the places we can see this reactive respectability being institutionalized, although, this time, in response to the contemporary moral panic of Black male crisis. Within this campaign, using masculinity to prove the rightful place of Black men as racial leaders and representatives to the white mainstream is no less riddled with anxieties and no less staked on proving the virtuousness of specific forms of sexual and gendered behavior.

With that in mind, this book takes a rather nonconformist approach when compared to many traditional sociological explorations of institutional cultures. One of the most common approaches to ethnographic or sociological studies of a particular group or organization is to focus on a single theme of social inquiry that can be elucidated by examining a site or case in depth. For sociologist Shamus Khan, that meant looking at one of the country's premier boarding schools to zoom in on how their cryptic interactions signal the transformation of American elitism.[19] Ann Ferguson observed a public elementary school in order to examine how Black boys were being socialized into deviance by a culture of disproportionate and discriminatory punishments.[20] *Respectable*, in contrast, does not pursue the ways a single social problem or dynamic manifests within a group of people; rather, it looks at how the institutionalization of a restrictive set of beliefs about acceptable forms of Black masculinity produces an array of social problems from constrictive class hierarchies, to a widespread campus rape culture that uses racial tropes to normalize masculine violence, to a narrowly constructed curriculum about Black male leadership that aligns with white conservatism and ostracizes Black liberatory politics. What I find fascinating is how Morehouse's cherished ideologies about Black manhood result in paradoxical and often contradictory messages and practices that take root and flourish when the college attempts to actualize those missives into the institutional practices that "make" men.

The Paradoxical Landscape of Morehouse College

An examination of Morehouse College is a particularly important and informative way of considering reactive respectability as a response to the perceived crisis of Black men and boys. From the moment of the college's founding until today, the mission of producing racial leaders and advancing African American men's professional success has been central to the institution. Located in southwest Atlanta, Morehouse enrolls nearly 3,000 undergraduates, 93 percent of whom are Black.[21] The college awards more Black male baccalaureates than any other college or university in the country. From its founding at the height of Reconstruction in 1867, Morehouse has been deeply vested within the social and moral politics of racial advancement (its founding specifically as a seminary should be contextualized within the postemancipation racial morality campaign Michelle Mitchell describes). Through the rhetoric of leadership and exceptionalism that is consistently articulated there, the institution fervently lauds a belief that Black advancement relies on the exemplary deeds of the race's accomplished men. Morehouse has well demonstrated its preeminent role in producing Black racial leadership, and its list of notable alumni includes many of the most revered men of the Black elite. Boasting of such stellar graduates as Martin Luther King Sr. and Jr., Samuel L. Jackson, former US Surgeon General David Satcher, civil rights icon Julian Bond, former Atlanta mayor Maynard Jackson (as well as his grandfather John Wesley Dobbs, the unofficial "mayor" of Black Atlanta's power structure), Shelton "Spike" Lee, lay historian and publishing mogul Lerone Bennett, Homeland Security secretary Jeh Johnson, US senator Raphael Warnock, Princeton professor and MSNBC commentator Eddie Glaude, former Surgeon General David Satcher, Olympian Edwin Moses, and hosts of CEOs, physicians, clergymen, entertainers, elected officials, and four Rhodes scholars, Morehouse lauds itself as "The College of Choice for Black Men." It both enjoys and heavily promotes its public reputation as a paragon for high-achieving college-educated Black men, and many African Americans regard it as setting the standard for the image of Black male success in higher education.

Like many other HBCUs, Morehouse's student body comes from an array of cultural and economic backgrounds. While low-income and working-class students who seek upward mobility and introduction into the middle class comprise a substantial number of its students, the college continues to uphold its historical reputation as a favored school of the Black bourgeoisie when preparing their sons for elite professionalism. Class acculturation at the college is not just a process of introducing low-income men to normative middle-class behaviors because many of Morehouse students' backgrounds are already in step with the expectations of aspirational class behavior that are standard on campus. Beyond socializing men into middle-class norms, the college infuses ideologies about race into performances and beliefs about class and gender throughout nearly every corner of campus life. Informed by its history of gendered respectability politics as a strategy for countering white racism, Morehouse stands as a nexus in men's life courses where "doing" Black manhood becomes adhered to expectations about racial uplift vis-à-vis the comportment and presentation of masculinity in the professional-managerial class.

In the wake of the recent national discussion of alarming gaps in Black male educational achievement and college preparedness,[22] Morehouse's leadership has positioned the college's national image as one that is emblematic of graduates who overcome troubling statistics about young Black men. The experience of being groomed within the walls of the college is not isolated from the worrisome condition of Black men writ large but is in essence a reaction to it. Nearly all US colleges—Morehouse not least among them—are feeling the effects of decreased pools of academically high achieving Black male applicants.[23] A study of experiences at Morehouse, then, captures a microexamination of the macroeffects of nationwide racial and gender disparities that feed the rhetoric of a Black male crisis. Morehouse is demographically unique in that it is the only institution of higher learning in the United States where Black men are neither a racial minority nor a gender minority within their race. The findings in this book do not map the universe of Black male thinking on this topic. Given the diverse range of the types of Black men in this population, contrasted with the dearth of attention Black men receive elsewhere in discussions of issues such as college cultural curriculums, campus sexual assault, and homophobic violence, this group presents an important lens through which we can begin to map the experiential terrain of how college experiences, race, and masculinity triangulate to shape forms of thinking that are particular to Black men.

The image of Black male success that Morehouse assiduously promotes and celebrates is belied by many of the realities that challenge the students on this campus. The college is exempt from none of the problems in Black male enrollment and retention that plague nearly all colleges and universities, and its own internal culture exacerbates these issues by responding to serious problems with window dressing rather than effective solutions. Unique challenges in academic curriculum and enrollment have also changed the structure and culture of Morehouse. Its proud distinction for leading the country in undergraduate degrees for Black men has been recently challenged by the rise of for-profit colleges like the University of Phoenix and Ashford University, which now confer more bachelor's degrees on African Americans than HBCUs.[24] While the academic performance of Morehouse students remains above average for HBCUs, its four-year completion rate is an alarmingly low 40 percent. In keeping with the trend across HBCUs, Morehouse's appeal to college-bound high schoolers seems to be diminishing. In 2012, only a third of accepted students committed to Morehouse, compared to nearly half in 2008.

Increasingly, Morehouse finds itself losing top-performing applicants to competitive predominantly white institutions. As a result, Morehouse is forced to accept often underprepared students who are harder to retain and costlier to educate. In response, administrators quietly implemented a recruitment strategy of targeting Latino boys by attending college fairs at predominantly Latino high schools—a decision that sparked backlash from many alumni.[25] The college's current recruitment strategy relies heavily on its cultural appeal to prospective students seeking a place where academically serious Black men are not the minority. Since 2002, the college's recruitment materials have employed the imagery of high achieving Black boys' isolation, including an extensive description of "the Morehouse Mystique," which promises that "ignored, stereotyped or marginalized" young men will find a home at Morehouse as "the heart, soul, and hope of a community. And where you are not alone."[26]

Respectable is driven by reckoning with paradoxes: the paradox of how a single institution sees itself making Black men who are the solution to a national Black male problem, and the paradox of being groomed to be the elites within one of America's most downtrodden groups. These men are racially marginalized and yet are primed to marginalize other expressions of Blackness. As a Black woman and feminist who graduated from Spelman, I also inhabit a paradoxical position. Simultaneously a sister and an outsider to this place, I set out to scrutinize how it inculcates masculinity. The college is itself highly paradoxical; its most glaring issues often stand in direct contrast to its most celebrated achievements.

Despite its self-promoted image of exceptionalism, Morehouse has been embroiled in a series of incidents that have shaken its reputation. National news about the college has oscillated between extremes of heights of achievement and unthinkable abhorrence. The attack on Gregory Love, for example, occurred while the college was celebrating the selection of its fourth Rhodes Scholar in 2003 (a record for HBCUs). In July 2006 an underclassman was murdered and stuffed into the trunk of his own car by classmates who tortured him for information about an insurance policy payment the victim was expecting.[27] As high-profile philanthropic donations from Oprah Winfrey, Ray Charles, and venture capitalist Robert Smith carried Morehouse's name into the national press, the college was also under investigation for a litany of Title IX violations that implicated misconduct and assault by students and employees. Homophobic harassment and violence within the student body has drawn increased attention in the last two decades, even as these incidents remain under-reported by victims and under-acknowledged by administrators.[28]

Gay students and a small number of transgender and gender-nonconforming students have become increasingly visible and organized on the campus in recent years. The administration's response has been a backlash, rather than a considered adaption, to change. In 2009, the college formally implemented an "Appropriate Attire Policy" (informally stated dress code policies had long been enforced by faculty, staff, and student leaders) that explicitly targeted and sanctioned students wearing "clothing associated with women's garb (dresses, tops, tunics, purses, pumps, etc.)" as well as style trends readily associated with low-income Black youth street culture such as sagging pants and metallic decorative dental "grillz."[29] In 2019, administrators authorized an admissions policy for transgender students that, while progressive on its face, drew sharp criticism from trans advocacy groups for requiring transwomen and gender-nonconforming students to appeal their case for continued matriculation to a predominantly cisgender board of male faculty and administrators or face immediate expulsion.[30] The college may rest its laurels on its claims to leadership, but its continuing efforts to enforce a constrictive norm of masculinity on its students come at a time when, nationally, colleges' policies on gender and sexuality are rapidly becoming more liberal toward queer, trans, and gender-non-conforming forms of expression.

The Morehouse of the last two decades has been a fount of institution-wide problems that have affected the shape and scope of my work. Since I began framing this research around 2007, a flurry of headlines about the college has made some of the issues I was concerned about more obvious, while in other respects the problems on campus have become more acute. When I began this project, I did so with the intention of getting men to assess and interpret what their Morehouse experience meant to their understandings of themselves and Black manhood. Thirty-three men, all Morehouse graduates, generously offered me not only their time but also their often-naked transparency about what they had experienced. I soon realized that these men's college experiences were set within a larger context that spanned their diverse childhood upbringings, their pivotal high school years when they came to see themselves as "exceptionally" college-bound compared to many of their peers, and their years since leaving Morehouse, when the world for which they were so urgently prepared confronted them with having to rethink and re-examine their college experiences. The men with whom I spoke all came of age during the era of Black male crisis, and thus, unlike the generation before them, navigated their entire social and scholastic pathways to college while forming an awareness that their successive educational achievements increasingly distinguished their group as a gender minority within a racial minority.[31]

Just as importantly, as Morehouse's problems continued to pour out into national news feeds, I understood that so many of the issues that were now breaking into the headlines had been brewing on this campus for decades and were situated within a larger context of how an entire civil rights era framed both the problems and promise of young Black men and boys. The same kinds of violence, hyperconscious self-image, and rhetoric about personal responsibility and rightful racial leadership that echoed throughout my interviews were but snapshots of a conundrum about Black men that communities nationwide seemed to be facing throughout my lifetime. A history of problems seemed to be eerily repeating itself even as the broader social climate around Morehouse was shifting drastically. It was clear that the experiences men were describing for me were the twenty-year-old origin stories of current issues. While the coverage seemed salaciously fresh, I knew that my participants were describing tensions and conflicts that were the culmination of a period from the early 1990s to the present. Only now can we assess what the moral panic of Black male crisis cost for an entire cohort of Black men who were coming of age.

Theoretical Grounding

Sociologists have long described race as a socially constructed classification system that has no biological bases but is formed within and through social and political conflicts. When these racial categories are institutionalized into what Michael Omi and Howard Winant call a "politically organized system,"[32] that process is what defines *racialization*. Racialization involves not only people but also anything to which we can attribute a racial formation, that is, the process through which social, political, and economic forces determine the importance of racial categories and hierarchies and in turn ascribe racial meanings to them. As Michael Walker puts it, racialization is "the increasing association of phenomena with meanings ascribed to race constructs; hence, we speak of 'black neighborhoods,' 'white sports,' 'Latino clothing,' 'Asian music,' and so on."[33] Thus we can racialize *Black* colleges. While the designation of a Historically Black College or University (HBCU) was defined by the Higher Education Act of 1965,[34] Morehouse's racial significance as a Black college is not based on the proportion of its students who are Black; rather, Morehouse is racialized because the college infuses ideologies about racial uplift and identity into its organizational structure and culture.

To date the field of organizational sociology has mostly accounted for race chiefly in terms of an individual characteristic, meaning that institutions and organizations have been approached as race neutral while any racial dynamics within them are ascribed to the race of individual members. Most recently, however, sociologist Victor Ray has pushed us to examine organizations themselves as being racialized,[35] in that organizations and institutions bridge our cultural rules about race to the material resources they do or do not allocate to members of racial groups. Organizations, therefore, are constitutive of race in that they make meanings about the material consequences of our cultural understandings of race. In sum, Morehouse, in keeping with Walker's view, is a racialized college because its students view going to Morehouse as signifying a Black experience. But Morehouse, in alignment with Ray's theory, is furthermore a race-making institution in that it organizes material and social resources around a specific idea of which meanings of Black identity and experience are acceptable for its students.

There are myriad studies on African American racialization that emphasize how meanings about race are made in interactions with other racial groups (most commonly these approaches highlight the power of whites to racialize African Americans by limiting resources and determining racial inequities). Yet our discipline's mainstream has a long history of intellectually marginalizing those who have called attention to the processes of racialization that occur exclusively within predominantly Black spaces, in which Black people across lines of class, ethnicity, nationality, complexion, region, sexuality, and gender are racializing each other. There have been phenomenal recent contributions by Black sociologists like Marcus Hunter and Zandria Robinson, Karyn Lacy, and Orly Clergé that have captured the places and processes where within-group racialization happens for us across diverse lines of region, class, and ethnicity, respectively.[36] Considering the legacy Black sociologists were bestowed from W. E. B. Du Bois, it should be no surprise that this work is very insightful. Nonetheless, I must admit that Black political scientists have provided the most powerful contemporary analyses of this process.

Political scientist Michael Dawson argued that Black voting patterns cut across class lines that were more similar than those among whites because African Americans shared a sense of "linked fate," the belief that our individual destinies are tied to problems affecting our race as a whole, and that Black voting patterns reflect how Black communities decide on collective racial agendas.[37] Cathy Cohen followed up with a simple but cutting question: which African Americans set these agendas? In *The Boundaries of Blackness*, Cohen used the HIV/AIDS crisis, which disproportionately blighted Black communities, to examine the tensions around reaching a consensus on a racial agenda.[38] Cohen's answer was that the race does not reach a consensus as a whole; instead, social hierarchies within Black communities relegate some of us to "secondary marginalization." The most vulnerable, economically precarious, and socially stigmatized among us are often blamed for our condition, while the least disadvantaged African Americans are viewed as the victims of racism and deemed worthy of the most attention. The urgency of the racism that affects these prioritized groups of African Americans is divorced from the intersectional social problems that compound racism for the most marginalized African Americans. Cohen saw the HIV/AIDS crisis as a "crosscutting issue" that drew on the multiple identities African Americans hold along the axes of sexuality, class, religion, and gender and organized those differences into within-race hierarchies that replicated the same forms of marginalization that white America has inflicted on us.

A plethora of tensions and crosscutting issues within Black spaces produce racialization beyond the physical presence of whites. Blackness is an active process that is made within our interactions with whites or dominant social institutions but also well beyond the reach of members of these dominant groups. We cannot escape our racialization by operating mainly outside of white spaces, since within-group hierarchies are intensified in spaces where we are organizing to set racial agendas and, in the case of Morehouse, to define the standard for racial representatives. *Respectable* complements Cohen's work by providing ethnographic insight into the heteronormative, upwardly mobile, college-educated Black men who are step-

ping into roles of dominance in which they are being primed to decide which Black people and which parts of Blackness should be seen
by a dominant white gaze.

Du Bois classically theorized that the process of racialization
for oppressed groups was formed by looking at the dominant world
from inside "the veil" of racial subjectivity. For the racialized subject
behind it, the veil prevents members of the dominant group from the
full recognition of the subordinate racialized group's humanity—a
term Du Bois tended to use interchangeably with manhood.[39] The
veil structures the world into a one-way mirror in which the racialized subjects who live behind it can see out, but the racializing white
subjects who live outside of it cannot hear, see, or properly recognize those within.[40] Black people in America straddle the constant
tension of two worlds in which the veil is oppressive and their own
community lends a source of support. Du Bois saw this tension in
Black life as particularly catalyzed by the experience of education,
in which he describes of himself, "I was not an American; I was not
a man; I was by long education and continual compulsion and daily
reminder, a colored man to a White world....I could not stir, I could
not act, I could not live, without taking into careful account the reaction of my White environing world."[41] Where Cohen picks up is
where Du Bois leaves off: she interrogates how Black spaces are contested when the veil provokes an anxiety of self-consciousness about
who should be recognized as representing those within it.

I maintain that some particularly anxiety-producing spaces for
Black racialization firmly press Black subjects up against the veil as
African Americans prepare to confront a white gaze, either real or
imagined. The hierarchy that Cohen describes is organized by determining who will be in front, flush against the veil, while sweeping
other Black identities farther back from view. In these spaces where
demarcations of Blackness are contested within the group, the veil
intensifies, as class, gender, and queerness are ordered by their suit-

ability to becoming visible to those outside the race. Morehouse deliberately prepares its students for the scrutiny of a dominant, mainstream, middle-class white world beyond the veil in which men are taught to "measure oneself by the means of a nation that looked back in contempt."[42] These men, who sit atop the hierarchy, set the racial agenda. But even their expected position of dominance within the race is no longer secure, as gender and class frictions increasingly trouble their assumption of power among Black people and in relation to whites. *Respectable* looks deeply at a place and time when Black male elites took the issue of a Black male crisis—in which deindustrialization and an unleashed war on drugs overwhelmingly devastated low-income Black men *and* women—and took full advantage of the veil to redirect the race's attention to an agenda that prioritized themselves.

In addition to providing an improved understanding of how legitimate economic and political crises within Black communities are metabolized by Black elites into reactive respectability politics, this book offers two central contributions to the sociological study of intersectionality (a subfield that many sociologists refer to as race, class, and gender when their studies centrally take all three into account) as well as the sociology of culture. First, it addresses how the larger sociological trends of Black social class mobility use gender as a cultural vehicle for class ascension in the way that housing or employment provide economic vehicles for this group. African Americans very rarely occupy the highest strata of American wealth and, when they do, they are disproportionately non-college-degree-holding athletes and entertainers who do not necessarily control the institutions and organizations that dictate race-specific meanings of class and prestige.[43] The cultural markers of Black elitism do not always align with the economic realities of wealth attainment.[44] Cultural meanings of class, then, fall heavily on gender performances because they can be learned, adapted, and enacted, but few sociological studies before this book have asked where and how the Black middle class adopts these gender scripts. This book contributes to filling that missing gap in cultural sociology and Black middle-class studies by finding that institutions like Morehouse set expectations for racialized gender ideologies that influence not only their students but also transmit the cultural standards of racialized gender ideals for Black elites' communities nationally.

Second, I have increasingly grown concerned that too few scholars in my field know or care to study how Black racialization occurs away from interpersonal interactions with whites. Those who study racialized organizations tend to default to examining how race and racism can be observed through the lens of how racialized subjects navigate white spaces. Subsequently, much of sociology's race scholarship consumes the entire Peoples of Color experiences of racialization through its relationship *to racism* or, most commonly assumed as relational to whites. The assumption by many mainstream white sociologists seems to be that race is static in all-Black spaces and that nothing of sociological importance happens with regard to intragroup racialization. When proposing my single case study on masculinity at a Black institution as a graduate student, I was told on multiple occasions by white faculty members that I should consider a comparison case of a predominantly white men's college as though what I was observing about college masculinity at Morehouse could not be validated without referencing it against a white standard. Many sociologists seem to miss what any Black person who has grown up within predominantly Black spaces can tell you: there are dynamics and meanings of Black life that have nothing to do with the presence of white people. Black people experience racialization and make meanings of race that lie deep beneath the surface of what our popular approaches to interracial racialization are currently capturing. A second contribution of this book, then, is that it locates how gender and class meanings are amplified and manifested behind the

Du Boisian veil of Black racialization. It is standard among sociologist of culture to signal Bourdieuan theories of habitus (that is, the way any person of a particular background imagines and navigates their perception of their social world) to explain cultural production and phenomena, particularly within the context of individuals and their relationship to institutions. This book, instead, revisits Du Boisian cultural theories and finds that the veil is as much a *cultural* apparatus as it is political. It creates intraracial cultures within it that amplify the ways that gender and class map onto meanings of race inasmuch as the inverse is also true.

The Study of a Place over Time

One choice in the framing of this study pertains to its conceptualization of place. Many of the classic works are oriented around a physical place and the people who interact within it, whether that be a neighborhood ethnic enclave, a community liaison office, or a criminal courtroom. The aim here is to observe a culture in process—what characteristics, activities, and shared assumptions make the people in that space into a group. But what if the qualities and contexts that made a group a group are in the past and pertain to a shared memory of an institution, a trauma, or a conflict? What if the time in their lives that made them a culture has passed, or the neighborhood that once bonded them no longer exists? Anthropologist Sherry Ortner grappled with these questions when she interviewed surviving classmates from her majority Jewish graduating high school class of 1958. When she conducted this study in 2003, the school's student body was majority Black.[45] For Ortner's middle-aged subjects, notions of success, whiteness, and upward mobility come into focus as they contextualized their experiences at one urban high school at a particularly significant historical point when inner-city American Jews experienced and imagined white racialization by mobilizing into the upper middle class and migrating to the suburbs.

Like Ortner's, my ethnographic site belongs not to a physical place but rather to a collective institutional memory whose participants' experiences contextualize a particular moment that spans the 1994 crime bill through Obama's presidency. For men in this study, college was not simply a coming-of-age experience but an incubator of ideas about race, class, and gender that continue to inform their meanings of manhood well into adulthood. An intensely institutionalized yet shifting belief in Black male respectability was being projected onto the lives of these men at a pivotal point in their budding manhood that has now passed. Thus, the perspective that shapes this book is retrospective.

This study is based on my telephone interviews with thirty-three men who were young alumni in their early thirties at the time we spoke and had graduated from Morehouse between 1998 and 2002. Each participant was interviewed twice within a span of five weeks. Having two interviews in succession facilitated the men's scrutiny of their memories, and often men would follow up in the second interview with an experience they had forgotten, wanted to reconsider, or about which they could offer more detail.

Choosing phone interviews had practical and methodological implications. On one hand, interviewing by telephone meant I had no access to nonverbal cues, so I could not base probes and follow-ups on facial or bodily expressions. It also meant that I at times awkwardly interrupted the respondents more than I would have liked when I was not sure if they had finished their thought or were merely pausing to find and formulate more thoughts. But the phone format also proved to be highly beneficial. I initially chose this approach because it allowed me to access men whose alumni "diaspora" had spread them all over the country. Phone calls also proved to be beneficial in ways I did not anticipate. Calling these men on their mobile phones greatly facilitated scheduling, as many of them had not only demanding jobs but also small children. Mort was tending his son in his nightly bath during one of our conversations—the bath was a loving ritual that seemed to put him in a very vulnerable mood as he thought back on his own coming-of-age stories.[46] Mingus was in the midst of talking freely about the time he ran for student government office when he asked me if I could hold on momentarily. A few minutes later he let me know he had gone through airport security en route to a business trip but wanted to continue talking. Men were far more flexible when they did not need to leave their work or family surroundings to be interviewed, and, as a result, most interviews ran without significant interruptions. Using the telephone also had gendered implications. For a female researcher, interviewing men always involves a careful negotiation of gendered space, sexual dynamics, and professionalism. Having a researcher on the phone meant these men did not have to explain my presence to their wives, partners, and coworkers. It also meant I did not need to manage my own appearance and body. Phone interviews muted much of these gendered and sexual dynamics.

Gender is constantly present in any interview dynamic, and thus our questions within studies of interview methodology are no longer *if* gender makes a difference in the interview dynamic but rather *how* gender affects all interview dynamics.[47] Being interviewed by women is a noted preference among male research subjects[48] and is commonly attributed to an assumption that men (presumed here to be cisgender) feel more comfortable telling women things they would prefer not to disclose to other men.[49] To this I would add that men often presume a level of emotional care-work with women that is enhanced by the intimacy of one-on-one interviews. In my disembodied voice over the phone, respondents at times seemed to enjoy a confessional-like quality to our conversations. When my conversation with Bird, a financial trader who was often up late to keep abreast of foreign markets, had reached its four-hour mark, he mentioned in passing that he hadn't talked to someone this in-depth in ages. When I asked if he had considered seeking out someone to talk to more regularly, he audibly gestured as though he were considering it.

Most ethnographers struggle with the quest to gain intimacy with their research site and subjects, but for myself, such familiarity was almost immediately established. As a single woman who was younger than all of the subjects, part of my consideration was in not having my participants interpret these interviews as social hangouts. Even on the phone these boundaries were challenged. In my first round of interviews with Nelson, the Wi-Fi connection I used for voice-over internet calls continued to drop. Nelson was becoming frustrated, as I repeatedly had to call him back, and at one point stated abruptly, "You know my whole life story and I don't even have your number." Our exchange seemed inequitable to him and wasn't operating under the guise of the new friendship he would understandably expect from one in his college community with whom he was sharing so much of his life story.

Both interviews with each respondent were semistructured and covered a wide set of questions about their college and postcollege experiences. The first took a life-historical approach and explored their family background, academic and social life on campus, professional training, and subsequent career. The second interview allowed for further exploration of experiences highlighted in the first, including additions, revisions, or explanations the men wanted to make and revisit and questions I wanted to further probe. The range of what I asked men and what they wanted to discuss followed a handful of themes. When, for example, I asked them what they knew about Morehouse before they applied, their responses typically included an ample discussion of Morehouse's far-reaching reputation within Black communities. Questions about their precollege high school days often covered the extra efforts they took along with their parents to keep from getting derailed from the college-bound track by racist schools. We talked about dating, historical moments like the Million Man March, and the analogue days of standing in line for hours to register to classes. We talked about the men who had power on campus and the ones who never did. They talked a lot about influences, from older students, visiting speakers, faculty, and administrators. They told me about the words of wisdom they remember and other things they heard and saw that still haunt them. They told me about things they'd do differently, and I asked them what they'd like to change most about the college for the men coming behind them.

The decision to interview alumni who were some years out from their college experience was the first of two critical decisions I had to make about my participant sample. When asking men to reflect on their manhood and including in that an aspect of how they were prepared to enter the white professional mainstream, it is important to interview men who have enough adult experience to apply to such a question. There is another project to be conducted with twenty-two-year-old recent graduates, but that question would be about another historical period and their understandings of another type of function the institution bears on their life course.

A second critical decision in the design of this research had to do with addressing that college experience as the unit of analysis. Back in the seminal days of proposing this project to my graduate advisor, I was initially determined to interview dropouts—a population that was disproportionately composed of low-income, queer, and gender-non-conforming students.[50] But a unit of analysis must be consistent to be compared, particularly when it is longitudinal. One cannot analyze what a Morehouse experience means in the life of men who were there for one or two semesters when compared to those who completed the college's intended process of being "made" into Morehouse men. This focus on student experiences is also the reason you will not find administrators, staff, or other affiliated bodies in this work. Where necessary, they speak through comments made available to media outlets, which enhances the context for how this institution operates. To do an analysis that equally weighted Morehouse personnel experiences with students, however, would also be a study with a drastically different orientation than this one.

In centering my analysis on men's experiences, I relied wholly on in-depth ethnographic interviews. Research by neuroscientists has repeatedly informed us that memory is notoriously imperfect and is wholly susceptible to bias, forgetting, and even the influences of group-thinking. But we also know from neuroscience that adolescence and our twenties are the times in our lives from which we tend to retain the most memories because we have the most "change moments" during this stage in the life course. Memories, however, are not veridical data compiled and stored in our minds like to a hard drive.[51] This doesn't mean that those with distorted memories are lying. Memories are as much sociological functions as they are neurological. They are culturally mediated and arbitrated, disputed, and reformed in collective endeavors by those with whom we share them.[52] They are essentially a dialogical relationship we have with our former selves through the social world as we see it now (in which our backgrounds inform what we *can* see and of what we can make sense in our recollections). Our expectations for ourselves (including our imagination of our future selves) and others play as much a role as our eyes and ears in determining to what we attend, what we see, and what we retain.[53]

Reflexive in-depth interviews are a key component of research on the remembered past. Some sociologists who belong to the ethnographic tradition in the field have claimed that what people observably do is more revelatory than what they say when we analyze how they make sense of their social world and their interactions within it. While ethnographers' observations of social interactions can help them to understand a social order, what people do is not necessarily an accurate reflection of what people *think*, or even what they think about what they do. Consider, for example, the gendered division of labor in working-class and low-income Black families, which has been shown to be fluid and gender egalitarian.[54] This observation may lead us to conclude that members of these households hold progressive ideas about gender. Getting them to talk reflexively about what they *think* they are doing, however, reveals that these men and women may endorse conventional beliefs about male breadwinning and female caregiving but lack the resources to put them into practice because economic discrimination requires female partners to earn money and the lack of affordable childcare compels male partners to take care of children. What *looks* nontraditional to outside observers is often regarded by these couples as a situational expedient.

Even the most detailed observational research can shortchange capturing the nuances, intricacies, shifts, or even contradictions in the ways people think about themselves. In setting out to provide a richly textured account of Black masculinity and to capture men's perceptions of a process that many feel made them into men, I have aimed to lay bare the beliefs, paradoxes, reconsiderations, and contradictions men are negotiating, both throughout their lives and in their conversations with me. In their reflexivity, these men are coming to terms with their former selves and actively deciding what parts of themselves they did and did not take from their college experiences, what has and has not worked from where they stand now, what they are glad to have learned, and what they are trying to unlearn. A small handful of men loathed their experience at Morehouse or were ambivalent about its various components, but far more waxed nostalgic about their experience and their alma mater. Notwithstanding the divergence in their attitudes, most of these men were leading quite similar lives with respect to what can be observed from their professional standing and class attainment.

Without talking to them, one could assume they were mostly similar in their outlooks. In-depth interviews are the most fitting and epistemologically rewarding approach to gathering data on how individuals interpret historical and biographical events, describe their perspectives, and make meaning of otherwise complex experiences at different points in their lives.[55]

Memory-based interviewing has implications particular to studies of men and masculinity. I approached the interviews with a battery of open-ended questions intended to invite narrative responses from men in interviews that were scheduled to last one hour each. Nearly every interview went for two hours or more, with two respondents continuing well into a fourth hour. Interviews lasted much longer than expected because the men spontaneously offered up far more than I asked them. That so much narrative data emerged without prompting points toward the effectiveness of memory-based interviews. Masculinity theorists have promoted the usefulness of reflexivity in allowing men to open up, since it "mediates the role that social circumstances play in influencing social action and thus is indispensable in explaining particular social actions, such as sexual violence."[56] Memories allow researchers to connect college masculinity to masculinity throughout the life course by assessing how college environments serve as rehearsals in men's minds for ideas about masculinity that they perform in adulthood. Memory positions men in a "two-ness" of seeing their lives then through the eyes of their lives now, inviting a second sight on gendered processes of which they are only made aware reflexively. This approach is invaluable for studies of the ways we make meanings of our experiences in hindsight.

On Being a Sister-Outsider

"Anything to help a Spelman sister," Blakey replied almost immediately to my email request for an interview. This response was common among the men I contacted, 80 percent of whom agreed to be interviewed. Their unusually high response rate reflects the fact that, often unbeknownst to me, I was not a complete stranger to many of these graduates. My older sister, Tulani, had been a popular Spelmanite in their cohort, and for some of them I was not just any Spelman sister asking for research participants (which would have sufficed for many), but was also a "little sister" of their friend who they felt needed their help. Multiple points of overlap within friendship and family networks were a regular feature of my relationship to my participants. The Spelman-Morehouse network of alumni is tightly knit, and the network is drawn closer by being bound inside the circles of affluent and middle-class African Americans who spend most of their lives within only a few degrees of separation from each other.

When I began recruiting participants, I surmised (from my take on the male friend groups of my own graduate network) that most Morehouse alumni had three or four long-term friends from college, so I asked each participant to recommend three other men for me to contact. With this approach, my sample rapidly snowballed. The success of this strategy produced a problem I had not foreseen, however. All my participants had signed a consent form stating that I would protect their anonymity, but within their own friend groups they routinely outed themselves to each other. Percy forwarded an email I had sent him to his former roommate with my contact information attached and told his buddy, "You should do it. It's pretty fun." I soon realized that giving up their anonymity was not a matter of these men being careless; rather, many of them did not *want* to be anonymous. Being a voice in a book about Morehouse was a source of pride for them, and I can only assume from many of their reactions that they saw "being chosen" for a book about their alma mater as a mark of distinction among their alumni networks.

Some of the men saw themselves as helping me out in the pursuit

FIGURE 1. The author
singing Morehouse
Hymn with students,
post-football game.

of an advanced degree, which they held in high regard since roughly half of them were recent graduates of law school, medical school, and other postbaccalaureate programs. Except for three participants who had written doctoral dissertations themselves, however, their interest in my intellectual aims and the scholarly implications for this study was minimal. I was, instead, a *Spelman sister*, familiar with our shared institutional culture and amenable to upholding the good name of our corner of the Black collegian community. The eagerness of a few respondents to participate gave me the sense that my relationship to "SpelHouse"[57] led them to assume that I was writing something that would promote the image the college.

This assumption was fed later, after I had completed interviewing, when men learned through our mutual contacts that I had not only been a senior columnist for the student paper but had also served as Miss Maroon and White—the scaled-down campus equivalent of Miss America—during my senior year.[58] "Wait a minute, you didn't tell me you were Miss Maroon and White!" Dolphy laughingly protested in a social media message months after our interview. Having experienced the campus's culture firsthand and having been involved in re-creating and challenging it, I am deeply connected to these men as friends, colleagues, and surrogate members of my own family, and I take tremendous personal pride in having watched them emerge over the past decade as nationally recognized voices on issues from police brutality to health care access equity for African Americans. Even beyond my interaction with these men during interviews, our mutual membership in a close-knit alumni community plays a significant role in how I navigate my own professional and social landscape. In many ways, the SpelHouse alumni community (and their parents) anchored me within a national network of well-resourced African Americans that has continued to provide me with opportunities and look out for me and my endeavors throughout my adult life. The SpelHouse extended family is one of the best gifts my education ever gave me.

At the same time, I am an outsider in multiple ways to a highly guarded Morehouse brotherhood community: as a woman; as a researcher at a predominantly white institution; as a scholar whose work speaks to a white-dominated field that has regularly misinterpreted and exploited Black life and experiences; and as an unapologetic radical Black feminist. My political standpoint only became known to many respondents after the fact, when they requested to become Facebook friends and became privy to my posted social and political thoughts. In studying my race and class peers, I have negotiated my insider-outsider status at every turn. While ethnographic studies have long been conducted by researchers who belong to the mainstream studying subjects on the margins, my position as a woman studying men who occupy positions of power in almost every realm of my social and professional life required a constant balancing of my social identities. While I acknowledge the risk my participants took in being honest and forthcoming about their experiences within a small and tightly knit community, I also felt a great risk of being ostracized from this community because I might tell an "unfavorable" story about the college or about them. Indeed, I have become known within the SpelHouse online community for being direct and vocal about what I feel are Morehouse's very serious and long-standing issues with homophobia, patriarchy, and sexual violence. These opinions have put me in jeopardy of losing friends, access to pertinent information about the college, and the resources of professional and social alumni networks.[59]

My recruitment methodology resulted in an oversampling of men who were still in regular contact with college friends. As a result, this sampling method favored men who still had an affinity toward their college friends and experience. The ages of the men in this study ranged from thirty-one to thirty-seven, with an average age of 33.5 years at the time of the interview.[60] Twenty-four of the thirty-two men held a postgraduate degree: eight held master's degrees in business administration, five held law school JDs, four had earned PhDs, and one held a medical doctorate. The remainder had earned various terminal master's degrees.[61] All but three of the men were employed in professional-managerial long-term occupations. Of the three exceptions, one had just graduated from law school days prior to his interview and was working part-time while on the job market, and two were career police officers. Twenty of the men were married, one respondent was divorced, and five were in long-term committed relationships (two became engaged within months of our interview). Of the married respondents, ten were fathers of at least one child. Among the unmarried men, one was divorced, and one never-married respondent had a child.

On the topic of risk, I feel obliged to note that none of the respondents were openly queer, inasmuch as none of them discussed anything in their experiences that made any indication of having same-sex romantic, sexual, or intimate contact. This does not mean that there were no queer men in my sample. In the years since these interviews, I've seen their social media updates about family and relationships. Now in their forties, some of them are living more out lives than they did in their thirties when I talked with them. As a point of research ethics, I would never ask a participant to out their sexuality. What I want to note, however, is that queer people can be out in some contexts and not in others—the closet is not a singular construction that requires coming out only once. The experience of invisibility and marginalization at HBCUs is common among queer students, and research shows that Black gay men who attend HBCUs more readily identify with their race than their sexuality.[62] In asking men to participate in a study that reentered them into their college memories and that invited them in through their friendship networks, more men than I know may have made the choice to keep that part of their lives from me—a woman in their alumni networks—and from this study, which would be read by an audience not of their choosing. Even searching for out gay participants may not have resolved this issue of representation, as I would have been deliberately putting queer men on the spot to tell stories about their college experience that potentially outed others. I do not feel it's my right to ask men who may be out to myself and others in some contexts of their lives to also reveal themselves as out in the context of this study. If I were to do this study over again now, I could simply leave a participant recruitment message on one of the social media pages of Morehouse's queer advocacy student group. None of this was available to me in historically reconstructing the experience of graduates from the previous decade.

In the ongoing insider-outsider debate among sociologists who do ethnographic research, insiders have been typically regarded as being advantaged in gaining rapport with respondents and understanding the unspoken nuances and cultural and social contexts of their ideas and actions.[63] Usually, insider status was grounded in similarities of race, gender, or background between researchers and their subjects. To be an outsider on any or all these grounds presumably meant having to extend more effort to achieve rapport, confidence, and cultural comprehension with respondents.[64] Furthermore, outsider ethnographies are regularly challenged as unreliable unless researchers can demonstrate the methodological rigor of their fieldwork as they transitioned from outsider to insider.

In contrast to many others in this field, I do not regard being an insider or an outsider as a strict dichotomy, since in this project I occupied both positions simultaneously. My participants understood that as well. They used insider language with me and did not pause to explain campus jargon or within-group references. They knew that I could identify the administrators, buildings, or popular social events on campus or within the city of Atlanta that they mentioned. At the same time, they understood me as an outsider and told their stories with an awareness that they were speaking to a woman about closed men's spaces. Ornette ultimately refrained from describing the college's most clandestine rituals to me. Dewey described times when his friends partook in graphic conversations about women, and then apologized to me as though I should not be subjected to hearing their secondhand locker-room talk, or at least should not have to learn how crass my Morehouse brothers could be.

Beyond disrupting this dichotomy, this project challenges the common assumption that ethnographers seek to become insiders and shed their outsider status. When ethnographers study a social problem, they tend to do so within communities that agree they have that problem. The unemployed know joblessness is a problem; the poor know that poverty is a problem. In my approach to Morehouse, in contrast, I was discussing the problems of a group of men who mostly disagreed that these phenomena were problematic. I was problematizing an institution that saw itself as "solving" a national Black male problem.[65] In this way, I practiced *outsider intentionality* in my ethnographic duality. Feminist standpoint theorists such as Patricia Hill Collins, Donna Haraway, Nancy Hartsock, and Sandra Harding have argued for the "strong objectivity"[66] that marginalized individuals provide in their accounts of social phenomena. Similar to the ways in which Du Bois's veil provided racialized subjects with insights into the world beyond it, which those outside the veil lacked, standpoint theory regards the outsider-within position as enabling subjugated individuals and groups with the vantage point to see patterns in ideas and behaviors that those in the dominant group are unable to recognize about themselves.[67] Standpoint theory situates feminist research by women as the optimal position for analyzing the dynamics of patriarchal masculinity that men either cannot see or are committed to maintaining. Even as my race and background privileged me with the rapport of an insider, my outsider feminist lens on men and masculinity in this setting is my epistemological claim to veracity.

Organization of the Chapters

Understanding the culture of masculinity that shapes men at Morehouse cannot begin with Morehouse itself. The first chapter probes the history of anxiety about Black masculinity that emerged from racial uplift ideologies that Morehouse has inherited and reproduced. By interrogating gender as well as class ideologies, chapter 1 reveals that Black men were elevated as the rightful heirs of racial leadership and the emissaries of racial advancement. From Reconstruction through the twentieth century, the status of the race's progress was set to the measure of its men and dictated by its educated male elites. That masculine-centered uplift endeavor was not only driven by anxieties about Black masculinity but also reinforced them in ways that precipitated moral panics at the historical moments that suggested declines in achievement among Black men. Morehouse's approach to young Black men actively participates in regenerating these kinds of anxieties about Black masculinity today.

The subsequent three chapters address three respective problems epitomized by Morehouse and its students. In exploring these pressing issues, I have let the alumni I interviewed speak for themselves and connected their experiences, perspectives, and questions to the college's public pronouncements. Chapter 2 focuses on the college's cultural curriculum, which organizes campus life and grooms men into the "Morehouse Brand." Chapter 3 unpacks men's racialized thinking about sex and sexuality, showing that it reinforces a culture of gender violence that is dually manifested in its racialized rape culture and deeply rooted homophobia. Chapter 4 problematizes the dominance of corporate influence on the college and shows how narrowly constructed ideas about young Black male success and racial leadership make for strange neoliberalist political bedfellows across right-wing and antiracist interest groups. Finally, the conclusion returns us to present-day Morehouse, when I served as a guest speaker to a class of eager freshmen who, through my now adult eyes, seemed more aware of these issues than the men I remembered as my classmates. I recap the theoretical implications of each chapter, and then provide practical next steps for addressing exigent problems within the institution. As the social landscape of Black manhood changes, so must the college reconsider its choices in a world that questions whether the brand of Black masculinity it produces is still useful for Morehouse men whose lives take them far beyond the gates of the college. I contextualize what it means to reconsider the "social contract" that Morehouse has with its graduates, and what it means that successive generations of Black male elites are reconsidering the meaning of Morehouse to Black men.

Respectable finds that the hierarchies of Blackness that Cohen and Dawson framed are not only organized by the prioritization of racial agendas but also by a belief about what kinds of Black people should be the most visible to the world beyond our race. In this book, Morehouse is a window through which we can examine current social constructions of Black masculinity, as this elite institution ordains itself as making men who are the solutions to the crisis of Black manhood. Within this construction, however, the college is also an active converter—metabolizing its own beliefs and those held by Black male elites into how it decides and prioritizes what Black men's problems *are*, all while refusing to recognize the problems that afflict its own students and others with whom they interact (particularly queer men, gender nonconforming students, and women). This strategy of racial advancement is taken up by the leadership of Black men who see themselves as both exemplary and amenable to a white mainstream headed by white political and corporate elites. It is through examining men who believe they are the most successful practitioners of this work that we paradoxically can expose the limitations and contradictions of an approach that is fundamentally based on demonstrating that African Americans deserve equality by reason of their virtue and good behavior. Just as importantly, this book's approach exposes how the straight Black male elites who sit atop the intraracial hierarchy of African Americans strategize how to dominate Black visibility in the same ways they organize to control political agenda-setting for African Americans. Thus, this belief about Black representation deepens class and gender divides and reinforces the idea that Black women, and marginalized Black men, are responsible for their condition. As you will see throughout this book, Morehouse is a place that is nearly obsessed with its own image. Through this book I also hope you will understand that this preoccupation neither begins nor ends at Morehouse. The college is merely a centerpiece in a social landscape where the politics of Black visibility have long been nervously dictated by the Black male elites who feel most entitled to represent the race to the White mainstream. Morehouse is simply the way that I invite you to see that story told.

1   *The Masculine Arc of Uplift*

The torrent poured on mercilessly. Hundreds of families huddled under umbrellas or held futilely soaked commencement programs over their heads. They had not the slightest intention of leaving or waiting it out in their cars. Sunday, May 19, 2013, was far too important to miss. On this historic occasion, the sitting president of the United States, Barack Obama, addressed the Morehouse College graduating class of 2013. The wide stage that sheltered faculty and prominent administrators had been erected in the heart of the campus yard, positioned as though it were at the head of a table of simple but enduringly proud classroom buildings and dormitories that looked back at it. Some parents had waited hours for the best seats from which to witness it all. Laughingly, they jested over their shoulders to each other that they had waited twenty-two years.

The president's signature charisma helped to make up for the weather. As he asked the nearly 570 graduates and their families to take their seats, someone shouted "I love you!" from the crowd. Without skipping a beat, he boomed back "I love you, too! That's why I'm here!" Obama's ground team had done their homework, and he spoke with such warm and detailed familiarity about the college that an outsider could have easily mistaken him for an alumnus. Perhaps this was the intention: to nod to the Black men in soaked-through gowns and regalia who looked up from rows before him that he, in essence, *was* them, so they *could become him*. Like so many African Americans, I watched the live stream of the speech with the same sort of giddy pride that had the starstruck faculty seated behind the president hoisting up their cell phones to record the moment like teenagers awing the presence of a pop star. From the bright glare of my laptop screen in my humble graduate school apartment in Ann Arbor, my feeling then was that even from hundreds of miles away I was sharing in this undeniably proud moment for our people—one of those occasions in which African Americans pause to take inventory that we were actualizing our ancestors' dreams. Given the stony road that had been trod in little over a century since Reconstruction, I thought to myself on watching that field of smiling brown faces that even with my criticisms of the president and the college, this moment felt like I was witnessing some sort of mile marker being placed for our people. The faces of all I watched in attendance looked awash with a beaming pride that seemed to say the same.

Unlike any commencements before it and all other commencements across the nation that season, this moment was distinguished by the only Black male president addressing the graduating class of the nation's only historically Black college for men. The graduates and the president fed off their mutual uniqueness. As his oration got underway, his message leaned heavily into what exceptionalism means in the life of a Black man. I listened intently as the cadence of raindrops on the graduates' mortarboards seemed to punctuate each of his words.

Your generation is uniquely poised for success unlike any generation of African Americans that came before it. But that doesn't mean we don't have work—because if we're honest with ourselves, we know that too few of our brothers have the opportunities that you've had here at Morehouse. In troubled neighborhoods all across this country—many of them heavily African American—too few of our citizens have role models to guide them. Communities just a couple miles from my house in Chicago, communities just a couple miles from here—they're places where jobs are still too scarce, and wages are still too low; where schools are underfunded, and violence is pervasive; where too many of our men spend their youth not behind a desk in a classroom but hanging out on the streets or brooding behind a jail cell.[1]

The message was familiar to the crowd that day, as it was to anyone raised in an African American community: the recycled trope that nested the often-hazy post-civil-rights-era struggle for Black advancement within a belief that racism—in the absence of the blatant legal discrimination facing the previous generation—could be offset by education and individual achievement against all odds. That this missive to young Black male America was being delivered by the beau ideal of Black male achievement-via-respectability, and one who epitomized the college's doctrine, elevated the words to a sermon-like quality based in moral authority. Throughout his address, the then president enjoined the graduates to practice personal responsibility and to consider the outcomes of their lives as consequences of their choices and work ethic. Riven by internal contradictions, this message speaks to the disparities of structural disadvantages yet suggests that the "brooding" Black men "hanging out" in these impoverished communities are at least partly responsible for their perilous state. While lauding the graduates as having more opportunities for achievement than any generation before them, Obama's warning is clear: as Black men, their lives are only a few poor choices away from marking the stain of the race. "We have individual responsibilities," the president continued. "There are some things, as Black men, we can only do for ourselves. There are some things, as Morehouse men, that you are obliged to do for those still left behind. As Morehouse men, you now wield something even more powerful than a diploma you're about to collect—and that's the power of your example."

The audience received these words with rounds of affirmations and applause. The loudest cheers greeted the individual graduates who rose from their seats to the whoops of their classmates as the president acknowledged them for their odds-defying stories. One graduate had dropped out of Morehouse and worked as a custodian to provide for his pregnant girlfriend before returning to finish college. Another was a former foster child headed toward Harvard Law School and a career of legal advocacy for youth who are involved in the social service system. Obama used both examples to underscore his directive that "excuses are the tools of the incompetent" and are meaningless for those entering the new and hypercompetitive global workforce. "Nobody cares how tough your upbringing was. Nobody cares if you suffered from discrimination," he declared. "Whatever you've gone through pales in comparison to the hardships previous generations endured."

The crowd surrounding them continued to roar in applause, but the good-humored levity that had greeted Obama vanished from the graduates as they listened to these sobering words. While straining to make out the brief camera cutaways to their crowded faces, I noticed the rain now took on a different mood. For as much as Obama praised them, he also admonished them for the shortcomings of their brethren and impressed on them that to meet the benchmarks of masculine respectability as fathers, husbands, and role models they must escape the pitfalls that trapped so many other Black men. The message was clear: racial advancement is an outgrowth of the individual advancement of African Americans who are propelled to achievement. For educated Black men, the daunting task be-

FIGURE 2. Graduating students listen to Obama as the rain warps their mortarboards. MANDEL NGAN/AFP/Getty Images.

fore them was a clean-up job of the embarrassment caused by their counterparts who would see a courtroom before they saw a college classroom.

In office, President Obama demonstrated his earnest belief in these ideals. A year after the commencement speech, his administration unveiled My Brother's Keeper (MBK), a White House initiative targeted at African Americans and Latino young men and boys. In its official literature, the White House described its purpose as addressing "persistent opportunity gaps" facing this group by focusing on K–12 education, college readiness, and career preparation, including education and workforce training for incarcerated youths. These programs were not federally subsidized government policies, however; they depended mainly on local public-private partnerships, voluntary organizations, and the individual mentoring of struggling Black boys by college educated Black men.

In the years since Obama's presidency, however, critics representing Black communities have pointed out that his administration largely ignored the policies and practices that devastated Black households during the Great Recession. MBK's individual-based initiative presented an effort to address the plight of young Black men and boys as an opportunity to deflect from the administration's notable lack of response toward African Americans during a sluggish economic recovery. In the years leading up to the economic crash of 2008, long-standing wealth disparities between Black and white families showed signs of narrowing. Since home value disproportionately accounts for the wealth of Black households (compared to whites),[2] the collapse of the housing market and the foreclosure crisis hit Black homeowners especially hard. Low- and middle-income Black households, which had been targeted by discriminatory housing and predatory lending practices, suffered a 40 percent drop in their median wealth; by 2015 they were, on average, $98,000 poorer than they would have been without the Great Recession. Throughout Obama's two administrations and thereafter, Black households recovered slower because they had fewer opportunities to rebuild wealth than white households.[3] Black women heads of household, who had been disproportionately represented among first-time home buyers before the crash, lost even the small gains in wealth they had previously made. As the Black middle class was catapulted into a precarious position, many of Obama's Black supporters, as well as his detractors, harshly criticized the administration for not taking a direct policy approach to ameliorating the structural and economic conditions of African Americans. In that context, My Brother's Keeper stood out as Obama's only race-based initiative at a time of historic Black economic setbacks. It also focused on Black young men and boys, a group that was not in an exceptional state of decline in that historical moment, over Black women, who had disproportionately taken the economic blow to African Americans households during the housing crash.

MBK's origin story is little known by the public. While the emphasis on high school completion and college readiness led many to assume that it was born in the Department of Education, the initiative began as the brainchild of Eric Holder, the nation's first African American attorney general. Through its incubator in the Department of Justice, it expanded as an alliance between several federal agencies (including the Department of Energy) and the White House with the help of its principal architects, which included Morehouse alumni and affiliates. In the wake of dozens of high-profile police shootings of young African Americans, Holder initially imagined a "Smart on Crime" program that would "restore broken bonds" between Black neighborhoods and law enforcement. His goal was to improve community policing by shouldering part of the responsibility onto the very Black male youth that discriminatory police practices were targeting. On the one-year anniversary of MBK, Holder explained how the aims of the initiative originated in his vision for enhancing policing and the penal system:

> I launched a new "Smart on Crime" initiative to help strengthen communities, to improve public safety, and to make America's criminal justice system more effective—and more equitable. Our actions under this initiative are born of the crucial recognition that growing both tougher and smarter on crime means investing in innovations; striving for more just and equal outcomes; and rejecting any policy or practice that has the potential to undermine law enforcement—or erode the sense of trust that must always exist between police officials and the citizens they serve....As the My Brother's Keeper Task Force reported to the President last May—months before events in Ferguson captured headlines—we need to do more to strengthen the relationships between law enforcement and their communities. America's law enforcement leaders must ensure that every community can see that we are firmly committed to the impartial and aggressive enforcement of our laws—and the unbiased protection of

everyone in this country. Bonds that have been broken must be restored. And bonds that never existed must now be created—because this is the fundamental promise that lies at the core of who we are, what we do, and what so many brave law enforcement officers sacrifice so much, every day, to achieve.[4]

In its rhetoric and policies, the Obama administration and the president himself had delivered an unmistakable message to Black men. While thousands of Black households floundered amid the economic crisis, the tonic for Black communities' ills seemed to lie in the ability of young Black men and boys to do better. For African Americans to advance, the cultural prescription of respectable masculine behavior was given priority over remedying material and structural inequalities.

Repeatedly I have asked myself the question: how did we arrive at this moment? Why has the arc of racial advancement ideologies since the end of slavery brought us to its current iteration as a clear yet contradictory edict that Black men are simultaneously the saviors of the race and the cause of its downfall? As historians have consistently shown, the project of racial uplift has been gendered since its inception in the late nineteenth century. While this burden of moral respectability, personal achievement, and gender conformity has been visited on both Black men and women, Black men have generally been imagined as the yardstick for the race's progress. Since the mid-1920s our racial attention focused particularly on the upward mobility of Black men into the college educated and blue collar middle class and the most visible posts of racial leadership.[5] The evolution of Morehouse's mission, and the problems it faces both internally and externally, have run parallel with this history. Through the historical process of racial uplift, the college has responded to and helped shape a belief extolled by Black leadership and communities that held that the dignity and respectability of Black masculinity was our most potent weapon against racism.

Black men, particularly those who were well educated and financially secure, have long been leaders of African American uplift movements, some by self-appointment, others through their ordination by white elites, and still others by answering the call of the organized masses.[6] Morehouse College as an institution is wholly invested in cultivating Black men to fulfill these roles. To understand the college, we must see it in its historical and contemporary context. This chapter examines three key dimensions of the interplay between race, gender, and class in the making of the Black male elite. First, I examine how Black male respectability was ideologically birthed from a belief about racial uplift strategies that expressly saw gender propriety and the dignity of Black manhood as urgent issues in the immediate aftermath of slavery and as and vehicles to Black social and political equality into the formative years of modern Black political thought in the early twentieth century.

Second, I unpack the concept of Race Men, that is, Black men who seek to disprove the inferiority of the race through personal achievement and/or the activist campaigns they regard as necessary for Black improvement. Interrogating how masculinist and patriarchal beliefs are integrated into multiple ideologies about Black advancement or, in many cases, are propagated by the men within these movements, is critical to understanding the process of racialization at Morehouse. Racialization, as the process of assigning meanings, resources, and identity to race is a diverse endeavor, and Morehouse men hold conflicting or even divergent ideas about it. It is essentially the process of *making* race, sociologically, in terms of what that means in relationship to structures, institutions, and one another. It is a highly varied endeavor that depends on social context, and Morehouse men hold highly varied ideas about what is best for Black communities and the role their lives play in that effort. These diverse racial ideologies, however, often share the common thread of masculinist constructions of advancement, which is key to comprehending how Morehouse men can undergo their college racialization experiences differently and yet arrive at shared patriarchal beliefs that center men and masculinist frameworks in the betterment of the race.

Third, I examine the contemporary context of what has been dubbed the "Black Male Crisis." This viewpoint is one in a long line of political ideologies about the state of the race, yet, unlike previous generations' interest in addressing the obstacles to equality in the dominant society, it focuses on the attention of Black leadership to the decline of Black males. Here I point out that the crisis was deployed by many prominent Black men as a gender-wedging issue that, instead of measuring Black men mostly against their white counterparts, assessed Black men's stagnant or deteriorating position in comparison to Black women's perceived advancement.

The story of the Black male crisis, which originated in the early 1980s and gained steam throughout the 1990s, is best understood in the context of the accelerating deindustrialization and mass incarceration of that period, which were both articulated by Black male leadership as targeting Black manhood. The decline of manufacturing devastated all blue-collar workers[7] but was popularly associated with male-dominated labor sectors. Similarly, the criminal legal system targeted both Black men and women but was justified by a fabricated moral panic around Black male "super-predators," a term coined by political scientist John Dilulio in 1995 on his work with the Clinton administration and popularized soon after in a speech by Hillary Clinton about her husband's anticrime agenda. That both issues were skewed toward Black male youth placed organizations, initiatives, and schools for Black men and boys not only on the front lines of the crisis, but it also seeded a social phenomenon into what anthropologist Janet Roitman terms a "crisis narrative" in which the problems facing Black men were reframed by leadership not as a pivotal moment but, rather, as a chronic condition that shored up meaning and identity to the new struggle for African Americans a generation removed from the clear-cut desegregationist aims of the civil rights movement.[8] The mission of contemporary Morehouse both shapes and is shaped by the rhetoric and realities of the crisis, but it also plays a principal role in the production and political imagination of the crisis narrative.

Up from Slavery through Sexual and Gender Propriety

In 1908, W.E.B. Du Bois wrote in his introduction to *The Negro American Family*, an edited collection of sociological studies of contemporary Black life:

> Without doubt the point where the Negro American is furthest behind modern civilization is in his sexual mores. This does not mean that he is more criminal in this respect than his neighbors. Probably he is not. It does mean that he is more primitive, less civilized, in this respect than his surroundings demand, and that thus his family life is less efficient for its onerous social duties, his womanhood less protected, his children more poorly trained. All this, however, is to be expected. This is what slavery meant, and no amount of kindliness in individual owners could save the system from its deadly work of disintegrating the ancient Negro home and putting but a poor substitute in its place. The point is however, now, what has been the effect of emancipation on the mores of the Negro family. The great and most patent fact has been differentiation: the emergence from the masses of successive classes with higher and higher sexual morals.[9]

Du Bois had committed his corpus to arguing against the cultural and moral defectiveness of African Americans, and he used his voice in *The Negro American Family* to contend that Black manliness and womanliness (the terms, in the Victorian era context, signified both sexual propriety and gender relations) had been destroyed by the exploitation and degradation of slavery and thus could be rebuilt with the economic and political restoration of Black families. Thus far in racial advancement, economic marginalization had allowed only a small population of relatively privileged Blacks to construct and maintain what Du Bois saw as normative households. Therefore, the logic flowed that economic justice would facilitate moral progress for the race. While many of his contemporaries inverted the logic of this argument and maintained that moral uplift would usher in economic progress, Du Bois saw moral betterment as a collective (rather than individual) project and dismissed the belief that "proving" Black morality to whites would accomplish anything politically or economically.

Every contemporary sociological question holds a century-old backstory in its answer. After emancipation, the Black movement shifted its priorities to attaining citizenship and economic independence and to defending the moral worth of African Americans. Beginning in the late nineteenth century and continuing through the Jim Crow era into the present,[10] the historical project of racial uplift has signified the collective struggle for social advancement and liberation from racial oppression.[11] That sexuality and gender remain so marginalized in the popular narrative of Black racial uplift is surprising, given the obvious embeddedness of these prescriptions within the historical record's formulations of uplift ideology. Gender relations were central to abolitionist disdain for enslavement as a violation of marriage and parenthood, and even sotto voce as the profit-driven incentive for the interracial rape of Black women (whose children born automatically as property would expand the slaveholders financial assets). Some white abolitionists argued that the exploitation of enslaved women in the cotton fields and other forms of heavy, physical labor was degrading; so was the use of enslaved men in domestic service and other demeaning tasks.[12] When African American men asserted their rights, whether through petitions in the Revolutionary period or legal suits in the antebellum era, they often rested their claims on their manhood.[13] As historian James Oliver Horton pointed out: "Clearly there was the hope, even the expectation among some black men that with freedom would come the possibility that black people could form their lives to approximate gender conventions of American society at large. Indeed, for black men the ability to support and protect their women became synonymous with manhood and became synonymous with freedom. Often slaves demanding their freedom used the term 'manhood rights.'"[14]

As African Americans considered the fundamental question of how to secure the economic, social, and political recognition of their humanity necessary to clench liberty, some race leaders advocated the promotion of individual morality, which they tethered to gender normativity and sexual propriety. Eager to rectify the sexual legacies of slavery, many Black elites and their white abolitionist allies promoted a condescending campaign of moral reform, social purity, sexual decorum, and marital reproduction as prerequisites for emancipated citizenship and Black improvement.[15] Historian Michele Mitchell points out that, of all the topics of racial reform that immediately followed the decades after emancipation, regulating intraracial sexual relationships was urgently prioritized as a means of ameliorating the subjugated condition of Black men, women, and children.[16]

Even though the agenda of post-emancipation-era racial uplift activists was not representative of the entire race, the abolitionist

elite's obsessive interest in sexuality set in motion a political and social campaign that affected virtually every African American. The
politicization of sexuality drew the topic out of the private sphere of
households and individual relationships into larger and much more
immediately consequential questions regarding labor, citizenship,
and sociopolitical recognition. By impregnating the political with
the sexual, middle-class sex reformers established a protocol about
Black family life with the intention of countering the pervasive stereotypes of Black women's excessive libidinousness and Black men's
predation. Perhaps most importantly, Black elites admonished others that these cultural norms should be attained through self-help
and thus implied that Black men and women on the bottom rungs
of the social strata should be faulted for their own lowly status.[17]
Moreover, politicizing sexuality allowed these reformists to target
a range of relationships and dynamics, from the choice of sexual
and marital partners and age at marriage, to courtship, intercourse,
rape, miscegenation, and reproduction.[18] Fundamentally, this trian-
gulation between class, sexuality, and social reform allowed Black
elites to promote a collective uplift agenda outwardly while simultaneously culturally demarcating and exacerbating class stratification
within Black communities.

The dire and dangerous conditions of Black life at the turn of
the twentieth century allowed elites to frame this sexual and gender
campaign in imperative terms. Black liberation through cultural assimilation was defined then, as it is now, in terms of Black men's and
women's ability to be recognized as full Americans and be granted
full participation in society. While Black men and women shared
similar risks of violence, racial terrorism, and a descent in social and
economic status for not upholding these expectations, the constitu-
tional marriage of manhood with citizenship meant that only men
would be advantaged by these norms.[19]

Only three years after Morehouse was founded in 1867, the ratification of the Fifteenth Amendment, which granted the vote to African American men, politically bifurcated the race into enfranchised "active" citizen men and disenfranchised "passive" citizen women.[20] The college and Black male citizenship came of age together through Reconstruction and the turn of the twentieth century, when a powerful conjunction of ideas of manhood, race, and imperialism reshaped political culture. Like so many historically Black colleges and universities (HBCUs), Morehouse was founded during the precipitous years immediately following emancipation, when formerly enslaved African Americans found themselves thrust into a citizenry still hostile to the novel idea of their humanity. The purpose and history of historically Black colleges contrasts to the histories of white higher education in the United States.[21] Although they vary greatly in size, specializations, and endowments, they share a common origin story that (for all but a few of them) began in the decades following emancipation and a history that reflects both white America's ambivalence toward the education of American Americans and the purpose that HBCUs uphold for Black communities. M. Christopher Brown and James Earl Davis explain that this duality defines the "social contract" of 103 original HBCUs and note that HBCUs are products of a segregationist belief in racially polarizing American education at all levels.[22] Out of whites' belief in Black inferiority, however, HBCUs committed to serving a primary role of conveying social capital to Black graduates and, consequently, the race. This social capital, Brown and Davis maintain, was imparted through the six common goals of HBCUs, which include: (1) the maintenance of African American cultural traditions; (2) the provision of racial leadership and responsibility of college administrators and faculty to community affairs; (3) fulfillment of economic responsibility to Black communities; (4) the provision of role models who serve as examples in their responses to social, political, and economic changes for African Americans; (5) to provide graduates who serve as political and social liaisons between marginalized Black communities and the dominant white populace; and, (6) to produce research, training, and information dissemination that prioritizes and benefits Black life.[23]

In its nascence, Morehouse's founders and early leadership interpreted this HBCU social contract through a masculinist frame. What would become Morehouse College was founded as Augusta Theological Institute in Augusta, Georgia.[24] The college came into existence largely through the efforts of Reverend William Jefferson White, a mixed-race carpenter and undertaker who had been propositioned to bring a seminary to Georgia by an enslaved Black man who had traveled extensively throughout the free communities of the mid-Atlantic with his master. Not only was the college forged within the racial and gendered ideologies of Reconstruction, but it also came of age nestled within the postwar urbanization that would so inseparably associate it with the emergence of Black leadership in the modern city of Atlanta. In the decades following the Civil War, Old South slaveholders turned themselves into New South developers by purchasing large tracts of land to form a wealthy white suburb of Atlanta whose streets were named for Confederate generals in order to attract white merchants and politicians to the unincorporated southwestern end of the city. In 1885, when the institute fled white terrorists in Augusta (its leaders had openly criticized the treatment of Black Augustans) and relocated to southwest Atlanta, it settled on a hilltop that was formerly a Confederate defensive outpost. The institute renamed itself Atlanta Baptist Seminary and was attracted to the location in part because of potential safety—it would be located nearby the newly established Spelman College—and partly because its new position on safe, high ground (the highest natural point in Atlanta) helped somewhat to protect its students from white terroristic violence beyond its gates.[25]

In its new Atlanta home, however, the college was beset with new

FIGURE 3. Graves Hall, built 1889 as Atlanta Baptist Seminary. The first building on campus; UNCF-member institution, Morehouse College.

challenges of the blight of turn-of-the-century Black urban poverty both in the city's Black communities and within its pool of prospective students. During this time, rural Blacks were increasingly fleeing white violence by migrating to the denser Black communal spaces of Atlanta. The challenges of educating this impoverished and often illiterate population resulted in the restructuring of the seminary into "preparatory" (remedial and basic skills), "normal" (high school and college preparatory), and "theological" (postsecondary) schools. By 1897, just three years after West End was annexed into the city of Atlanta, the school had eliminated the preparatory and normal divisions and had officially become a college, thus limiting the institution's impact on and accessibility to West End's Black poor and emphasizing its affiliation toward the Black middle class.[26]

This turn away from remedial learning and toward classical theological education differentiates Morehouse's institutional origin story from the charters of many other Black colleges that commonly kept the path of preparing newly freedmen with practical skills and basic literacy.[27] In forging its way as a school of ministry, Morehouse would have immediately become a distinguished destination for aspiring Blacks, as the clergy was one of the most prestigious and learned nineteenth-century professions to which Black men could aspire. Given the moral panic that shrouded Black advancement throughout the turn of the century, a school to instruct the formerly enslaved in the ministry attracted white Northern missionaries and upwardly mobile Black social activists who insisted that the social panacea for the twentieth century's advancement of the Black race would rely both on the schooling and the moral instruction of newly freed Blacks.

White developers' plans for the West End depended on racial segregation from the beginning, and unofficial racial boundaries were soon established that divided the Victorian avenues of West End's prominent white residents from the infant Black colleges that had also taken root in the area.[28] Morehouse, Spelman, Morris Brown College, the Gammon Theological Seminary,[29] Atlanta University, and Clark College (the latter two would merge in the 1980s to form Clark Atlanta University) distinguished West End as the South's premier cluster of Black learning and intellectualism. The Atlanta University Center (AUC), as the consortium of schools would later be formally named, was the intellectual force driving development in post-Reconstruction Black Atlanta in ways that elevated its premier faculty and administrators—like John Hope, W. E. B. Du Bois, James Weldon Johnson, Walter White, and Sadie G. Mays (a proto-feminist University of Chicago trained Atlanta University professor of social work)—to equal prominence with the city's Black business and civic leaders. Founded in 1865, Atlanta University was the nation's oldest graduate institution for African Americans. It initially granted bachelor's degrees and trained teachers and librarians, but by the 1920s turned its curricular focus exclusively to graduate training—mostly for continuing Morehouse and Spelman graduates. So esteemed were its faculty and programs that Du Bois, who served as Atlanta University's chair of sociology from 1934 to 1944 and spent twenty-three years writing many of his most preeminent works there,[30] once scoffed that the consortium was an isolated "ivory tower of race."[31] But the AUC's educators and alumni closely strategized with Atlanta's civil rights community throughout the early twentieth century, and the city's Black power structure drew from Morehouse's graduates and administrators for many of its most prominent leaders in politics, business, and religion.[32] The reach of the AUC into civil rights movements magnified Morehouse's seminal and lingering influence on Black progress and politics in Atlanta.

At the turn of the twentieth century, the political, intellectual, and social gains made by African Americans during Reconstruction and throughout thriving spaces like the AUC were met with a vicious white backlash.[33] The Black male representation in local, state, and federal offices was swiftly erased by the Black codes and Jim Crow laws that effectively nullified the Black male citizenship enscribed in the Fifteenth Amendment and abrogated the equal protections promised by the Fourteenth Amendment. Jim Crow proved particularly injurious to the patriarchal validation that middle-class Black men sought. Men of the Black bourgeoisie,[34] who were deeply invested in having their manhood recognized in the name of racial dignity, confronted the fact that segregation limited their gender privilege to intraracial relationships. Men who could formerly exercise some semblance of manhood and racial leadership found the denial of their masculinity (and thus their claims to citizenship) legally encoded into every interaction with whites. As historian Martin Summers describes, political disenfranchisement from the 1890s through the early twentieth century attenuated the bonds between Black manhood and citizenship. The gendered subtext of Jim Crow had specific legal, economic, and social ramifications in the lives of Black men. Summers says further that: "Economic discrimination and the inability of most black families to survive solely on a male breadwinner's income militated against a patriarchal organization of the black household, further making it difficult to obtain manhood by dominant cultural standards. The ever-present threat of lynching and mob violence, which purportedly sought to police an aggressive black male sexuality and often incorporated the horrific act of castration, made any assertion of independence or brazen behavior a potentially perilous action."[35] Successive generations of Black men, as well as women, continued to encounter deeply entrenched ideologies about racial hierarchy that denied them citizenship and moral recognition. The aspiring young college came of age when this issue took on new urgency, and those who led it were well aware that the institution's posterity relied on its ability to address this issue within the lives of its students. How could they ensure that their graduates had forms of manhood that would be immediately recognizable as entitling them to their rightful citizenship?[36] The problem had already hit tragically home: during the 1906 Atlanta riots, two Morehouse students were murdered by a white mob because they "dared to behave like men and not according to Southern tradition."[37] What was then still called Atlanta Baptist Seminary had already made a relatively defiant statement in its choice of curriculum. Unlike many Black secondary schools and colleges of the era founded under Booker T. Washington's accommodationist "Tuskegee model" of racial progress, which stressed normal and industrial training, self-help, and Black acquiescence to the Jim Crow racial order,[38] Morehouse's ministerial instruction and liberal arts curriculum would both presume and declare Black men's moral fitness and intellectual capacity.[39] The choice of Morehouse's curriculum would have been well understood by Black communities of the era as a defiant political statement of Black men's intellectual and moral aptitude. Du Bois was highly critical of efforts to limit post-

FIGURE 4. Class in chemistry, Atlanta Baptist Seminary (Morehouse), 1925.

Reconstruction Black training to industrial and technical fields and wrote in *The College-Bred Negro* that "there ought to be maintained several negro colleges in the South. The aim of these colleges should be to supply thoroughly trained preachers, professional men, and captains of industry."[40] In its founding, Morehouse kept with Du Bois's insistence that "the object of true education is not to make men carpenters, it is to make carpenters men."[41]

Henry Morehouse, the white Baptist leader after whom the college was renamed in 1913, envisioned higher education for Blacks as a means of "indirectly Americanizing the masses."[42] During the dawn of US imperialism (roughly the late 1800s through the years following World War I), racialized notions of masculinity-as-citizenship took precedence amid the military assertion and moral validation of US imperialism, which all the while was bloodily stained by lynching and white mob violence.[43] White elites espoused racist ideas of social Darwinism that equated masculine dominance with imperial conquest and feminine inferiority with conquered peoples of color.

By law, custom, and violence, whites enforced racial hierarchies by using masculinity as the measure by which races were ranked and civilization was recognized. To be fit for citizenship and capable of civilization was to be manly, and to be manly was to be white.[44]

In its first century—with a centennial that coincided with the apex of the civil rights movement—the nascent college took a vested interest in repairing Black men from the lingering effects of slavery and Jim Crow. As alumnus Edward Jones wrote:

> Morehouse College, since its humble, inauspicious beginnings as Augusta Institute (1867) in Augusta, Georgia, has been dedicated to the task of building men: first by enlightening their minds, then by freeing them from the shackles of a psychological conditioning brought about by nearly two hundred and fifty years of slavery. The task of these first educators was not simply one of inculcating knowledge, which of itself tends to make men free, but also one of rehabilitation—of repairing the psychological damage done to the souls of enslaved men who needed to be taught self-respect and dignity even in a degrading environment where the social and political status quo, by laws and mores, was diametrically opposed to such teaching.

Academic discussions of racial uplift ideology have nearly exhausted the iconic debates between Booker T. Washington and Du Bois.[45] Washington's accommodationist strategy appeased white segregationists by enjoining the African American masses to accept their inferior station and toil as manual and industrial laborers. While Washington viewed this temporary subordination as a necessary concession in exchange for white support for economic and educational projects, Du Bois saw accommodation as a betrayal of Black liberation and called for a simultaneous struggle for wealth accumulation, education at all levels, and "a development in culture and the higher things of life."[46] The debates between Du Bois and Washington would famously shape much of the arc of the twentieth century's Black advancement strategies, and the matter of the role of education for African Americans was center stage in this tournament. Regarding the decisions of Black colleges and universities to offer students liberal arts rather than an industrial education, Du Bois wrote: "We daily hear that an education that encourages aspiration, that sets the loftiest of ideals, and that seeks as an end culture and character rather than breadwinning, is the privilege of white men and the danger and delusion of the black."[47] Morehouse's commitment to propel its graduates to preach morality from the pulpit and serve more broadly as racial leaders defined its mission and marked its place in the terrain of race politics throughout the twentieth century. The institution set out to uplift African Americans by producing successive generations of educated Black men who would shepherd the race.

While the fin de siècle years and early twentieth century birthed stark class and ethnic divergences within political approaches to Black improvement, a common thread across these movements was the belief that producing educated Black men represented a path to full civil equality. Despite their organizations' appeal to working-class people, Black nationalists, too, shared this model of progress. Marcus Garvey, the iconic founder of Universal Negro Improvement Association (UNIA), which at one time had the largest membership of any single Black organization in the United States, agreed that the path to advancement lay not in industrial education and political accommodation but in liberal education and political agitation against disenfranchisement, segregation, and the exploitation of labor. Furthermore, it was the responsibility of the educated elite to act as the advance guard for racial progress. While Garvey did not engage directly in the debate between Du Bois and Washington and did not share Du Bois's determination to struggle for civil equality within existing nation-states, Garvey and the UNIA leadership conducted massive educational programs on history, culture, and politics for the membership. Part of the UNIA's early agenda was that the "intelligent must lead and assist the unfortunate of the people to rise."[48]

Across the historical arc from Reconstruction through the interwar period, a belief took hold within Black community politics that the race depended on its successful men. Manliness was a preoccupation among the white middle class at the turn of the century.[49] For the group whose claims to manliness provoked the violent assaults of Jim Crow, this fixation was slow to recede as the civil rights of Black men—even of military veterans—were denied. Modern political and social campaigns for Black male respectability have been carried on almost entirely by organizations and institutions. The employment of Black men in urban industries brought forward new ideas of Black male dignity forged by organized labor. In this effort, Morehouse and other HBCUs stood alongside the Brotherhood of Sleeping Car Porters, the all-Black union of men who worked in Pullman cars on overnight trains and chose the socialist writer A. Philip Randolph to lead them; the Prince Hall Masons, the Black fraternal order that took its name from a Revolutionary leader of Black emancipation campaigns; and the UNIA. Together, these groups confronted the degradation of Jim Crow with a new and wholly modern construction of the "race man."[50] The race man proved to be more than a belief that the fate of the race was harnessed to Black male success. It became a call for real men to oblige themselves to see their bodies, dress, comportment, achievements, and personhood as microsites of the entire race's advancement.

Race Saviors

Ask any freshman to rattle off the names of esteemed Morehouse graduates. He will begin with the indisputable headliner, Martin

FIGURE 5. Martin Luther King Jr. (*front row, third from left*) listens in class at Morehouse College.

Luther King Jr., and follow immediately with an honor roll of marquee celebrities, businessmen, elected officials, and public figures. A new crop of alumni has made the list recently, ranging from film and television stars to network news pundits and correspondents to elected officials. Then there are the sons of A-list African Americans, whose presence demonstrates that Morehouse not only propels men into the Black elite but is also a preapproved destination for young men from the most well-heeled Black families.

For Morehouse students, these lists confirm the fact that fame, power, and wealth are affiliated with their college. They confer a sense of racial pride and authenticity derived from men whose individual achievements are seen as bestowing greatness on the race. Some names are quietly omitted, such the late Herman Cain (a farright former Republican presidential candidate and businessman who died in 2020 after contracting COVID-19 at a campaign rally for Donald Trump). A great alumnus is not required to reach the level of reverential selflessness set by King or Julian Bond, but his political leanings cannot be openly viewed as injurious to Black communities and therefore racially inauthentic.

Who does (and does not) make the list reflects the college's claim to the "race men" among them.[51] This cultural and political archetype first took loose form in the canonical works of St. Clair Drake and Horace Cayton. In *Black Metropolis* (1945), Drake and Cayton described a racial pride rooted in the historical need for African Americans to disprove the inferiority encoded into their second-class citizenship by demonstrating superiority in their respective fields of achievement. The race man metaphorically fused race pride, racial solidarity, and racial consciousness into a human personification whereby "the success of one Negro" becomes "the success of us all."[52]

Reciprocity exists between the race man and his masses: he must see in his achievements a declaration of his race's aptitude, and his race must also read a meaning of shared racial pride into his success. The accomplishments of Herman Cain, for example, were marred by his ardent support of Donald Trump and multiple allegations of sexual misconduct toward women who were his subordinates while he was CEO of the American Restaurant Association. Many Black women and some men regarded these acts as unbefitting of a race man. As cultural theorist Hazel Carby pointedly put it, "What a race man signifies for white segments of our society is not necessarily how a race man is defined for various black constituencies."[53] In popular Black racial consciousness, the race man's achievements—at least in the absence of blatantly immoral misdeeds—are credited in and of themselves as rightful forms of racial representation and often provide a culturally accepted prima facie form of racial leadership. The cultural and political construction of race men and the authority vested therein overwhelmingly favors Black elites, who have held the power to attach racial uplift ideology to their self-interest.

The self-interest of the Black bourgeoisie reimagined the call to educated African Americans from the social justice movements led by Du Bois, Randolph, and Garvey. Among college educated African Americans, one of the most commonly quoted passages in Du Bois's writings on racial advancement comes from "The Talented Tenth," his introduction to a 1903 collection of essays written by "representative Negroes"—that is, those who represent the highest achievements of the race and are recognized by elite whites. He pronounced in that magnum opus that "the Negro race, like all races, is going to be saved by its exceptional men. The problem of education, then, among Negroes must first of all deal with the Talented Tenth." He envisioned this educated tier of the race as "guiding" the masses away "from the contamination and death of the Worst, in their own and other races."[54] He further implored educated African Americans to move on this obligation to the Black masses as a social and moral imperative by asking, "Can the masses of the Negro people be in any possible way more quickly raised than by the effort and example of this aristocracy of talent and character? Was there ever a nation on God's fair earth civilized from the bottom upward? Never; it is, ever was and ever will be from the top downward that culture filters." His use of the term "talent" was, in the heyday of the American eugenics movement, synonymous with intellect much like "character" was synonymous with morality. "The Talented Tenth rises and pulls all that are worth the saving up to their vantage ground," Du Bois proselytized. "This is the history of human progress."[55]

Today, the talented tenth ideology persists as a rallying cry for Black achievement and serves as the political validation of the conviction that their individual accomplishments, wealth, access, and status tend automatically to improve conditions for the race. In explaining how elites deployed this strategy, Kevin Gaines observes, middle-class African Americans offered racial uplift ideals to whites in the form of cultural politics with the hope that Black men's suffrage had already made the case for their political citizenship rights during Reconstruction. "Elite Blacks," Gaines writes, "believed they were replacing racist notions of fixed biological racial differences with an evolutionary view of cultural assimilation, measured primarily by the status of the family and civilization."[56]

College educated African Americans may tout the talented tenth as their creed and believe that the mighty Du Bois crowned their ilk as heirs apparent to race leadership, but such a self-congratulatory announcement requires the selective hearing of what is clear in his body of work: Du Bois did not feel that Black elites were endowed with any spiritual, ethical, or cognitive superiority over their working-class brethren. Rather, it can be argued that with the talented tenth Du Bois established one of the earliest iterations of what political theorist Michael Dawson termed "linked-fate theory,"[57] which explains the consistency of Black political trends across class lines by emphasizing that African Americans understand their personal prospects as essentially yoked to the progress of the race. Black exceptionalism, in Du Bois's view, is not a birthright predetermined by privilege, but rather a matter of the social service that well-resourced Blacks owe to the socially marginalized, to whom their fates are married. For Du Bois, the responsibility of the educated class to chart the lot of the race was derived primarily from their literacy, not any putative cultural superiority (the very term "talent," in the context of the era's eugenics jargon meant learned). Their working- and lower-class counterparts, he believed, were socially and economically strangled by the illiteracy and abject poverty caused by racism.

Race Men as *Men*

This book scrutinizes how Morehouse racializes its men to understand their lives in relation to the condition of Black communities. What they believe Black men should be doing and what these communities need, however, can be varied and conflicting. For some, becoming a race man is staked in Black men's individual ability to achieve personal success and defy ideas about Black inferiority in white-dominated professions and corporations. For a vocal minority, race men uphold a form of pro-Blackness that is rooted in a more radical Black nationalist tradition. These approaches may seem divergent, but they share a common thread: Morehouse men overwhelmingly use these frames to make meanings of their own manhood and rely on masculinist frames in assessing and describing their approach to achievement and race progress. In addition to considering how the race man ideal became conflated with Black elites, we must consider how the race man came to be defined as *a man*. If the "success of one negro" stood for the success of us all, then how did the success of the race become harnessed to the strides made by its exemplary *men*? Black leadership has long been defined in masculinist terms, regardless of the conservative or progressive leanings of its politics.[58] Two ideological traditions, the gentleman scholar and Black nationalism, both wagered Black progress on cultural imperatives for Black manhood.

Benjamin Elijah Mays, Morehouse's iconic first Black president and husband of esteemed Atlanta University social work professor Sadie G. Mays, famous for his forward thinking about Blacks in higher education as well as his mentorship of Martin Luther King Jr., instilled in the college a legacy of conducting oneself as a "scholar-gentleman." The race man's essential defiance of Black inferiority lies at the core of this construction. In his charge to the 1961 graduating class, Mays stated:

There is an air of expectancy at Morehouse College. It is expected that the student who enters here will do well. It is also expected that once a man bears the insignia of a Morehouse Graduate, he will do exceptionally well. We expect nothing less....May you perform so well that when a man is needed for an important job in your field, your work will be so impressive that the committee of selection will be compelled to examine your credentials. May you forever stand for something noble and high. Let no man dismiss you with the wave of the hand or a shrug of the shoulder.

"As an educator," alumnus and *Ebony* magazine editor in chief Lerone Bennett once remarked, "Mays addressed himself to the major problem of oppression—manhood. He did not intend, he said, to make lawyers or doctors or teachers—he intended to make men."[59] Within the legacy of Black scholarship Mays inherited from Du Bois before him, he did not have to choose between these endeavors. Du Bois's Black intellectual tradition, which lives on in successive generations of its male disciples, is a seminal ground for constructing the race man on a cultural claim to masculinist intellectual authority. Du Bois fervently advanced his belief in the masculine marrow of Black intellect, and while he championed Black women's economic contributions to household budgets and their social and political activism within Black communities, he unequivocally rejected the significance of Black women's intellectual contributions to theories and strategies of racial emancipation and was reluctant to include Black women in the academic societies and publications he controlled.[60]

Most shortsightedly, Du Bois refused to publish Anna Julia Cooper's essays in *The Crisis*, although he eventually published a portrait of her in her doctoral regalia. While Beverly Guy Sheftall, Cheryl Gilkes, Shirley Moody-Turner, and other historians of Black women's thought have rightfully asserted the feminist intellectual contributions of Du Bois's female contemporaries, particularly Anna Julia Cooper, philosopher Tommy J. Curry claims that Cooper herself invested, to some degree, in the popular vision of masculinist uplift. Curry argues that patriarchal gender norms were a form of racial uplift endorsed by both men and women in the Progressive Era. In his reading, Cooper subscribed to the idea that Black manhood and womanhood were interdependent, and that "the fundamental nature of womanhood was to develop in the race a patriarchal manhood capable of protecting the Black woman and the Black home."[61]

In this minority opinion, Cooper's presumed fealty to Black male racial leadership cannot be reconciled with contemporary Black feminist critiques of race patriarchy, but as historian Glenda Gilmore reminds us, Cooper's ambitions for Black women's liberation were staked in the idea that the advancement of men need not limit women's achievements. "If women were gaining in the race of life, men should run faster," Gilmore explains of Cooper's stance.[62] Cooper herself argued that educating and raising the status of mothers would, in turn, influence their sons and daughters, repeating the old and widely used saying that "a stream cannot rise higher than its source."[63] This key insight importantly points to the model of partnership that many Black feminists, before and after Cooper, espoused and exemplified in their work for racial uplift. It also reflects the class sensibilities and weight that gendered norms of respectability held for Black elites' notions of leadership. In this view, middle-class Black women charged Black men with shielding Black women and girls from the gendered insults and sexual assaults of white men. "If racial ideologies of whiteness were crucial to bourgeois aspirations of non-blacks," Gaines expounds, "then gender ideologies of manhood informed African Americans' middle-class ideology of racial uplift."[64]

In *Race Men*, Carby devoted an entire text to reading the masculinist constructions of racial leadership and iconography.[65] Du Bois himself, she explained, disqualified Washington as the descendant of racial leadership in the vein of Toussaint Louverture, Nat Turner, and other militant rebels on the grounds that the Tuskegee Institute founder lacked the valiant manliness embodied by these liberatory figures. Du Bois insisted that Washington's policies of submission and accommodation were intrinsically unmanly and "bound to sap the manhood of any race."[66] In public exchanges, Du Bois impugned his rival on the grounds that Washington's concession strategy failed to exert manliness. Thus, Du Bois lambasted Washington's own masculinity as insufficient and rendered him invalid to inherit the helm of racial leadership for which they both jockeyed in the wake of Frederick Douglass. "Mr. Washington's counsel of submission," Du Bois wrote, "overlooked certain elements of true manhood...[un-like] the great form of Frederick Douglass, the greatest of American Negro leaders."[67]

Carby reads their iconic feud through this lens of competition for "true Black manhood."[68] The connection between racial leadership and robust forms of masculinity is more than a mere residue of Du Bois's concept of Black intellectualism. Carby argues that Du Bois's preoccupation with masculinity rested on the harmonious relationship he saw between Black intellectualism and the embodiment of cultural nationalism. Du Bois marked the male body of the intellectual by a particular masculine style of dress.[69] His vision of a well-educated male with a finely clothed Black body, Carby argues, worked "to secure [the] qualities" of critical intelligence and moral action "as irrevocably and conservatively masculine."[70] Du Bois assigned the race man a uniform that established a well-fitting suit as an artifact of intellectual authority; he "would be treated as he is dressed."[71] To fall short of this tailored, authoritative aesthetic was to manifest disrespect for himself and invite indignity. For Du Bois, his many male intellectual disciples, and the bodies of gentle-men-scholars to come, adherence to sartorial style held more racial meanings than merely seeking white approval. For the successive generations who are products of Benjamin Mays's vision, the gentleman-scholar's ascendance to the status of race man in their own eyes and in the eyes of other Black men is a process stitched onto their bodies.

The roots and contemporary iterations of most varieties of Black nationalism have been no less masculinist than gentleman-scholar constructions. In their pursuit of a cultural identity that countered Western Eurocentrism, Black nationalists such as William H. Ferris, a Garveyite, Yale alumnus, and editor of the *Negro World*, promoted manhood and the symbolism of powerful patriarchal authority as the grounds for a rightful claim to Black nationhood.[72] Black feminists like historian Ashley Farmer have highlighted the masculinist organizational hierarchies, leadership aesthetics, and militaristic strategies of Black liberation organizations such as the Black Panther Party, even though women constituted most of its membership, grassroots organizers, and full-time staff.[73]

In another example, the Black cultural nationalism of the Congress for African People set out to "re-Africanize" gender roles by defining Black womanhood as a cultural contribution accomplished through childrearing, education, and homemaking. The structure of Black families was upheld as a cornerstone of these masculinist movements. Historian E. Frances White criticizes the cultural nationalist US Organization for calling on Black women to take submissive roles in order to support and inspire Black men.[74] The group also practiced polygamy under the guise that it refuted Eurocentric family constructs and honored African traditions. These family ideologies relied on an essentialist idea of African cultures and reinforced dominant Western gender constructs.[75] For Historian Scot Brown, these models "fortified a Moynihan-inspired argument"[76] that surmised that Black families suffered from a shortage of men."[77] Masculinist movement prescriptions did more to mirror and reify Western gender roles than challenge them.[78]

Although radical Black nationalism bears little resemblance to the gentleman-scholar rhetoric espoused by Du Bois and Mays, a common thread of masculine anxiety pervades both understandings of Black progress. Overwhelmingly, the beliefs about racial progress voiced by my respondents can be sorted into these two schools. That the experience of racialization men undergo at Morehouse divvies them into these bicameral Black masculinist politics, rather than to numerous other currents of Black political thought, begs the question of how deeply masculine anxiety anchors the institution's messages about Black progress. This anxiety is folded into a belief that while Black men may claim authority in leading the race to a better future, they simultaneously stage and perpetuate a fear that they may also be the race's ruin.

Race Ruiners

In "Of Our Spiritual Strivings," the essay that opens *The Souls of Black Folk*, W. E. B. Du Bois voiced the provocative question that often remained implicit in the various questions he was asked by whites when matters of race arose in conversation.

> To the real question, How does it feel to be a problem? I answer seldom a word.
>
> And yet, being a problem is a strange experience,—peculiar even for one who has never been anything else.

Although Blackness has long been viewed as a problem by whites, patriarchy has not always been regarded by Black people themselves as a problem that imperils the race. Successive generations of African Americans arose from slavery and Jim Crow holding fervently to an ideology that Black citizenship would be secured by men who could fully achieve masculinity. Paired with this ideology was a belief that the fate of the masses of the race lay in the hands of men whose achievements at the frontiers of class ascension would propel them forward. How, then, did we land so swiftly—in just the turn of a post-civil-rights-era generation—on commencement speeches that lambast Black men for threatening to bring about the downfall of the race? How have Black men been repositioned from the saviors of the race to its ruination, whose perilous condition demands our urgent and nearly exclusive attention?

The notion that young Black men are the primary detriment to the race is novel. In 1965, a report authored by Secretary of Labor Daniel Patrick Moynihan, titled "The Negro Family: The Case for National Action," described the "pathological" condition of the Black poor and routinely blamed Black poverty on Black women heads of household from their supposed hyperfertility, promiscuity, and "out of wedlock" teen pregnancies to their putative laziness and dependency, which was subsidized by an overly generous government. The Moynihan report's hysteria over "emasculating" single mothers who prevented Black men from becoming breadwinners and heads of household was repackaged by the Ronald Reagan presidential campaign in the form of nefarious "welfare queens" who scammed government subsidies to indulge in luxuries all while unemployed.[79] Similarly, the War on Poverty, which had been launched by President Johnson and relentlessly vilified Black womanhood, spawned another gendered campaign as it swiftly morphed into a War on Crime.[80] Stereotypes of poor Black women's maternal and moral defectiveness made for convenient political football, but in actuality Johnsonian and Nixonian policies that were designed to stamp out the perceived threat Black resistance movements posed to state property and control expediently railroaded disproportionate droves of Black men into jails and prisons. In the mounting days of the crack cocaine epidemic, a new way of talking about Black communities emerged among white politicians and policy makers. Selective hearing on the part of Black male elites in media, civic and clerical leadership, and politics, however, insisted that what was most urgent for a race in peril was to improve the condition of the male half of it. "The Crisis of the Black Male" had dawned.

No single, definitive moment marks the beginning of this public rhetoric of crisis. Many factors contributed to the contraction of opportunities for Black Americans to attain a modicum of economic stability, although they affected women as well as men. The decline in labor-intensive manufacturing during the 1980s greatly reduced stable, blue-collar employment for African Americans, whose unemployment rates even in periods of growth were consistently double those of whites. The disproportionate loss of manufacturing jobs that provided livable wages for many working-class Blacks in industrial cities made a college education urgently necessary for eligibility for more stable and higher-earning white-collar jobs. This devastating loss of jobs for Blacks in urban areas was compounded by a mounting war on the Black poor that took the form of mass incarceration. As a political project of the carceral state whose blueprints were drawn by the Nixon and Johnson administrations, mass incarceration directly responded to white hysteria over the Black Power movements and social unrest that arose in American cities during the 1960s and 1970s. In an even harder blow to the Black poor and working class, mass incarceration married this broader economic downturn and the contraction of the social safety net with targeted antiradical surveillance, an expanded criminal code, and longer sentences for nonviolent offenses.[81]

The rhetoric of Black male crisis could have been framed as one gendered outcome of the state's race and class warfare against Black political movements and the Black urban poor, but its framers' insis-

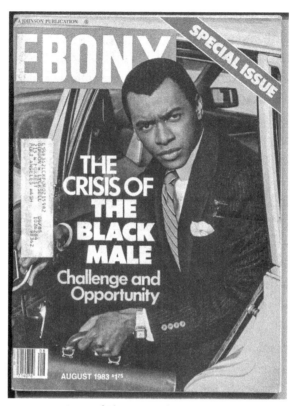

FIGURE 6. Cover of *Ebony* magazine, August 1983.

tence that Black men were under siege and falling behind everyone
else—including Black women—swiftly captured public imagination.
The crisis was readily absorbed into Black cultural ideologies and
changed the ways African Americans thought about an entire generation of Black males.

The panicked outlook in the popular discourse is perfectly exemplified in a 1983 special issue of *Ebony* magazine with a striking
typeface declaring "The Crisis of the Black Male: Challenges and
Opportunity" and featuring the stern and piercing eyes of a young
Black man in a dark business suit emerging from a yellow taxicab
holding his briefcase.[82] The visual language of the power-suited cor-

porate executive was no mistake—it expropriated any attention to-ward the realities of the crisis as an assault on the Black urban poor and refocused the lens on Black male professionals as its most urgent victims. In this messaging, the everyday humiliations suffered by clean-cut Black men in suits who can't hail a taxicab in New York City are at least comparable to (if not more important than) whatever else was happening to Black people under the Reaganomics-sponsored class warfare of the 1980s. In the heyday of print glossies, the Black-owned and operated *Ebony* reigned as the equivalent of *Time* or *Life* magazine among African American households. With its patchwork spreads highlighting news, business, entertainment, culture, politics, and Black intellectual thought, *Ebony* both interpreted and set Black America's agenda. Morehouse alumni played a direct role in propagandizing this repackaging of the crisis. The publication's editor in chief was none other than alumnus Lerone Bennett Jr., who praised Benjamin Mays for his mission of inculcating and defending masculinity.[83] Bennett's editorial introduction to the special issue underscores the plight of Black men. "The Black male is at a crossroads in his relations with American society, in his relations with Black women, and in his relations with himself," he said in his full-page screed. "He has always lived on the knife edge of danger, and the institutions of American society have been systemically and mercilessly manipulated to keep him down."[84]

Bennett went on to pick out a set of ominous indicators of Black men's employment, education, and health to buttress his claims. He pointed to "dismal statistics" of a "criminally high rate" on unemployment for Black men as proof that they were losing ground to white men, white women, and to Black women in both colleges and their careers (he included a statistic that "Black female-male ratio at some colleges is three, four and five to one"). He then cherry-picked other indexes such as mortality to argue that Black men have a higher adjusted death rate than any other group.[85] Tacitly echoing Moynihan, he framed the crisis of Black men as indirectly injurious to Black women, while ignoring the direct impact of state economic warfare on Black women: "Black women in particular have expressed the view that Black males are scarce and getting scarcer. That view, unfortunately, is not entirely incorrect. The Black sex ratio—the number of Black males per 100 females—has been declining since at least 1910 and was reported at a low of 89.7 in 1981. In the crucial marriage and childbearing ages of 25-44, the sex ratio is only 85.7. Sociologist Robert Staples says that if you exclude married men, imprisoned men and homosexuals, there is only one acceptable Black male for every five unmarried Black women."[86]

Finally, Bennett pointed to the social conditions that had placed Black men in this alleged predicament and called for "immediate social action and additional support systems for young Black males." The statistics, he proclaimed, were not reflections of Black masculinity "but of a society which is, in some respects, an organized conspiracy against Black masculinity."[87] Bennett joined a chorus of voices in sounding the alarm about Black masculinity at a time when White officials were playing political football with hypercriminalized images of Black men. The manufactured hysteria over Black male "super-predators," echoed the Jim Crow myth of "the Black rapist" that had served as whites' specious rationale for lynching. It aroused public fears about Black youth and crime throughout the George H. W. Bush and Clinton administrations with remnants loudly resounding still today.[88] In the 1980s and 1990s, a chorus of Black voices—including intellectuals, clergy, and organizational leaders—propagated this panicked rhetoric and stigmatizing image to both academic and popular audiences. Discussions of Black men and masculinity were permeated by an almost axiomatic emphasis on crime and incarceration, the product of a toxic mix of urban poverty, educational underachievement, unemployment, and social marginalization—all with a differentially severe impact on Black males.[89]

The perception of some of these issues was undoubtedly based on material realities. The soaring incarceration rates for poor urban Black men belied the court-ordered desegregation and civil rights legislation of only decades before. Yet facts about the dismal situation of Black men that needed no exaggeration were often misrepresented and arranged to overwhelm public concern with the damaging rhetoric of the crisis. The mistaken idea that there were more Black men in prison than in college, for example, has been debunked.[90] Over half a million more Black men were in college than were incarcerated in 2014. The murky prediction that one in three Black males will be imprisoned in his lifetime has been repeated profusely by advocates for Black boys.[91] Yet, in fact, this projection was based on a Bureau of Justice Statistics study conducted by two white male researchers who actually claimed that one in *four* Black men had a chance of imprisonment in his lifetime, and that figure applied exclusively to males born in 2001 and was based on a model of what would happen if 1991 crime rates held steady throughout their lives. Black men born in 2001, at the time of this publication are now around twenty-one years old, and neither the crime rate nor their rate of incarceration is consistent with the model's predictions.[92]

Furthermore, while it is inarguable that Black men have been incarcerated at rates far exceeding those of their white counterparts, the gendering of the mass incarceration narrative has often ignored the fact that the war on crime was equally injurious to Black women. Black women who remained in targeted Black communities contended with a lack of fair and affordable housing and forced displacement.[93] The Clinton administration's welfare reform legislation converted entitlements into "workfare," relegating the mothers of young children to low-wage, part-time, dead-end, and unstable jobs without health insurance or affordable childcare. A wave of crack cocaine addiction was neglected by underfunded public health services, while a medically unfounded panic about "crack babies" led to the forced legal separation of numerous Black newborns from their mothers. Black women suffered along with Black men as the state criminalized their poverty-induced problems. In couching the mass incarceration narrative of what it did to manhood, much of the public rhetoric in Black communities obscured the scope of the war on drugs as an all-out assault on the Black poor.

Bennett's editorial points to another source of urgency in the rhetorical construction of Black male crisis. While the post–civil rights generation of Black men faced a newly enhanced and draconian carceral state, the timing and urgency of the crisis rhetoric can be understood as a confluence of mass incarceration with another "epidemic" perceived by Black male leadership: the social and economic advancement of Black women. Bennett posits the crisis as coming on the heels of women's liberation movements, and his claim that "the Black male is on the list of endangered species"[94] was not based on any evidence that Black men were falling behind their fathers or that racial disparities with white men were widening. The younger generation is in crisis, Bennett leaves readers to presume, because they are losing ground to Black women. By positioning a zero-sum game between the advancement of Black women and that of Black men (as if Black women's gains came at Black men's expense) Bennett implies that the "organized conspiracy" against Black men may be—at best—beneficial exclusively to Black women at the expense of Black gender relations and was at worst an outcome of their collusion with white racism.

The urgent tone about Black men's condition that permeates much of the public messaging of Black male crisis has been described by legal scholar Paul Butler as the phenomenon of *Black male exceptionalism*.[95] Butler's work bedrocks much of the analytical framing of this book, as he argued that Black male exceptionalism is a way of thinking about Black men and boys as though they, by any measure of education, employment, health, or opportunity, fare worse than any other group. Black male exceptionalism, Butler argues, converts intersectionality into expressly antifeminist and male-serving aims, and shapes the discourses that appeal to interventions in Black communities by not only prioritizing that community resources tend to the problems disproportionately affecting Black men, but also by misrepresenting issues, statistics, and epidemics that affect the race overall as affecting Black males exclusively. He makes clear that Black male exceptionalism does more than appropriately acknowledge that racial discrimination may take gendered forms that effect Black men and boys differently than women and girls. Rather, the issue lies in how Black male exceptionalism prioritizes racial justice interventions on behalf of Black males and evaluates racial injustices based on the extent to which they affect Black males. Effectively, this form of exceptionalism, of which Bennett was one of the loudest public voices, validates the necessity of gender discrimination against Black women and girls when drumming up the "endangerment" of Black males. Butler, for example, explains that "statistics about African American males are used to support the necessity of special interventions for Black men, with no description of what the corresponding data is for Black women," and that the *Ebony* letter by Bennett used "data about African Americans that includes both men and women [to] support the case for special interventions for African American men."[96]

Like many of his contemporaries, Bennett relied heavily on the views of Robert Staples, the sociologist and vocal antifeminist whose 1982 *Black Masculinity* proclaimed and analyzed the crisis.[97] Staples's argument quickly disseminated throughout popular discourse. He acknowledged that institutional racism and social environments shaped by poverty had impaired Black men's ability to fulfil normative masculine roles as breadwinners and heads of households. Negative stereotypes had reduced Black men to "being socially castrated, insecure in their male identity, and lacking in positive self-concept." The racial subordination of Black men, he claimed, "cancelled out their advantages as males.... Unlike white males, they have few privileges in this society except vis-à-vis black women, and that advantage is being eroded by black women who have a competitive edge over some black males for certain jobs."

Much of the evidence Staples cited, however, unintentionally belied the stereotype of the emasculating Black matriarch by reporting that few Black women out-earned their husbands; indeed, 85 percent of low-income husbands out-earned their wives.[98] The jobs for which Black women were favored over Black men referred to subordinate nonmanual positions that are stereotypically feminine and low paid. Bennett's interpretation of the crisis involved an empirically unfounded assumption: that striving Black women were "getting ahead" of their male counterparts by pushing them down, or at least aside. Black male leaders' preoccupation with the perceived crisis of Black masculinity is primarily the result of elite Black men projecting their class-gender anxieties onto a period when a growing minority of educated Black women were making their largest strides ever into the middle class.

One of the manifold legacies of this crisis mentality is the current public focus of racial issues such as police brutality on visibly gender-conforming men.[99] In the thirty-five-plus years since the publication of the special issue of *Ebony*, the ideology of a Black male crisis has been preserved and absorbed by a wide range of public and private institutions, from the Department of Justice and the White House to higher education and K–12 charter schools designed for Black boys.[100] Because Black male elites projected their class and gender anxieties onto the rest of the race, the institutions such as HBCUs that they dominated took up the charge of addressing the crisis they declared. Efforts to solve the Black male crisis have focused on the barriers that keep Black men from advancing into the middle class and into environments where they can fulfill conventional—although now somewhat outdated and stereotypical—"masculine roles." Deindustrialization increased the demand for technical, managerial, and professional employees and made college degrees the price of entry into the middle class. Failing to secure the path to college and subsequent professional-managerial employment was akin to failing masculinity.

While the demand for college enrollment among African Americans overall is at an all-time high, the problems for Black males begin in the pipeline. US public high schools graduate only 52 percent of Black boys in four years, compared to 78 percent of white boys. In thirty-eight states and the District of Columbia, Black males have the lowest graduation rate of any group.[101] Consequently, US colleges—Morehouse among them—are facing small pools of academically high-performing Black male applicants. Currently there is no college or university in the United States, including both HBCUs and historically and predominately white institutions, that does not have a Black male "problem" regarding disproportionately low enrollment and retention. Black male college completion rates are the lowest of all groups in US higher education.[102] Only 6 percent of Black men age twenty to twenty-four have a two- or four-year college degree, while another 37 percent have some postsecondary education. African American males are overrepresented among the lowest performing college students, those who are forced to withdraw, and those who report negative college experiences.[103]

These statistics, while alarming, do not fully explain the gendered anxiety derived from these findings. For the first time since the 1970s, Black males are being out-enrolled in colleges and universities by their female peers. Black men made up 55 percent of Black undergraduates in 1955. Between 1976 and 2000, that figure shifted dramatically, not because of any decline in Black male enrollment, but because of a sharp increase in Black female enrollment. While completion rates and the proportion of Black male high school graduates who enroll in college are lagging compared to whites, Black male college enrollment has doubled since the 1970s. Ironically, as the crisis discourse escalated between 1980 and 1990, Black male enrollment rose by 7 percent.[104] The gender gap in higher education remains smaller among African Americans than the national average and may reflect gender trends among colleges and universities overall.[105] Currently, Black women earn nearly two-thirds of all bachelor's degrees awarded to African Americans and account for almost as large a proportion for all Black enrollments.[106] Yet, their return on their college investment is among the lowest. College educated Black women are far less likely than both Black men and white women to go into higher paying fields like engineering and management, and education does not shield them from racial gaps in pay and wealth.[107]

A growing number of qualitative researchers have sought to understand the lived experiences of Black male collegians.[108] These scholars have provided a context for treating gender and masculinity as definitive variables in Black men's college experiences. Research on variations of class, gender, and sexuality among Black male collegians is notably absent. While a few studies have examined Black college men's conceptions of masculinity, cultural research on Black masculinity has typically focused on boys or compared Black men to white men. The small body of work that is available, however, has shown that Black male experiences in college differ widely, depending on the type of institution they attend; whether the racial composition of the student body is congruent with their K–12 background; whether they are a student athlete or attend a university with high-profile Black male athletes; and whether they feel supported by their institution and peer groups.[109]

Despite being the nation's largest annual producer of Black male baccalaureates, Morehouse has serious struggles with its students. The economic setbacks felt by many middle-income Black households as a result of the Great Recession have increased Black enrollment in for-profit colleges and lowered completion rates.[110] While Morehouse graduates still fare better than those of many other HBCUs, its four-year completion rate is an alarmingly low 40 percent. Increasingly, Morehouse finds itself losing high-performing applicants to top-tier predominantly white institutions (PWIs); only a third of its accepted applicants it enrolled in 2012, compared to nearly half of applicants in 2008.[111]

The challenges Morehouse faces are tethered to the larger context of Black males in higher education, but the college's institutional culture contributes as much to larger ideologies about the crisis as it is structurally affected by some of its realities. Since 2002, the college's recruitment materials have employed the imagery of high achieving Black boys' isolation, including an extensive description of "the Morehouse Mystique," which promises that "ignored, stereotyped or marginalized" young men will find a home at Morehouse as "the heart, soul, and hope of a community…where you are not alone."[112] Imagining Black manhood simultaneously as a vehicle of racial uplift and a population at risk, with dangerous consequences not only for Black men but also for the future of the race, shapes the institution's mission and how men understand the mission.

This shift in the focus of racial uplift ideology may seem like an about-face. Whereas middle-class Black men were once championed for rescuing the race from the peril of white assaults, they have now been tasked with fixing the "problem" of Black masculinity from within the race. This prescription, however, is consistent with historical patterns. During periods when the race is declared in crisis—whether that be the violent repression that white supremacists meted out to freed people in the aftermath of Reconstruction or the war on drugs of the post–civil rights era—the cultural responses from the Black middle class have been disconcertingly similar: in times of greatest unrest, racial anxieties are projected onto gender and sexuality. The color line, which Du Bois pronounced to be "the problem of the twentieth century," may be the problem of the twenty-first century that stands between white oppression and Black liberation, but within the race, respectability-infused meanings of manhood and womanhood have long been at the core of the uplift strategy that Black elites communicate to the Black masses.

2   *Branding the Man*

A flurry of national and international headlines followed the college's April 2019 announcement of a new transgender student admissions policy. Only a year prior, neighboring all-women's Spelman College had announced its own trans admissions policy that progressively committed to protecting the rights and continued education of students who transition to men during their matriculation. Naturally, attention swiftly turned to Morehouse, the last of the three single-sex Black colleges without a proposed action on trans applicants. After a fifteen-month task force surveyed alumni (the official release does not mention whether trans students or advocacy groups were consulted), the decision to admit born females who identified as men upon application received celebratory press across outlets such as the *New York Times*, *Forbes*, and the *Guardian*. At a cursory glance, it seemed as though a college long reputed to be hostile toward queer and nonbinary students had evolved on one of the most pressing civil rights issues of the day.[1] A closer look, however, reveals why trans advocacy groups swiftly responded that it "needs work": the policy underhandedly doubled down on gender conformity.[2]

> In furtherance of our mission, tradition, and values as a men's college, and in recognition of our changing world and evolving

understanding of gender identity, Morehouse will now consider for admission applicants who live and self-identify as men, regardless of the sex assigned to them at birth. Women will not be eligible for admission at Morehouse.

We will also continue to use gendered language that reflects our identity as a men's college.

The statement went on to specifically address students who "transition while enrolled," meaning those who are born male and whose gender identity shifts during their college years—a distinct category from students who are born female and already identify as men on applying. As the policy stated:

Once admitted, every student will receive the individualized support that is an essential part of the Morehouse experience. However, all students are expected to continue to self-identify as men throughout their matriculation at Morehouse. If, during a student's time at Morehouse, a student transitions from a man to a woman, that student will no longer be eligible to matriculate at Morehouse.[3]

In defending the use of "gendered language," the statement's framers undermined their claims to providing student support. Their insistence that they reserved the right to gender all students as men through the widespread use of institutional literature, rituals, and curriculum disregards individual students' gender identities or preferred pronouns. They expounded:

Morehouse will continue to use masculine pronouns, the language of brotherhood, and other gendered language that reflects its mission as an institution designed to develop men with disciplined minds who will lead lives of leadership and service.

Like so many elements of Morehouse's institutional culture, the rhetoric of the projected policy is belied by its actionable substance. At the time this book was published, trans men (those who transition from being born female to identifying as men) have been almost entirely absent from the college's applicant pool. Essentially, the policy gained public accolades for addressing a nonexistent or not-yet-existent issue.[4] Those who comprise nearly all of Morehouse's small number of trans and nonbinary students are femme (males who may express themselves as highly feminine, wear makeup, heels, and form-fitting clothing while deemphasizing some or all masculine features), woman-identified, and gender nonconforming males (those whose gender varies beyond conventional masculinity or femininity and who may wear makeup and heels, or not, while wearing facial hair and barbered haircuts, or not). The gender fluidity and/or transition of these students often begins or accelerates during their formative young adult years in college. Instead of addressing the trans students toward whom Morehouse has a long-established history of violence and exclusion, the policy shores up its right to remove them and erase their visibility on campus. More alarmingly, these official statements reinforced the compulsory gender conformity to which queer students had long objected. As education scholars Steve D. Mobley and Jennifer Johnson note, the policy openly targeted both "women's garb" and attire stereotypically (and wrongly) associated with street life and "thugs," thus equating gender nonconformity with criminality and made unmistakable that students who fall outside expectations of both gender and class have no place at Morehouse.[5] Anthropologist Jafari Allen, an openly gay former student who left in the 1980s, described the institution's attitude toward queerness as "'the perfect storm' of homophobia—racial and class anxieties of 'exceptional Negroes,' masculine gender trouble, class conflict and fundamentalist religious baggage (or as some might say, 'heritage' or 'tradition')."[6] Transphobia looked to be the new frontier in the college's long-drawn-out assaults on student queerness, and one that, due to its single sex status, could be openly sewn into official policies instead of tucked into campus customs and hidden curricula. For administrators, the policy was a stubborn declaration that students might change and change the world along with them, but the college's beliefs and instructions about manliness would remain fixed.

One of the most unsettling clauses in the policy pertains to trans women who wish to continue at Morehouse, even though the policy calls for their expulsion:

> Exemptions from this rule may be granted by a three-person committee appointed by the President after a written appeal is submitted by the student. If the student disagrees with the committee's decision, the student may make a final appeal to the President of Morehouse.

In this clause, total discretion over the continued enrollment of students undergoing a highly nuanced emotional, physiological, social, and legal process is granted to administrators who have no training in LGBTQIA issues.[7]

Like so many in my Spelman-Morehouse alumni community, I learned about Morehouse's policy via news coverage and internet feed traffic from my classmates. It was surprising to see a vocal (albeit very small) minority of my Morehouse siblings celebrating the decision. One friend remarked that it was a step toward the twenty-first century for the college and that they supported their queer classmates. Another friend, who seemed exasperated by the transphobic backlash he was witnessing from the larger Morehouse alumni community, repeatedly stressed that the policy was making concessions for what would amount to only a handful of trans students, as if to suggest that the transphobic uproar was disproportionate to the small number of students the college would actually need to accommodate to be trans inclusive. For myself, though, I couldn't help but think that once again Morehouse was taking a step back as it simultaneously took a step forward. The policy was a Pyrrhic victory for queer students and their allies that seemed to play both sides of acknowledging trans students and yet doubled down on what the college felt was its right to not change any of its culture to recognize and protect them. What soured me most was the part of the policy that mandated trans students "plead their case" before the college's president. It cruelly mirrored another item circulating the news cycle at the time that I found equally unjust: the clemency hearings for felon voter reinstatement in Florida in which hundreds of Black people, mostly men, had to plea for their civil rights before then governor Rick Scott, who sat before them as both their judge and jury while single-handedly denying their appeals one after another.[8] Surely my Morehouse brothers could articulate why subjecting a disempowered marginalized population's rights to the subjective judgment of those in power who had historically kept them disenfranchised was unjust. At the most visceral level, it affronted both my senses of logic and justice that administrators and the majority of alumni would not admit the parallels between that form of racism and what they were doing within the race to Black trans and nonbinary students.

All schools have a hidden cultural curriculum, which conveys the institution's unwritten, unofficial, and often unintended values to students through set cultural expectations. With their trans policy, however, Morehouse administrators confirmed a larger point about many of our existing approaches to Black male schooling. Institutions that are modeled on Black male success programs share an almost universal quality of supplanting the primary curriculum (which for most schools is academic) with a cultural curriculum of gender instructions. Trans students prove that normative adherence to manhood at Morehouse holds equal footing with academic instruction because manhood can be *failed*.[9] Those who read the headlines may mistake the policy as a contemporary convention necessitated by a newfangled issue that the college faces from a wind of change across higher education. The story of how manhood emerged as a primary curriculum, however, is clearly visible within the narratives of men who walked these grounds decades before. Their stories unveil how beliefs about "good" Black men are staked in the bodies, behaviors, and minds of students whose every interaction is judged against the "Morehouse Brand" of racialized and gendered success.

If we have arrived at a point where young Black males are at once upheld as saviors of the race and feared as its nemesis, how does that goal look in action when it must be operationalized into all of the components that make up daily life on a college campus? Stamped with the heavy responsibility of defying the odds and righting the wrongs afflicting their demographic, this chapter shows how these men navigate a cultural curriculum that molds them into a single imagined ideal of race and gender propriety. These are not, as conventional sociological wisdom would have us believe, men who are simply held to white masculine standards and deemed defective. Morehouse is a site where racialization uses gender as a cultural vehicle to infuse masculine standards into meanings of Blackness by which many and most variations of Black masculinity will come up short in comparison. In the interplay between the individual and the institution, men at Morehouse receive unmistakably gendered messages about racial advancement. These expectations are not met organically but, rather, are groomed through a rigid structure that turns the raw material of boys into the manufactured product of men.

In my years of talking to Morehouse men about their experiences, ultimately I have come to understand that this grooming process occurs primarily in two ways that I present in this chapter. First, I examine how men understand the college's expectations by exploring an idea they each discussed explicitly: the Morehouse brand and the accompanying Morehouse Man. The brand offers more than a set of guidelines about how to comport oneself on campus. It is emblematic of ideals of Black masculinity writ large and a measuring stick by which men compare themselves with others. Second, I look at how men experience the process of *being* branded. Alumni share their memories, frustrations, appreciations, and new understandings of fraternity-like hazing rituals, rules that resemble those of boarding schools, and a system of strict edicts and oversights. As adults reflecting on their formative years, these men make sense of the extent to which branding did and did not work on them, or *for* them. As the variation in their resources, backgrounds, and identities dictates how they navigate the process, men ironically experience being made the same although quite differently. The college's tacit contradictions in branding such a varied group of men speaks just as loudly as anything it says openly about its curriculum of manhood.

"My First American Experience"

Throughout its history, the lore of the Atlanta University Center has been described on oasis-like terms—a thriving space for Black thought beyond the reach of the blows of injustices suffered from the white world beyond its boundaries. James Weldon Johnson, the famed activist, poet, novelist, and lyricist and Atlanta University alumnus,[10] called the hub of HBCUs "a spot fresh and beautiful, a rest for the eyes from what surrounded it, a green island in a dull red sea."[11] Over half a century later, that sentiment of Black oasis lingered for the men with whom I spoke. "It was like a movie. It was like *A Different World*," Horace, a Detroit native, remembered, referring to the pioneering 1990s *Cosby Show* spinoff about lively campus life at a fictitious historically Black college based loosely on a mashup of

Spelman, Morehouse, and Howard University. Even as a graduate of a large predominantly Black high school and product of nearly all-Black neighborhoods, Horace felt the electricity of being engulfed in an epicenter for Black young people with backgrounds and interests he never imagined his peers having.

For a high-achieving Black male in a typical American high school, being able to associate with a variety of like-minded young Black male adults is a rare experience. Arriving at Morehouse offered Horace and others an opportunity to, for the first time, assess the differences and compatibilities between themselves and their peers and organically sort through choices in potential friends as well as rivals. In controlling for the race and gender markers that otherwise had guided the default formation of high school friendships, Morehouse provided revelation about the range of possibilities for being a Black man. Horace described his high school as being filled with plenty of academically advanced Black males with similar neighborhood backgrounds, but he found the array of students at Morehouse to be markedly different: "While everyone [at Morehouse] is Black, there's so many different perspectives on being Black. Like there are people who have done things that I just never…I had never been to Martha's Vineyard. Hell, I didn't even know what Martha's Vineyard was. There were kids who went to Martha's Vineyard every summer. Like there are kids who do camps every summer. I didn't do that growing up. So being able to hear them talk about it and the things they'd done…your sense of the world evolves."

Milt and Monk were particularly struck by the cultural diversity among Black men from across the United States and beyond. Milt, a midwesterner who followed the path of his father and uncles to Morehouse, was nonetheless surprised when it was his turn to be immersed in the spectrum of differences that defied his previously narrow expectations for how Black men acted and what interested them. "[I grew up] the stock African American male character," Milt began. "[I] wore jeans a certain way, listened to a certain kind of music, and wanted to drive a certain kind of car, [wore] sagging pants.... So the idea that you met a Black guy who was a rocker and wanted to skateboard everywhere was a new phenomenon." He ended by telling me how that first semester "opened my eyes to diversity within African American men."

Similarly, Monk, who described his racially diverse and socially liberal Californian upbringing as considerably different from most of his classmates' backgrounds, found an exciting challenge in seeking common ground with other students who were so varied that he couldn't rely on stereotypical assumptions about young Black male interests when talking to them. He seemed almost tickled when remembering the vastly unexpected hobbies and interests of his peers. "One of my boys liked horseback riding, one guy played soccer, one of my best friends was a native of Nigeria, another one's from a small town in Georgia," he laughed, while also sounding proud that the experience challenged his comfort zone and forced a form of substantial engagement beyond activities-oriented socializing. "I was like, we have these different socioeconomic cultures.... So I had to learn how to relate to men differently outside of just basketball and skin color, right?"

Fitzgerald, another Californian who had grown up in a nearly all-Black working-class suburb of Los Angeles, was aware of well-heeled Black families as well as those who struggled far more than his, but Morehouse was the first place he experienced a meeting ground for these wide-ranging class backgrounds. He made one of the most profound comments on the meanings of diversity. "My roommate was a psychology major, he was fourth- or third-generation college. [I] never experienced Black people [like] that," he began. So that I understood what a stark contrast he experienced in the backgrounds of his college friends, Fitzgerald pressed on me that "I had a friend whose mother was a crackhead. I had a friend, my best friend, whose father was a judge in North Carolina. Things I never experienced before."

Many of my fellow HBCU alumni will tell you that one of the most modal criticisms from non-HBCU alumni we heard when making our college choice was something to the effect of *Black colleges don't prepare students for the real world where they will have to encounter and negotiate diversity.* What I experienced, and what was consistently echoed across the interviews, repudiates that criticism. Black colleges are where many Black people learn how vastly diverse Blackness is. If the grossly disproportionate white and class insular spaces of the Ivy League can prepare elites for the world, then Horace's praise for how Morehouse widened his eyes should force critics of HBCUs to reconsider why Black college experiences are so often dismissed as monolithic. "It was nice to have diversity within Morehouse even though we were all Black males," Fitzgerald continued to chime. In fact, he credited the environment's racial homogeneity for allowing him to more meaningfully appreciate the differences among his classmates and to understand himself in a space where he was relieved from having his own experience swallowed by assumptions about his racial difference. He said pointedly: "You really learn diversity when you take off color. I was able to see differences between Black people and then apply those to differences between white people. An all-Black environment removes the burden of being a representative Black person. You come face-to-face with who you are at your core. You can collaborate and compete with others who are also judged by their merits. For me, Morehouse was my first American experience."

The process of racialization that African Americans create for themselves within homogenously Black spaces amplifies parts of their identities that might be muted in spaces where racism consumes all their attention and dictates the attention paid to them. There is an irony to Fitzgerald's insight: HBCUs were created in response to white America's educational exclusion, and yet Morehouse permitted him, for the first time in his life, to feel a sense of individualism and meritocracy otherwise reserved for whites. Fitzgerald also captured a grossly understated feature that racially veiled Black spaces provide for Black racialization. It was through witnessing a vast diversity of Black life that he understood white people's differences beyond his limited and one-dimensional childhood interactions with them. Understanding nuances of class, region, and ethnicity within whites is undoubtedly crucial for successfully navigating the American mainstream. Without being immersed in a richly diverse Black space, he might have continued to apply a one-dimensional lens to a world beyond the veil well into young adulthood.

In so many of our conversations, men brought up revelations about their experiences that felt as though we were reliving the past together. This was the case with their awareness about how vast differences in financial support among their classmates dictated many of the differences they observed among their friends. I came to the AUC comfortably middle class, if not a bit more comfortable than middle-class friends whose parents seemed to be shorter than mine on wealth and were determined to scrape ends together for their tuitions. The splash of cold water to my face compounded class with transitioning regionally from sleepy rural-adjacent Kentucky to the fast-paced teen life of friends from posh suburbs whose upper-middle-class signifiers were expressed through the amenities brought within reach by major metropolitan areas (I did not know what a commuter rail was or that teenagers hung out downtown without their parents. I had almost no point of reference for retailers exclusive to large cities like Tiffany jewelers or Neiman Marcus). Unlike remote campuses where student activities are almost entirely provided by student services, socializing on an urban campus requires spending money, and city life makes it obvious from nearly day one which students do and do not have disposable cash. Ornette, whose Bronx childhood had also not been marked by any financial strains, reminded me how it can be gobsmacking to realize just how vastly different a lifestyle can be afforded by affluent Black college kids who approached luxuries in the city of Atlanta much the way one might expect overindulged white students at UCLA or USC approached the lifestyle of Brentwood and Beverly Hills.

I let out a perhaps too eagerly audible affirmation when Ornette leaned into the self-consciousness he felt when realizing he simply couldn't afford to hang out with his wealthier classmates whose tastes in restaurants, night life, and cars neglected all stereotypes of the broke college student. Looking back on my own memories, I'd say many of even the flushest students were trying to one-up and impress each other, and that competition weighed on men in particular. For example, transportation to and from off-campus events often fell on "the boys" and their cars (thus securing a prominent place in any friend-group for guys with large capacity SUVs). The way I remember it, off-campus house parties and the liquor they provided were nearly always paid for and organized by "the boys," which bent the gender-power dynamic of our social lives and the popularity pecking order toward those men who dictated the economics of the social scene. The guys in my friend group sometimes picked up or split the bill for mixed-gender group dinners and bar tabs, perhaps to impress us women or because they felt grown-up by imitating their parents. But more likely it doubled as a subtle test in those early semesters to see which men in our group were equally yoked financially. I wouldn't say that the wealthiest students at Spelman and Morehouse are automatically the most popular. I would say that it is very hard to be unpopular if you are wealthy.

Even low-income and working-class respondents had a preexisting vague notion that such moneyed Black families existed from television shows like *The Fresh Prince of Bel Air*, but living among the sons of these families in an up-close residential atmosphere un-

unfamiliar to other African Americans beyond a certain milieu, but in other contexts, Black Americans can often speak a shared language of class markers that is completely imperceptible to whites. Racialized modes of class distinction bring nuanced and Black-specific meanings to interactions, language, and observable traits that would not be read the same way by anyone who hasn't substantially interacted with Black institutions.

Overall, respondents easily read classmates "who had money" (as Ornette labeled them) via unsurprising visual cues, such as those who lived in expensive apartments or always had money for shopping or nightlife. However, for students like Waller, who grew up in an often unstable single-mother household, Black class differences were detectable even in family structures. "One of the things I found out was how many people had two-parent households," he chuckled in recalling his earliest days (throughout our interview, he spliced his phrases with light-hearted chuckles that didn't read as nervous because I had known him for years). "People would have folks come and move them in [to the dorms] and give them all this stuff...and I was like 'wow! You know your father?' Like I never really knew my father that well."

Observations like this capture the racially specific cultural capital that African Americans both learn and sense. "I don't know if that's a class difference," Waller contemplated, chuckling again, this time as though weighing his thought half-jokingly; "that's definitely, like, a family difference." Back home in Detroit, Waller's social environment was split into two worlds. His mother struggled with addiction, and his family, like their neighbors, teetered on the edge of poverty. At the elite parochial boy's academy he attended, however, his schoolmates included sons of Detroit's most well-to-do two-parent white and Black families. Becoming racialized in a homogenously Black space, however, tuned his recognition of unspoken and nuanced race-specific cultural markers of class that went beyond the stark economic differences that were obvious in his prep school.

Race also shifts demographic class categories for African Americans when compared to whites. Sociology's most cited scholars on what class means in the lives of African Americans stress that Black class categories have always been inflected by racial caste, and thus can be even harder to distinguish on economic terms alone, particularly compared to their white counterparts.[13] Given that Black families inherit disadvantages with regard to wealth and occupation, social and cultural capital often make up the difference in significant material distinctions. With these nuanced noneconomic markers in consideration, I constructed class categories for the thirty-two men I interviewed based on the ways they described their own backgrounds and frequently talked about themselves and their parents' resources and occupations in comparison to their childhood peers.

Fourteen of the men were born to families in which both parents (or sometimes one) were white-collar professionals with baccalaureate or postgraduate degrees. These men were mostly products of predominantly white high schools and had been raised in either racially mixed or predominantly white suburbs.[14] Nine more of the men could be classified as lower middle class given that they had only one parent (typically their mothers) with at least some college education. Their fathers tended to be employed in blue collar or civil service jobs. These men were mostly products of predominantly Black neighborhoods where they attended majority-Black schools alongside the Black poor but saw their own households as distinguished by home ownership and dual income married parents. Men in this group often understood their home life as comparatively stable, but on the periphery of neighbors who often fell below the poverty line. "My family was definitely a little more well-off than other families" that were "very, very poor," Roy said, in a statement typical of men in this group.[15]

The remaining nine men commonly described their families as "making ends meet."[16] The children of these low-income families mostly attended school alongside their blue-collar counterparts in hypersegregated Black neighborhoods. Most came from single-female-headed households with mothers who had been briefly married or never married to their fathers. Their mothers were mostly educated beyond high school, for example, in licensed professional nursing programs or associate degree programs. It may be surprising to some that nearly half of the lowest income men's mothers were four-year college graduates. College education is no panacea for the economic consequences of gendered racism for Black mothers. But for these men, educated mothers were a resource that made the difference (compared to many of their low-income schoolmates) in terms of the expectation to attend college and the know-how of mothers who could navigate college preparedness even amid chronic financial struggles.

With such a diversity of students, then, how is it that freshmen begin this experience so differently and emerge as graduates with astounding similarities across the ways they speak about, think about, and embody Black manhood? Existing ethnographic approaches to Black men's mobility tend to explore the pathways from where men start (typically in the Black urban poor) and follow the ways their lives either repeat the cycle of poverty or are able to escape it. Understanding how men experience matriculation at Morehouse requires us to reverse this approach. Morehouse allows us to see a process of making-men from students who begin at vastly different origin points of class, culture, and understandings of Black manhood as they are all packaged and shipped to the same destination point: living out their adulthoods as *race men* in the middle-class cultural mainstream. The process of institutionally branding men uses mechanisms, structures, and racial and gender ideologies to gather up men from vastly different walks of life and levels of cultural capital and funnels them onto a path that conflates "good" Black manhood with white-collar professionalism and gender, conformity, and sexual propriety. "One of the things that makes Morehouse unique is that you are not just leaving with an education, you are leaving with a social contract," Ornette explained. Upward mobility carries a social obligation. Branding presents a curriculum of manhood and gender respectability as a vehicle to class aspiration and the achievement of the college's restrictively defined terms of successful race men.

Brand Compliance

Davis had a sense of humor about how little he challenged the college's expectations for conformity. In his life since graduation, he sees himself as ideally fitting the Morehouse mold and applying the lessons from his college days as life principles. "It's funny that I do PR now, because I learned brand management when I was at Morehouse," he began. "I live by three words," he explained. His tone filled with deliberation as though holding his own one-on-one press conference with me: "Manage the brand. [That] has to do with everything from how you look, how you carry yourself, the words that come out of your mouth, how you treat people. And it's reputation management. It's all about people's experiences with you. So what happened in the classroom, how do your professors think of you? Because we learned that if your professors think well of you, scholarships start to fall in your lap. Internships and interviews start to get on your calendar. These are the things you learn when you learn to manage the brand."

Similar to what I heard from nearly all the men, the description Davis provided of the "Morehouse Brand" captures a set of institutionalized cultural understandings about how men should behave, present, and comport themselves within the space of the college and, just as importantly, how they should think of themselves within this space as a rehearsal for how they will behave in view of the white masses in the future. For Percy, a proud Chicago South Sider from one of its poorest neighborhoods described the brand as "everywhere." He endorsed it as a model for success that ensures potential employers of his aptitude. "I'm an ambassador of the college," he told me. It's "a name brand. When you go out and you want a yard tool or instrument, you're going to get a John Deere. That's what you get; it's like you know I'm riding a Deere, like this is not going to fail me. And I feel like it's the same thing. When people hire a Morehouse man they're like, okay, we've got the right guy."

Far from a mere shibboleth, the brand is a screed about race men adapted to contemporary anxieties about young Black manhood. In an era of a perceived Black male crisis that has pervaded public rhetoric about everything from educational underachievement to "Black on Black" crime, Morehouse increasingly postures itself as an institution whose graduates overcome these troubling national statistics and counter the racist stereotypes du jour that are pinned on young Black masculinity. The experience of being branded within the walls of Morehouse is not removed from the Black male condition overall but is, in essence, a reaction to it tailored to the times. In the face of Black male underemployment and economic immobility, the brand promotes a hard-working professional whose personal ethos can skillfully navigate racial barriers. In times of widespread rhetoric about Black families' instability and the waywardness of Black boys resulting from the absence of male heads of household, the brand promotes an obligation to exemplify breadwinning Black husbands and fathers. At the age of panic about Black male criminality, the brand reassures Black communities that Morehouse men stay out of trouble.

As I listened to men describe the brand and the man, I was struck by the extent to which both were riddled with ironies and contradictions. The countless different ways that their classmates could be Black men that had awed them on arrival was supplanted, within their imaginations of the brand, by an idea that they now shared an exclusive way of doing manhood that made them similar by distinguishing them the Black male masses. In their minds, a branded man was representative of Black masculinity not because he was common, but, to the contrary, because he was exceptional. The Morehouse brand exemplified the signifiers of leadership, professionalism, intellectualism, responsibility, and propriety that were echoed throughout their ideas of what more Black men *should* be. A chorus of men voiced a similar sentiment that the brand is a set of cultural expectations. Their descriptions, however, tell us more than just how many times they discussed the brand. From this tapestry of their narrative excerpts we can see dimensions and layers to their understandings of what the college's expectations mean to them and for Black manhood:

> When you tell someone you're going to Morehouse the first thing they say is "so you're going to be a Morehouse man?" and you hear the expectations of a Morehouse man are very different. [Horace] | It's just the ethos of the school. If you are, at the time, a man of Morehouse, you are expected to conduct and comport yourself in a manner befitting those that have come before you. Point blank period. [Tadd] | A Morehouse Man is about achieving professional excellence.... It's just ingrained in the system. [Hubbard] | The perception is that Morehouse produces responsible Black men for the community.... That's what I associate with being a Morehouse man: someone who handles his business, someone you look upon with respect. [Chet] | You just thought of Morehouse men as the impressive prototype of what a Black intellectual should be.... It seems like my life was all about the expectations: the expectations of a Morehouse Man. [Coleman] | The Morehouse Man is—I hate to use the word mystique—it's an archetype, a blueprint for what a man should be

and what a man should do. A man should take care of business, his family, a man should be a leader and be respectful. He should be knowledgeable and able to speak. [Elvin]

I kept hearing words like *excellence, leader, success,* and *prototype* echoed throughout men's flowery descriptions of the brand. All of the respondents referenced the brand, and almost always within a context of describing the students branded by it. Nearly two-thirds defined the brand or the Morehouse Man in their own words, and the extent to which they felt groomed to aspire to the brand, or saw it as a prototype for manhood, was one of the most recurring topics across all of our conversations. What remained consistent across this imagery of professionalism, well-spoken-ness, and responsibility for leading the family and community were the mythic proportions of the idealized Morehouse Man.

These narratives consistently articulated in minute detail how the Morehouse Man walks, wears his head and facial hair, what he does for a living, and even his height, so I envisioned this image as analogous to the Marlboro Man: a cultural icon of an aspirant manliness that provides a gendered visual language for what the tobacco brand embodies. The iconography far exceeds what any Marlboro advertisement has ever claimed in words, or, given its compelling imagery of boot-strapped, dust-kicking cowboy swagger, even has to articulate. Like the classic Marlboro ads, the Morehouse brand is replete with its own slogans that men rattled off with ease. "You can always tell a Morehouse man but you can't tell him much," chirped Tadd and Elvin. "A Morehouse man always carries a pen," Clifford recalled proudly. Both men uttered these memorized maxims as though they were chanting along with an auditorium filled with their classmates.

The modal term I heard in descriptions of the brand was *expectation.* Like the Marlboro Man, the Morehouse Man is a fictionalized beau ideal of an unattainably flawless kind of race man. Even as real men may approximate some of his characteristics, the Morehouse Man is not really a means of men seeing themselves; rather, it is a measuring stick to which men assess their manhood by ceaselessly aspiring to the ideal but also perpetually coming up short of it. While real Morehouse graduates may approximate different traits of the *Man* and may even represent a close proxy for their classmates (several of Mingus's friends, for example, praised him this way), the brand and the Man are cultural carrot sticks dangled over the heads of students without ever actually coming within reach. "Real men try to emulate" the Morehouse Man, sighed Elvin, a Florida native from a highly educated family who had followed the footsteps of his future brother-in-law to Morehouse. "But they're constrained in many ways."

Because the Morehouse Man is a fantasy, the real-life rituals, structures, and institutional mechanisms that initiate new students can defy the kinds of logic that legitimate forms of academic assessment would typically follow. Student orientations at a typical university, for example, might stick to a script that says students need to know where they are going, be familiar with front-facing student services, and get acclimated to campus life so that they will be adjusted and academically successful once classes start. When manhood is the emphasized curriculum, however, what results is that Morehouse's New Student Orientation (NSO) rolls out a week-long series of rituals, institutional history lessons, and brotherly bonding experiences that resemble a fraternity initiation. Ramsey rattled off the demands that orientation makes of new students: "Upper classmen led the rituals and made [freshmen] learn history, dates, names, founders, the charter, the number of students in the first year," he moaned. Those maxims about the brand that men chanted are not merely picked up from classmates over the years but are an outcome of the drilling new students endure. "You get the propaganda from upperclassmen during orientation week," Elvin expounded.

If NSO has any semblance of academic preparation throughout its activities, this is not what men remembered about it. "We like to say Morehouse is a school you have to pledge to get into," Tadd kidded with more than a hint of pride behind the joke. "You get to be part of this fraternity, almost, of people who have come through here, so it felt like pretty big shoes to fill." The events of that week mark men for a lifetime. Certain NSO activities are highly secretive, and even after many years had passed some men were reluctant to disclose the more clandestine rituals to me. It was the only topic in our conversations about which they were admittedly withholding. "To this day I'm not supposed to say what happened," Ramsey confided. "It was like joining a cult or something. There was a night where we were up in the [campus] yard until like 3:00 a.m. and the old heads [upperclassmen who served as orientation leaders] were yelling. It was like a cult or a fraternity."

Rites of passage have increasingly grown in popularity as a component of Black Male Initiative (BMI) programs across community organizations and higher education.[17] Black Male Initiative programs envision brotherhood, mentorship, and the additional support resources that specifically address Black male needs. Ceremonies within these programs often marry these goals with (the somewhat Moynihanian) belief that Black male success, and efforts to keep them off streets, are suffering because there are not enough elder Black fathers available in our communities to guide young men and boys through maturation and manhood.[18] As NSO week commences with a family parting ceremony, new students, as Dexter recalled, are told to "look at your parents, tell them goodbye, we're going to give them back to you Morehouse Men." Curiously, in this claim to brand "men" out of the material of raw "boys," a notable contradiction emerges. NSO is not led by elder men but rather by peer student leaders, many of them upperclassmen who were initiates only the year prior. Rites of passage tend to have strong cultural connotations about reclaiming Afrocentric gender rituals, but NSO's practice of college-aged men initiating each other into manhood resembles the hypermasculine cultures that sociologist Michael Kimmel captures in *Guyland*, his study of the world of excessive drinking and reckless youth for mostly white men age eighteen to twenty-four.[19]

In the world of Kimmel's *guys*, that is, postadolescent young men, the era of deindustrialization and a widening wealth gap marks colleges as a holding ground for young men—"guys"—who in previous generations would have likely graduated from high school directly into the industrial labor force. Young men with class privilege (often found on college campuses) are suspended between childhood and the milestones of adulthood such as full-time work and marriage. In the spaces where "guys gather to be with each other" unchecked by women or outside authorities, extreme behaviors prevail as men perform violence and dominance for each other. Tadd, a physician who gave me a fairly buttoned-up impression of himself over the phone, described himself as a willing participant of NSO even as he watched the climate "getting out of hand." Through adult eyes, he reconsidered its appropriateness but was forthright in admitting he had no objections to these tactics as a student. "They're pulling your behind out of your dorm room. Line you up, line your brothers up, and running your behind around the college. Getting your chants down. Putting you in a tent," he described in a way that felt matter-of-fact and almost unemotional. It was consistent with what I gathered of his cerebral way of talking through his recollections. "It was all a ritual," he continued without missing a beat. "It's a complete indoctrination process. I was absolutely in step with it."

Chet remembered NSO in much the same way but was far more impassioned when recounting the intense energy that enveloped both the initiates and the initiated ritual leaders. He made his voice brasher when mimicking the bellowing of NSO leaders and recalled that "we had to march through campus holding each other while upperclassmen yelled *do you have your brother's back?!*" Yusef, who outright called NSO a hazing practice, confided to me that "it was just a little too much." While a handful of men like Mort (a transfer student) and Archie (a six foot six athletic recruit who transferred in halfway through his freshman year) found ways of getting out of NSO activities with few consequences, Ramsey felt coerced into taking part. "We didn't have the option not to participate in NSO. I didn't want to be out there at four in the morning with a million dudes. I don't think any of us would have tried it with the [upper-classmen] we were dealing with. To my knowledge, nobody tried that," Ramsey noted in reference to challenging the authority of NSO student leaders or objecting to participation.

Unbeknownst to those respondents who were tight-lipped about this experience, I participated in NSO in my senior year when I served in the capacity of Miss Maroon and White, the ceremonial campus queen who traditionally addresses the class of new students as part of the official orientation schedule and can accompany them to NSO's evening activities. There are only two feminine entities that have a ritualistic role in the Morehouse Mystique, and the first is the college itself, which is always referenced with feminine pro-nouns. The second entity is the college queen—the only nonstudent member of the Student Government Association and the only fe-male coed who has a designated function in campus rituals through-out the year.

I was quite fond of the freshman class I helped shepherd and re-member many of their faces and personalities distinctly. They were eager, adorably green, and very sweet to me. Part of embracing the fraternal culture of Morehouse involves being taught by upperclass-men that Miss Maroon and White is your "Queen," and most of the new admits addressed me as such and performed the expected level of awe in front of NSO leaders (pretending that Morehouse anoints royals just comes with the hype of the indoctrination, but I was also wearing a weighty rhinestone-crusted satin sash and three-inch crown to a lot of these events). In the abrupt departure of their mothers and near nonattendance by adult women in hands-on NSO activities, however, I felt not so much regal as I did maternal toward them, even if I was only four years their senior. When it was time for the infamous ritual of Spirit Night, the most secretive of all NSO rituals, I sat with the freshmen in the bleachers, curiously anticipating experiencing all of the camaraderie along with them. I also felt a bit protective because I could feel the intensity of the student leaders and the crowd rising under the cloak of a darkening nightfall and an even darker crowded gymnasium with no adult staff in sight. Before much of anything kicked off, an announcement from the floor called for me to be politely escorted out. Women are not allowed at Spirit Night. The shocking accounts from men like Sonny and Tadd alerted me as to what can happen when "guys" are left behind closed doors to exert dominance and force over each other in the name of manhood. I knew Sonny well before our interview, and his discomfort about recounting what he observed seemed eased by our closeness. He began his account by bringing me into the world of Spirit Nights of yore that I had missed:

> We're sitting there, we're all under the tent and it's really late or whatever, and this dude starts walking around and he's like "Brothers, I fear there is one amongst us! I have heard there is one amongst us!" and we were like "Who?! Where?! Where?!" ... Because then I'm nervous that it's me! I don't know what *it* is but I'm like *"I'm it!"* ... So they brought a brother up to the front and I remember specifically to this day, he had more an *S*-curl [chemically processed hair style] type of thing, and they started singing the song and it was like

"Jheri curls and shower caps, Morehouse men don't look like that!" [re-peating]…and in a matter of like thirty seconds the entire tent was chanting that, so then they pulled out some clippers! I don't know if they were battery operated, but they shaved that boy's curl!

Before the word became part of activist lexicon, Sonny was what I would consider a feminist ally. But like so many of the men, at eighteen he was still finding his voice as a newly arrived freshman who was witnessing things he felt were disturbing. Halfway through re-counting this story he began laughing hysterically, and I realized he was doing what perhaps many men do when admitting to being a by-stander in an act that intentionally humiliated someone: he created a bit of cognitive dissonance, in this case through laughter. When I asked about the young man's reaction, he explained that he didn't have much of a reaction. "If you're a seventeen-, eighteen-year-old kid and there's about six hundred or seven hundred people—because you also have upperclassmen there chanting some shit to you—you're not gonna have much of a reaction at all," he reasoned. "He was probably morbidly terrified!"

Almost any African American who lived during the mid-1980s and early 1990s remembers the Jheri curl, a popular permed hair treatment initially worn by entertainers like Michael Jackson, Rick James, and the notoriously defiant rap group NWA. It later became associated with both the rural and urban working-class and Black poor soon after the trend had waned. It was swiftly cast as racially backward and buffoonish, comparable to how whites might mock a mullet.[20] NSO leaders, who were well underway in the branding pro-cess, fluently spoke that nuanced class language in which noneco-nomic markers are recognized in racially specific contexts. Studies of boarding schools figuratively describe how the "raw material" of student boarders is similarly discarded in order to groom them into "soldiers for their class."[21] Upperclassmen instantly deemed such a class marker unacceptable in a culture of aspirant Black men and decided that it warranted a forced removal, which, done publicly, sent a clear message to others. As the chants grew to a fever pitch, the humiliating act bonded everyone but the victim.

That such extreme measures could be deemed necessary in the context of Spirit Night brings to mind how brand compliance is accomplished through varying the extents of control exerted by the institution. Erving Goffman, the foremost sociological theorist of institutionalization, observed that "total" institutions, that is, organizations that "cut off" their members from "the wider society for an appreciable period of time," disrupt and undermine the very actions that, in civil society, inform us that we have command over ourselves.[22] He further explained that structural "tissues of constraint" envelop residents of the institution, rendering compliance to the path of least resistance. NSO adds an understanding to this theory: these institutional tissues of constraint expand and contract at different points in the institutionalization process. Taking in the "raw material" of new students stokes anxieties about the force and exertion Black male teenagers require to be pruned and groomed to success. The cultural curriculum dictated by NSO deploys the tissues of constraint to intentionally overwhelm "raw" students with the college's values about class, gender, and the men who wear its brand.[23]

"It Wasn't Rules to Them"

The majority of our institutional approaches to young Black males are paradoxically banked in a shared ideological belief that the successful schooling and enhancement of young Black men and boys necessitates a rigid and controlling organizational structure. In contrasting studies of Black male punishment in public schools and in schools that target Black male success, both Ann Ferguson and Freeden Blume Oeur found that Black boys' behaviors and academic performances were consistently framed around disciplinary cultures and structures.[24] Beyond the initial rituals of NSO, the culture of branding bleeds into a campus life that has an unusually abundant amount of rules for a college campus. If the brand is a cultural curriculum for grooming students, rules are the shears that shape men to the brand in their daily comings and goings.

Morehouse's culture of rules is more akin to that of a preparatory school than a liberal arts college. Some rules are explicit, such as the prohibition on overnight dorm guests (which has been lifted in recent years but was in place while respondents were enrolled). Others are venue-specific such as conduct and dress codes in the chapel, the disallowing of women in study halls, or the removal of hats inside classrooms and administrative buildings. The majority of the rules, however, are implicit and made known to men only as they are violating them. The difference between implicit and explicit rules involves when and how they are enforced, on whom they are enforced, and what the consequences are for men who either have or lack the resources to circumvent them. While an explicit rule dictates simple guidelines such as "no hats inside buildings," or "pajamas are not to be worn outside the residence halls," the implicit enforcement of these rules means that styles of hats that are associated with low-income street culture are more frequently sanctioned than those associated with golf. While a student may arrive at convocation compliant with the explicit dress code of a shirt and tie, they may be turned away for violating the implicit code by wearing cornrowed hair, baggy pants, or sneakers.

Men like Waller and Bird, who themselves were from low-income urban backgrounds (as were most of their friends), talked about the rules as being too rigid. Coincidentally, both men had attended elite all-male private high schools where they wore uniforms and adhered to strict codes of conduct and honor. With high school behind him, however, Waller was expecting to be treated like an adult. He pointed out friends who dropped out due to feeling constricted. "I think they made it to sophomore year and they just didn't really respond to the atmosphere," he said. "They hated hovering administrators and the lack of freedom. They just felt like *I'm in college, I'm a grown ass man.* They had already handled responsibility well as a young adult or manager in their home life, and so to have these parental figures or these figures of leaders who were more domineering than their actual parents just didn't gel well with them."

Bird, who contrasted Morehouse's murky conduct codes to the transparency of his prep school, had no desire to defy rules, but, rather, just wanted them to follow a consistent logic that was relevant to a set of life skills. "Why do I have to take my hat off inside the building?" he asked rhetorically. "Yeah, it's a tradition, but it's not my tradition." Bird had grown up with an educated and stable schoolteacher mother who could not shield his brother from a common fate on the poorest side of his city. By the time he was in high school his older brother was doing his first stint in prison. He adamantly wanted to avoid that turn for himself. Bird spoke fondly of his prep academy and its straightforward system of demerits. Prep school culture functioned transactionally for him, with punishments and rewards he could anticipate and link directly to specific behaviors, but at Morehouse he found that the system of rules operated like a language he didn't speak. "At Morehouse...it was more implicit," he harped in frustration. "If you're here, we're [administrators and authority figures] just going to expect all of this. There was no punishment like there was [in prep school], but it's more like you're here, we just expect more."

Institutions are gendered not so much by the gender composition of people within them but because of how they are structured and operate. Joan Acker theorized that gender maps onto the ways that institutions function and organize, be it masculine top-down hierarchies or feminine cooperatives and collectives.[25] Morehouse is a masculinist organization not only because it promotes competition, self-control, or hierarchical ideas about leadership in its students, but also because of the substantial control it exerts over them. We may think of college as a time for the independent self-exploration and risk-taking that provides key lessons in a young person's development, but dominant society's racist beliefs about the "natural" delinquency of young Black men pervade the administration's approach to a rigid and academy-like structure of student life. The rhetoric of manhood is actually undercut by an infantilizing practice of dictating areas of student life that would be left to free choice on most other campuses. Clifford, who also grew up low-income in an almost entirely Black neighborhood, felt the restrictive culture of being "parented" by staff and administrators undermined the college's purported mission of maturation and rites of passage. "They call us men and here we have a curfew," he said with detectable resentment in his voice.

Morehouse is not unlike many HBCUs that have long clung to a practice of enforcing rigid codes of conduct, even since the youth countercultural movement of the 1960s and 1970s that loosened the reins on dress, behavior, political expression, and gender segregation at many historically white schools. It is still common to find HBCUs that impose curfews (sometimes earlier for women than men), gendered dress codes, and/or that forbid certain hairstyles, as Hampton University did in 2012 when banning locked hair and cornrows for their business students.[26] As old as these practices that value the obedience of students over their independent thinking are, however, are also the critiques of them. In a little known 1916 response letter to Harvard professor Paul H. Hanus, Du Bois expressed his frustrations with what was then known as Hampton Institute (not coincidentally the alma mater of Booker T. Washington) and an approach to schooling students a generation removed from Reconstruction that he viewed as "deliberately educating a servile class for a servile place." For Du Bois, Hampton's emphasis on obedience and servility came at the immediate expense of the intellectualism and free-thinking necessary for promoting African Americans to the managerial caste. "Consciously or unconsciously, they propose to develop the Negro race as a caste of efficient workers," he admonished. "Do not expect them to be co-workers in a modern cultured state."[27]

Consciously or unconsciously, the vestiges of this curriculum of docility-inducing rule restriction remain in our contemporary approaches to Black male schooling in which Black male youth are viewed—even by many Black educators—as essentially damaged, problem prone, and inclined to deviancy.[28] As I repeatedly heard respondents speak to the aspirational laurels of the talented tenth and the responsibilities of Black intelligentsia they saw themselves as shouldering by becoming Morehouse men, the irony was not lost on me that the cultural approach to their education was far more in line with the Booker T. Washington's Atlanta Compromise than it was Du Boisian intellectualism. In their descriptions, the curriculum of Morehouse manhood is reduced to a technical education of modeling cultural and behavioral templates and following rules, with the promise that such instruction will be necessary to survive and assimilate under the gaze of a white professional world beyond graduation. Theirs was a curriculum for the making of *white-collar Washingtons* that more closely resembled a professional-class version of an industrial normal school than a liberal arts education.

Nonetheless, students break rules all the time, and learning what rules to break and what you can and cannot get away with guides how they navigate the institutional structure. Thus, the rules serve another function for branding beyond the administration's claims to keep men on the straight and narrow. Just as the tissues of constraint expand and contract *at different points* in the branding process, so do these tissues become operationalized into rules that expand and contract *around different individual men* differently. "Morehouse isn't very strict," Hubbard, a studious and straight-laced son of first-generation Caribbean merchants, insisted. "You can't have women over but in terms of professional rules there wasn't anything else. If you weren't doing well, you were out." When Yusef complained that living in the residence halls felt too much like being babysat, his father, a well-off corporate executive, purchased him a single-family home in a nearby neighborhood. In buying his way out of the rules and setting up his own bachelor pad, he also elevated his social capital on campus, which allowed him to borrow and exchange more resources with other students. As one of the only students who owned his own place and one of the earliest to move off campus in his class, Yusef earned instant social capital in friend groups where he was the consistent house party host. Dictating that social scene earned him easy favors from classmates who shared notes and assignments from missed classes that would have otherwise crippled his grades, helped him network for internships for his business school aspirations, and broke him into the social circles of women he wanted to date who had status and pull of their own. Elvin had few complaints but acquiesced that at times it "felt like a boot camp." Milt, a suburban midwesterner whose father and uncles were all alumni, felt the rules were mostly straightforward (it didn't hurt that one of his close relatives was a senior administrator while he was enrolled). He shrugged that Morehouse was likely no stricter than any other college.

"This is just what they did. It wasn't rules to them," Lucky asserted with words that loudly resonated his keen sense of how middle-class men were navigating the college with a different cultural map than his. Well-off suburbanites like Hubbard, Yusef, Milt, and Elvin entered the college already congruent with the desired cultural outcomes of the brand. Effectively, they had a shorter cultural distance to travel in order to be brand compliant. Lucky, in contrast, had grown up in an apartment complex just a few short miles from campus and excelled in his public magnet school. Much to the relief of his single mother, an LPN (Licensed Practical Nurse), he was accepted to Morehouse on one of its full-tuition scholarships. Lucky spoke with one of the most quintessential Black Atlanta accents I had ever heard. He had spent his entire childhood within walking distance of Morehouse's front gates but talked about his first encounters with his schoolmates as though they were foreign exchange students. "In Atlanta, we don't really finish words," he deadpanned, after deducing that I was similarly foreign. "That's not a slight against my city, it's just I noticed that when I was talking to [classmates] they would *e-nun-ci-ate every single syl-la-ble* in every word. *An en-ti-re word*," he gibed with a deliberately drawn-out exaggeration that made me observably chuckle.

Lucky's college interactions were marked by an inventory of class dissimilarities he detected between himself and his peers. His roommate slept in designer pajamas, and when boasting about his risky behavior back home, shared a story about stealing his parents' car and being caught by the family housekeeper. "Wait, you got caught *by your maid*?!" Lucky exclaimed incredulously when retelling the story. "Why would you steal a car when the fuck you got a maid?! I don't understand that. That was one of the stranger things. You had kids with money trying to act like kids with no money."

Lucky himself could hardly be described as rebellious. He approached college with every intention not only to graduate but to also reap the full benefits of the alumni brand for his future mobility. A vocal minority of the participants (a group skewed toward two disaffected low-income men in particular) scoffed at the brand as all hype and little substance, but Lucky shared none of their cynicism. He wanted to comply with rules not so much to be obedient, but because he believed Morehouse could have a culturally and economically transformative effect on his life if he just did it *right*. The culturally foreign language of unspoken rules frequently frustrated Lucky, yet he spoke not of the college's responsibility to be more transparent, but rather of his own liability in "making mistakes." He viewed administrators as forgiving. "I won't say I got in trouble, but it was always like *here's what you're doing wrong, here's how to correct it.*"

Significantly, what Lucky regarded as "mistakes" were often derived from the tangible material resources he lacked. At eighteen and fresh out of high school, he had not anticipated a campus dress code that required business casual attire so often. "At Crown Forum [monthly convocations and sometimes special events spliced in between] you had to go in a shirt and tie the first couple of weeks," he remembered (new students attend weekly Crown Forums for the start of their first semester). "You know, for me, I'm in some jeans and tennis shoes. You telling me to put on some khakis? Are you going to buy those for me? Because I really don't have that kind of cash on me, you know what I'm saying?" His take on the administration's patience with his "doing wrong" was perplexing because he simultaneously talked about the rules in ways that left the impression that they were unfair.

I tried to reconcile the ways Lucky saw the dress code as impossible to meet and yet talked about the college as though it helped him take personal accountability for this shortcomings. I later understood that he was *not* interpreting the rules as unfair, but, rather, as having a justifiably disparate effect on students. In his view, there was nothing unfair about the affluent students having the easier road to branding when his own aim was to get from Morehouse everything he needed to become one of them. By his mid-thirties, Lucky had apparently accomplished that goal. When we spoke, he was working as a financial services oversight officer for a federal agency. "Morehouse has things they want you to do," he reflected fondly. "And in hindsight you look back on it and they were preparing you for a larger world that probably you're not as used to as the kids from a different socioeconomic background." Lucky was keenly aware of the disparities with which men were experiencing the institutional structure, yet in his view he was learning how far he needed to travel culturally to get the rewards of the cultural curriculum.

Branding the Body

We can measure the progression of branding at Morehouse by tracing students' paths from their early years, when the rules actively enforced a structure around their bodies and behavior, to the point in their experience when brand compliance is internalized and manifested in their behaviors and ways of thinking. Just as the iconography of the Du Boisian three-piece suit is inseparable from the masculinized image of the race man, so "sartorial excellence" (as men lightheartedly described it) is ingrained in the Morehouse Man and the brand. "I always thought the Morehouse Man was really big on the look," said Mort, whose job as community health outreach organizer rarely required more than t-shirts and jeans. "It was a certain look, it was the aesthetics, you had to speak a certain way, you had to dress a certain way." Coleman, a convivial public sector attorney, described the Morehouse Man as "a brother wearing a sport coat and tie and giving a speech that's going to sound something like a sermon." He laughed before adding, "I always thought of him [the Morehouse Man] as highly intelligent, clean cut, dapper." For Waller, even images of famed alumni were selectively presented to students to emphasize style and dress. "In terms of modeling after [Martin Luther] King, I think of that in terms of being debonair, a worldly type of guy." Faculty and administrators, he explained further, "try to model that after being impeccably dressed. Every picture you see of [King] he was very presentable, wearing a shirt and tie." Still, for others like Davis, dress was a means to mirror the Morehouse Man with his own body, not simply to observe how suits composed the icon. "If you were to see me now in my blue single-breasted suit with double vents," he declared more matter-of-factly than boastfully, "I'm what they put in the brochure."

Morehouse's dress code, and critiques of it from both within and outside the college, has received significant coverage since the 2009 announcement of the Appropriate Attire Policy, which formalized many of the college's implicit practices by requiring "modest, casual or business casual attire" in campus common spaces and business attire for interviews, and specifically prohibited "women's clothing." In statements to reporters, mostly queer and nonbinary students expressed outrage that the policy's trumped-up rhetoric of professionalism and appropriateness was a thinly veiled attack on gender expression.[29] Moreover, the ambiguity between the implicit and explicit rules that even cisgender students like Bird complained about was particularly weaponized to leave the "appropriateness" of student dress almost entirely up to the interpretation of a staff and administration known for their homophobia.[30] The policy, which extends to what students wear outside the classroom and other official functions, "infringes on the student's freedom of expression," said senior Devon Watson in a 2009 statement to CNN.[31]

In popular depictions of college students, the prevailing image is often of slovenly twenty-somethings who could not care less about looking presentable, let alone wearing a suit and tie voluntarily. Since the 1970s, very few nondenominational liberal arts colleges still dictate student dress, and elite day schools have increasingly moved toward more relaxed attire for students and faculty alike. In contrast, narrowly framed dress codes have emerged as one of the most recognizable features of Black male schools, and many of them require uniforms. Beliefs about "dressing for success" persist in our approaches to Black Male Initiatives. Dress carries substantial consequences for Black men, and the rhetoric that young Black men can hope to evade endangerment and the more violent and hostile consequences of racism in public spaces by "pulling up their pants" has been echoed by Black celebrities, public school superintendents, police chiefs, and even the Oval Office. In her observations of gender and masculinity among high school boys, C. J. Pascoe observed Black male teens taking meticulous care of their shoes and clothing; in sharp contrast to their white counterparts, they understood tidiness and dressing well as a ritual of masculinity baked into the value they held for attaining name brand shoes and clothing with sometimes limited resources.[32] Dressing maturely and presentably is a means of inscribing the cultural language of the brand onto the body. Moreover, men not only internalize and express the brand in the ways they dress but also take on the role of institutional authority figures when, as Davis and Chet recalled, upperclassmen routinely policed the clothing of younger students.

Being seen during class hours in attire suitable for a business meeting is understood as a rite of passage in the transformation of high school boys into college men. Mingus recalled: "My brother, he came back from Morehouse sharp as a whip. He was wearing stuff and I was like, man, who are you!? He came back from school crisp and clean, so that said Morehouse to me." Dress gives the impression of the event for which a man is dressing. Freshmen may wear the streetwear and athletic gear of a typical adolescent roaming a suburban mall, but upperclassmen and student leaders are distinguishable by their crew-neck sweaters, button-down shirts, and sport jackets. Those with the best job prospects are distinguishable by the suits and ties they wear to and from on-campus interviews, meetings, and business classes. They are dressed as though they have somewhere to be. This performance expresses their imagination of themselves as much as it does their status among their peers. They have come of age within this cultural curriculum and look and act the part proficiently.

But how students dress is also a declaration of the kinds of Black masculinity the brand rejects. Beyond the obvious heteronormativity of this sartorial culture, clothing and style signals those noneconomic cues about class that far exceed one's ability to guess the cost of the clothes themselves. Take, for example, how timeliness is read onto the dressed body. For Black men in particular, differing understandings of time have long been observed in the everyday construction of social class. In *Tally's Corner*, Elliot Liebow's classic study of Black men on the street corners of 1960s Washington, DC, men spend their days loitering with seemingly nowhere to be. Flatbed trucks pull up sporadically with driver's offering a day's worth of work, and corner men regularly wave it off and return to their meandering conversation or dice game. To the observer, these mostly unemployed low-income men seem to be wasting copious amounts of time standing around uninterested in a day's work. But the work they are offered is erratic, shows up when and where it demands their backbreaking labor, and disappears as fleetingly as it arrived. A day's manual labor is not a job, and there is no long-term prospect of stability or reliability. The task is simply not worth their time.[33]

Similarly, Alford Young Jr. observed that socially marginalized Black men on the West Side of Chicago had completely different conceptions of time and schedule from more mainstream Americans. Their days revolved around socializing and dillydallying, and they had nowhere in particular to be. When he scheduled interviews with them, some arrived six hours early merely to linger in the lobby, while others never showed. In the absence of employment or other responsibilities that structured their days, they had a very fluid sense of time and few material rewards for being scheduled.[34] In contrast, everything about the cultural priority of timeliness at Morehouse seemed to renounce the association of Black men with out-of-work idleness. Mantras about time are drilled into NSO initiates, and learning to appreciate punctuality is repeatedly stressed by staff and administrators. "To be early is to be on time, to be on time is to be late, and to be late is inexcusable" was a maxim I often heard from my classmates; it was parroted by Chet, Clifford, and Dewey.

As the Man of Morehouse progresses through the college, his body becomes an account of where he is on the clock of his matriculation. The upperclassman in business casual attire tacitly repudiates the images of laziness and instability associated with the low-income counterparts. Clothing denotes more about social class than the garments one can afford. How and *when* men are dressed can provide their most immediate means of distinguishing themselves from Black men who loiter on street corners. A student's sartorialism tells us how far he has been groomed away from the pitfalls of endangerment and low achievement that will trap other Black men. Only Black men who are unimportant, or, more kindly, are unproductive, are dressed as though they have no place to be.

"Look to Your Left, Look to Your Right"

The construction of the Morehouse Man is as much about who he is *not* as who he is. As new students gather in their first freshman convocation, a ritual occurs in which the dean of the chapel dauntingly peers over his podium at the successive rows of green and easily intimidated adolescents and instructs them to "Look to your left, look to your right, one of you will be gone." The saying is a scare tactic meant to get new students serious about the challenge ahead of them, but there is also a haunting truth to it. Only 60 percent of those who matriculate at Morehouse graduate within six years.[35] While the college may boast about its renown, it loses one-fifth of its first-year students by their second year, an attrition rate that is on par with the national average and twice as high as that at Spelman.[36] "The entire time I was in King Chapel I was like *it won't be me!*" Bird exclaimed. He had taken a couple of years off to work before he graduated, and when he finished, he recalled the words again with relief and elation. "The whole time back [after his leave of absence] I was like *it wasn't me!* I know some niggas who it happened to, you know? Everybody is like *it ain't me!*"

Among these push-outs and dropouts, low-income men and scholarship recipients are overrepresented. So are out gay and bisexual students and nearly every one of the school's gender transitioning students, even before the passing of the trans student policy. After hearing that students were experiencing the structure, rules, and constraints of the campus culture differently along lines of class, gender, and sexuality, I gathered that it was not coincidental that push-outs were overwhelmingly the same students who were inhibited by the college's desired conformities of manhood. Such a high attrition rate significantly shapes the experience for those who graduate. Roughly two-thirds of my respondents spontaneously referred to attrition or students who left. "I came in with something like 800 and maybe, I don't know, 600 graduated maybe," Dewey explained, as he mentioned waning scholarships and college-wide budget cuts. "I think we went from 500 of us, something like that, then it dwindled down to maybe 300," Fitzgerald estimated while sounding unfazed at this suggested 40 percent loss. Ramsey was simply resolved to accept this fact. "It was pretty clear everyone was not going to make it. [Staff and administrators] told you [at] freshman orientation. You're competing the moment you get there." From year to year class sizes dropped so dramatically that men talked about students' departures as though those men simply disappeared. "You'd look up a couple of years later and they'd be gone," Waller shrugged.

Like so many colleges and universities—particularly HBCUs—Morehouse struggles with Black male student retention.[37] This systemic problem for Black males in higher education should be redressed, for it is a structural issue related to racial wealth disparities in inequities in K–12 resources. When an institution relies on a cultural curriculum to teach its students to succeed, however, it also draws on common cultural perceptions about race and gender to explain and rationalize both its unique problems and those compounded by larger structural inequalities. While a majority of the men who mentioned attrition readily named finances as one of its leading causes, they often, and in the same breath, listed personal behavior, immaturity, and a failure to live up to the brand's ethos as reasons why many students needed to be gone. When recalling the first time he heard "*Look to your left, look to your right*," Dewey immediately became adamant about the kinds of men who did not belong on campus. "Well [the saying] was true," he insisted: "There are a lot of those people who would just frustrate the hell out of you your first year and a half and maybe they were the fake thug or the guy who didn't want to be in college or a guy who was just not thinking about education.... There are some fools on that campus.... Your first, at least, two years are spent around these fools.... At the time there were a lot of fake thugs. I'm sorry, real thugs do not take the SAT."

Davis was sympathetic toward students who had financial problems but was critical of those who did not take advantage of resources and fit themselves to a professional mold. "I'll admit to you that for me I would judge what's the reason behind [not graduating]. Is this because [of] money? Then can't nobody help that," he shrugged before his tone turned sharply to an indictment of individual poor behavior. "But is it because you're fooling around? Or you're making babies, whatever?...So, for me, 'didn't fit the prototype' means that you didn't kind of buy into what the college was about.... Like it killed you to put a suit on and go to Crown Forum?" he asked regarding the regularly scheduled campus-wide convocation that requires a suit and tie. "When it's time to interview, you know we're going to the career placement center and you want to do an S&P [shirt and pants] combination with some khakis? Put on a suit. Get a haircut. That kind of stuff."

The sheer numbers do not support the case that this consistent attrition rate is simply a matter of personal responsibility, but men talked so often about those who could not properly behave their way to graduation that I named this topic "riff raff" in my data analysis (after Dewey used the term to deride an element of students he observed). It was fast apparent that in a time when images of Black male crisis saturate our ideas of troubled Black male youth, the brand is a built-in means of staking Morehouse men's worthiness for racial leadership in a repudiation of other kinds of Black masculinity. The idea that the Morehouse Man is not defined solely by who he is, but perhaps more by who he is *not*, was built into the institutional rhetoric. The idea that there are men who will not make it to graduation is essential to student belief in the brand. As Lucky put it, "There are men who went to Morehouse and then there are Morehouse men. And that's a stark and vast difference," referring in the former to those who attended but did not graduate, or even finished but do not embody the college's desired traits. Percy, too, made this clear distinction between those who had been successfully branded through to graduation, and who has simply attended. "A man of Morehouse is someone who went there. Like you went there and maybe you didn't graduate. Maybe you were there for a couple of semesters, or maybe you just didn't quite get that this is bigger than you."

The notion that the Morehouse brand is built on "grit" echoed throughout our conversations. Grit was formerly the kind of rhetoric typically applied to noneducational settings, such as becoming a US Marine or surviving prison, but it has been increasingly applied to the schooling of Black students who must cope with socioeconomic disadvantages. And, as Freeden Blume Oeur reminds us, the emphasis on grit tends to be reserved for Black males[38]—an assumption that Black males suffer the worst in society and therefore must be equipped to endure the most challenges. The belief that the measure of a Morehouse man lies in how he survives the gauntlet of his own college conceals an intrinsically academic problem—the difficulty in enrolling and retaining Black male collegians—behind the mask of masculinity, which serves as a cultural logic for explaining away the college's most pressing educational issues. Further, this masculine mythology incentivized graduates to keep the culture as is instead of being receptive to discussing its problems. If it is a competition they won, what fault should they find with it?

This cultural logic extends beyond explaining attrition; I heard it repeated as men discussed their preparedness for high-stakes professional competition after graduation. For all of Morehouse's pomp and circumstance, there isn't much hard evidence to support the conclusion that Morehouse graduates fare better in the workforce than Black men who graduate from other selective liberal arts colleges and reputable universities. I asked Percy to explain to me how he made sense of the successes of other Black men who worked alongside him but had not been subjected to NSO, strict dress codes, or restrictive rules about their comings and goings. His answer fell back on cultural reasoning. It was succinct and unwavering, because he was so strongly convinced of its truth: "But they're not the same kind of man we are."

For over a decade, Morehouse has struggled to recruit top-performing Black male seniors. Part of its declining appeal to this highly sought-after group is due to the regimented academy-like culture on which it rests its laurels. As it struggles to be selective and yet fill its classes to capacity, the college's rankings have suffered substantially. It is ranked 154th on the *US News and World Report*'s 2019 list of the best national liberal arts colleges, compared to Spelman's 57th place ranking (the best college rankings in *US News and World Report* are the most influential).[39] So why does Morehouse hold on to a branding process that is so inconsistently experienced by students and that may be costing them applicants (and presumably graduates) every year when recruits compare it to less restrictive campus cultures? The answer lies in recognizing that the cultural curriculum functions not only as a belief that the institution imposes on students; it also provides the institution with a rationalization about itself.

Percy's notion that the Morehouse man is distinguished from other men not because of his tangible accomplishments but because of the way he does manhood was not born of his individual invention. Across all these interviews, a vocal minority of men reluctantly admitted that selectivity of admissions and some aspects of the academic curriculum fall short of what they regard as ideal.[40] The fact that Morehouse accepts 74 percent of applicants (compared to only 40 percent at Spelman and 49 percent at Howard) refutes any notion that the college is highly selective.[41] As Morehouse struggles to prove its academic bona fides, the gender curriculum has been offered both to students and to the outside world as compensation. In official recruitment language, the college's rhetoric about what it offers in brotherhood and culture is heavily laden with references to the marginalization of Black manhood.

> So, why do black men still choose Morehouse? No doubt, it is the excellent liberal arts education and an environment that is conducive to academic, social and spiritual growth. But there are many great schools out there, so there must be something more?
>
> We call that something the "Morehouse Mystique." The phrase is not easily defined or understood, but it's also not just a clever slogan. The Mystique is joining a brotherhood like none other. And after being ignored, stereotyped or marginalized, it's about finally finding that "home" that, deep inside, you always knew existed, where you are the heart, soul and hope of the community. And where you are not alone.[42]

Nearly all colleges and universities subscribe to a manufactured self-image about what they offer with regard to their own competitiveness, importance, and reputation. The brand of the University of Michigan, Dartmouth, or Oberlin might not be inscribed onto the bodies and day-to-day behaviors of their students, but as colleges increasingly move toward functioning as corporations, these institutions are no less driven by an urgency to continually market themselves to student and parent consumers.[43] Historically and predominantly white institutions, however, direct their status anxieties mainly toward perennially ascending in the most important rankings. At these institutions, decisions about student life, admissions, and efforts toward retention are no less emphasized than at Morehouse, but the structural logic to which they subscribe focuses obsessively on the question, *how will this impact our ranking?*[44]

To ask why Morehouse articulates its institutional anxieties through a cultural curriculum is to recognize that Morehouse is both an American college clamoring for prestige and status and an institution informed by a larger history in which Black masculinity has always been fraught with anxiety. Morehouse uniquely stands at the intersection between its shared history with other HBCUs of disproportionately serving racially first generation and low-income students and its exclusive focus on Black men, who are widely marginalized within K–12 education and seem to struggle in all forms of higher education. As scholars of Black colleges like Melissa Wooten have noted, the racial inequality that is baked into the segregationist origin stories of HBCUs also inhibits their abilities to adapt to demographic and economic shifts in higher education.[45] As both an HBCU *and* a single-sex institution, the college straddles two higher education legacies. Where same-sex institutions were once the norm in colleges and universities, now there are only four men's colleges. Administrators and devoted alumni alike are challenged in justifying the appeal of the Morehouse Mystique when many in higher education question the goals of men's colleges and the necessity of historically Black colleges.[46]

I do not fundamentally object to men's colleges, and I certainly find questioning the necessity of HBCUs to be inherently racist, because, as Wooten maintains, such a question presumes the inferiority of Black college educations. What is sociologically interesting is not the question of whether Morehouse serves a purpose, but, rather, how it organizationally adapts to a cultural narrative of the new purposes it serves within the changing landscape of higher education. The Morehouse brand is but an adaptation strategy that draws on the cultural resources the college does have to compensate for the structural capacity and financial capital they lack. The brand is a shield, at least in the minds of many students and administrators, with which the college sustains its cultural contribution to the race via the molding of Black male leadership. Black male crisis, then, serves as a necessary foe within a cultural narrative that the college's continued existence is vital for improving—if not saving—Black men.

Cultural manhood, the *manliness* that scholars have shown has been central to social campaigns ever since emancipation, is the story Morehouse tells itself to assert that it produces uniquely valuable graduates in a nationwide socioeconomic context where it controls so little else about the Black male condition. Morehouse's predicament signals the challenges inherent in an all-male Black college that burdens the culture of its students with its own anxieties about racialized masculinity when the structural challenges of educating Black males prove daunting. Morehouse is an especially vivid example (that is scaled campus-wide) of the problems that face minorities of Black men at other HBCUs and PWIs as well as many secondary schools when they approach the schooling of Black men and boys with a cultural agenda about crafting them into exceptions to the stereotypes of their group. And, yet, when it comes to schools that specifically serve Black men and boys, Morehouse is a standard-bearer, not an exception. For these institutions, outside structural in-equalities are reimagined and filtered through institutional race and gender ideologies, resulting in an emphasis on instilling an ethic of personal responsibility so strong that this cultural agenda threatens to supplant the academic curriculum that provides the educational foundation for the schooling of every other kind of student.

3   *Of Our Sexual Strivings*

In 1996 the assault of a first-year Spelman student by four Morehouse basketball players became a national cover story for *Emerge* magazine.[1] When I graduated in 2004, in a stinging demonstration of injustice, more than one of my classmates watched as her rapist walked honorably across Morehouse's commencement stage. The affront to us was repeated in 2006 when two Spelman women reported separate assaults made by different Morehouse men. The following September over 150 women marched to Morehouse's gates where they held a speak-out in response to these events.[2] In 2013 we realized how little had changed when three Morehouse basketball players gang-raped one woman while a football player alongside them raped another.[3] In May 2016 an unidentified Spelman freshman took to Twitter to reveal that she had been raped by four unnamed Morehouse students, and attention to her case launched the #RapedAtSpelman and #RapedAtMorehouse awareness campaign hashtags.

These were just the stories that some of the women and a few of the men who were violated had the courage to report, but they were titillating and well-timed enough to get the attention of the local and national press. It had been over fifteen years since it happened to anyone I knew, and yet every two or three years an account of an as-

FIGURE 7. Cover of *Emerge* magazine, August 1997.

sault would escape from the rug under which it was swept. Damage control on the part of administrators—rather than disciplinary consequences for the perpetrators—inevitably followed each incident. Morehouse students and administrators consistently met Spelman students' expressions of outrage and demands for accountability with denial and victim-blaming. The patterns and the protests drew long-overdue attention to the deeply entrenched structural problems that kept Morehouse from addressing the issue and the victims from getting justice. Behind this impunity lay an attitude of exceptionality and entitlement: Spelman documentarian Laura Rahman captured an off-color comment by a Morehouse student who snarked that "at least it was Morehouse sperm."[4]

An exposé of Morehouse's Title IX investigations revealed a Catholic Church–style culture of top-down mishandling of victims' allegations by campus police and administrators, which exploded onto *BuzzFeed News* in 2016[5] (the same organization that exposed Donald Trump's "quid pro quo" Ukrainian scandal which led to his 2020 impeachment),[6] and the *New York Times* in 2017.[7] My former undergraduate advisor Professor M. Bahati Kuumba explained the long-running tensions regarding gender violence between the two campuses: "It's been perpetual since I've been here. Every year, every incident, we have to revive that movement in some way."[8] The results of the Title IX investigation were alarming. When a report by *Chronicle of Higher Education* named a "culture of hypermasculinity" as the source of Morehouse's sexual misconduct problem,[9] the story revealed that overwhelmingly male administrators were stifling the authority and effectiveness of the Title IX coordinator, the employee responsible for the college's compliance with the federal laws that prohibit sex-based discrimination in any education program that receives federal financial assistance.[10] According to the same *Chronicle* report, in the three years between 2016 and 2019, the college turned over seven Title IX coordinators, one of whom resigned within thirty days of her appointment. Both Spelman and Morehouse students complained that coordinators blamed victims, accused them of lying about their assaults, and urged them to drop their cases out of concern that they would ruin the perpetrator's career.[11]

Systemic changes since the 2019 Title IX investigation have been proposed but await implementation.[12] Time will tell what structural effects such changes will have on the college, but in its recent past and in the present the student culture surrounding these incidents continues to concern and, most times, the denial, thinly veiled victim bashing, or coddling of Black male perpetrators on the part of alumni and administrators (who readily assume that Black males suffer more hardships than Black women) incensed me.[13] While Spelman students have become increasingly politicized about this issue, Morehouse's campus-wide reaction to rapes perpetrated by its own students remains unchanged. Administrators and students alike display an unwavering preoccupation with their college's image and how rape allegations stain the Morehouse brand. This undue burden of worrying about how these cases make Black men look is even passed on to assault victims. As one Morehouse freshman victim told reporters, he didn't report his assault because the college groomed him to not seem weak. "You're supposed to be a man, you're supposed to be stoic," he told a *Chronicle* reporter. "You're supposed to solve your problems quietly."[14]

In an era of #MeToo activism and a surging nationwide demand for accountability, Morehouse's current media maelstrom seems to be making the institution pay the price for its decades of passing the buck on sexual misconduct. In 2015, then Vice President Joseph Biden brought the issue front and center when his "It's On Us" sexual assault prevention program visited Morehouse on one of its four national stops. In addressing a crowded Morehouse gymnasium on his visit, the vice president acknowledged the importance of holding men accountable for prevention. "We have a cultural problem," he told the overwhelmingly male crowd. "We have to change the standard of decency by which we measure ourselves."[15] Outside the arena, protestors—some of them assault survivors—gathered on the steps to draw attention to how Morehouse administrators' public stance on taking sexual assault seriously was greatly contradicted by their in-house handling of assault investigations. Sophomore Timothy Tukes sat in silent protested atop the mattress on which he was raped, with duct tape sealing his mouth. A sign in his hands called out the college's "queer erasure" of male victims of assault

FIGURE 8. Morehouse student Timothy Tukes, accompanied by friend Kim, engage in a silent protest outside Biden speech. This handwritten plea also appears in the cover art for this book.

and read "My perpetrator is still here."[16] In the aftermath of Biden's appearance, then Morehouse president John Silvanus Wilson, who had joined Biden on stage, communicated a different message than the initiative. He harped on concern about the negative image of Black men as sexual predators. While Wilson publicly committed to urgently addressing the issue, he cautioned reporters that "there's a stereotype [about] black males and you can walk right into it with a story like this."[17]

The White House's attention to the issue was well warranted. While national sexual assault rates have fallen by more than half since 1993,[18] campus sexual assault rates have not declined in fifty years.[19] College campuses remain unsafe spaces for women with the most accurate recent studies estimating that between 5 percent and 25 percent of college women have experienced sexual violence in some form while in school.[20] When turning the focus from women victims to male perpetrators, the statistical picture is even more alarming. An estimated 10.8 percent of college men have committed at least one rape by the end of college,[21] and men commit 99 percent of campus sexual assaults, including those against other males.[22] From 2001 to 2014 the rate of reported forcible sexual offenses doubled on college campuses.[23] While this rise may be attributed in part to increased reporting, the frequency of campus sexual assault is not declining with the rest of the country, even as the rates of all categories of campus crimes except rape, murder, and negligent manslaughter lowered from 2001 to 2017.[24] Across researchers, policy makers, activists, and victims alike the question remains: what is so different about college campuses when it comes to sexual violence?

In answering that question, many scholars and prevention experts have looked to the ways that campus sexual assault is sustained by *rape cultures*,[25] that is, societies or environments where rape is more likely to occur, where it is more likely to be normalized or trivialized, or where perpetrators are less likely to be held responsible.[26] They are not defined merely by the presence or number of perpetrators but are male-dominated cultures (backed by institutional policies and practices) that are underpinned by the particular contexts, spaces, and behavioral settings in which men are more likely to victimize others. Rape cultures don't mean that all the men who participate in them will rape, nor is being a rapist a prerequisite for belonging to a rape culture. Women, too, can participate in rape cultures by helping to keep men from being held accountable for sexual violence or by blaming victims, but rape cultures serve a particular purpose for men and their masculinity. As Ayres Boswell and Joan Spade argued in their study of college fraternities, rape is not a matter of individualized bad behavior, but, rather, has a social basis in the shared creation of masculine and feminine gender identities in relationship to each other.[27] In other words, as a form of socialized gender violence, rape culture serves a function for men in that it extends the benefits of masculine power and dominance to all men, even if they never commit an act of assault. On college campuses, where young boys are often forming their footing about their emerging manhood, rape and rape culture play prominent roles in the construction of gender and masculine expectations about how women and others will be gendered in relationship to men. Essentially, rape cultures play a prominent role on college campus because rape is part of how college men *do* gender,[28] meaning that they inform all men who participate in them that masculinity is partly defined by physical and sexual power over women, and that femininity, conversely, is defined by an ability to be overpowered.

The litany of assault cases and mishandlings of allegations inarguably qualify Morehouse as an institution with a noteworthy rape culture, but in my years of studying Morehouse students and the alumni community and observing how their beliefs about gender violence and responses to it were tightly bound to ideas about racism, Blackness, and Black manhood, I realized that when it comes to those "contexts, spaces, and behavioral settings" that determine rape cultures, race is one such critical context that has been grossly overlooked in both scholarly and popular examinations of campus sexual assault. Though our public accounts of high-profile college rapes from Stanford University swimmer and convicted rapist Brock Turner to the 2018 Vanderbilt University assault mistrial of four accused football players point to how sexual predation is a common occurrence across racial categories of college men,[29] our knowledge of rape culture on college campuses (and thus how to prevent it) remains lacking, in part because our existing approaches have studied college men and their conceptualizations of gender as though they were a racially homogenous group. I see Morehouse's rape culture not only as a deeply rooted problem, but also as a way of advancing how policy makers and scholars think about solutions to sexual assault by acknowledging that our "one size fits all" approach to sexual assault prevention does not encompass how men do and understand rape differently across different racial contexts.

Take, for example, that days after Biden's visit, a resident of

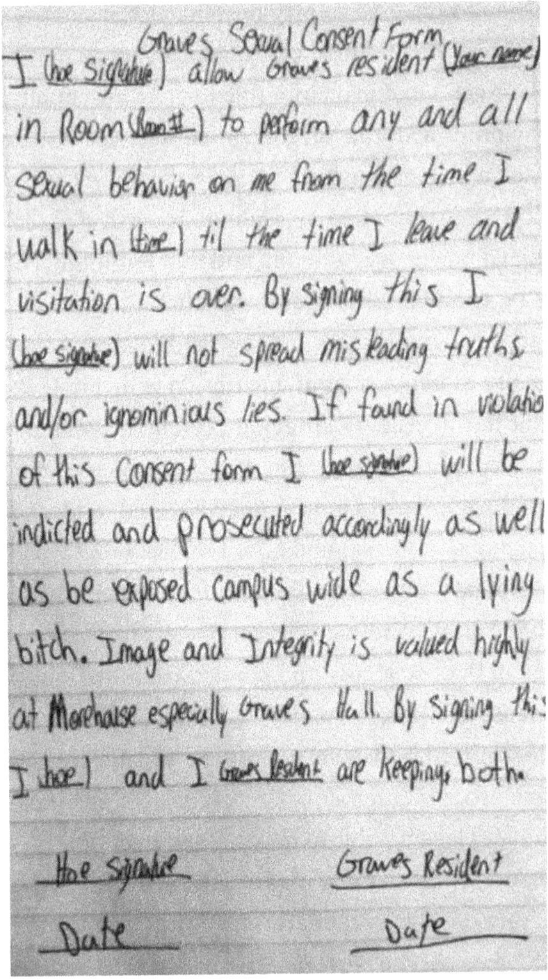

FIGURE 9. "Hoe contract."

Graves Hall, the largest freshman dormitory, circulated a handwritten "hoe contract"[30] meant to both mock the support of recent assault victims and the solemn tone around consent set by Biden's address. The note quickly went viral across student social media platforms and read:

I (hoe signature) allow Graves resident (Your name) in Room (Room #) to perform any and all sexual behavior on me from the time I walk in (time) til the time I leave and visitation is over. By signing this I (hoe signature) will not spread misleading truths and/or ignominious lies. If found in violation of this consent form I (hoe signature) will be indicted and prosecuted accordingly as well as be exposed campus wide as a lying bitch. Image and integrity is highly valued at Morehouse especially Graves Hall. By signing this I (hoe) and I (Graves resident) are keeping both.

In reaction, a Spelman freshman shared on Twitter that her roommate had been raped in their first semester. A Morehouse student immediately admonished her for smearing Morehouse's image. The Spelmanite shot back an inconvenient truth that her male peers and their administrators alike seemed long reluctant to hear: "The rapists that are on your campus are who's tarnishing your image sir."[31] The mocking, threatening, and discrediting of victims is a definitive quality of any rape culture. The student may have been seeking cheap favor among his peers but his emphasis on image denotes a double consciousness in which he is aware of how rape makes Black men at Morehouse look. He may be trivializing rape, but he takes protecting Morehouse's image to the outside world quite seriously. Couple this with President Wilson's aforementioned statement that, instead of acknowledging how sexual assaults harm Black women, emphasized the cost that *reporting* such assaults held for Black men.

What has been evident to me across reactions from administrators and alumni, in viral student responses like the "hoe contract," and within my conversations with respondents, was a phenomenon I believe has been completely left out of the theories scholars use to explain rape culture. In this chapter, I argue that these men, who see every way they are perceived in college as fastened to the fate of the race, are not only doing gender through rape culture, but are also doing race, and that campus rape cultures are *racialized rape cultures*. Racialized rape culture is not a *type* of rape culture, for there are no rape cultures that are not racialized. Rather, examinations of racialized rape culture call for a centering of the ways that race serves as a modality through which gender violence operates. For Morehouse men, their understandings of rape, sex, and women are primarily oriented toward how the racial implications of these issues position their own race-gender subjectivity. They see themselves as constantly vulnerable to images of Black male criminality, sexual impropriety, and misconduct that they cannot control in the eyes of the white world's racial veil. Thus, I use this chapter to draw the Du Boisian lens around Morehouse's particularly amplified rape culture because that culture is dominated in this space by Black men and fueled by their beliefs about Black masculinity and the tensions the veil imposes on their ideas of how they are seen as Black men. As we have seen previously with the anxieties that surround the brand, Morehouse men are prime for studies of double consciousness phenomenology (that is, the ways that racial subjugation constructs our consciousness and meanings we make about ourselves and our relationship to our social world).

Double consciousness theory, if we recall from the introduction of this book, describes a phenomenological process of self-formation via racialization[32] in which the veil prevents the full recognition of humanity and structures the world into a one-way mirror in which the racialized subjects who live within it see out, but the *racializing* (white) subjects who live outside of it cannot see, hear, or properly recognize those within.[33] Second, double consciousness invokes "two unreconciled strivings, two warring ideals in one dark body," in the racialized subject that visits everyday lived duality on them.[34] In this claim, race is not simply a variable of difference to be observed but provides "fundamental media through which we experience human otherness" and construct cultures.[35] Double consciousness is indeed a way of seeing, but I also believe that Morehouse men provide us with an urgent case for reckoning with how that twon-ess organizes gender and sexuality troubles within the race as well. When issues about Black men harming Black women and queer Black people through gender violence erupt within Black spaces and communities, Du Boisian double consciousness cannot be sold short as merely a relational theory between Black people and the outside world. How rape culture is racialized tells us that the veil is constitutive and actively prioritizes and reframes issues of violence between members of the race based on gender, class, and sexuality hierarchies within the race. Understanding how gender operates requires us to recognize that racialization both amplifies and dictates gender power. By unpacking racialized rape culture through this theoretical approach, this chapter expands on Du Boisian theory by positing that racially subjugated men may not control how they are seen *outside* the race, but they manipulate what they project onto the veil by using rape culture to sustain gender dominance *within* the race.

Sexual assault, like all violent crimes, overwhelmingly occurs within the racial group shared by both perpetrators and victims, but Title IX data does not track the race of campus perpetrators or victims, thus there are few studies to date that have examined race in campus sexual assault. Those few focus almost entirely on female victims at HBCUs.[36] Beyond the college context, we already know that race delineates Black experiences of sexual assault. Sociologist C. Shawn McGuffey extensively surveyed Black women victims of sexual violence and abuse and found that race "contours the perceptions of survivors" by largely determining the structural inequalities that either constrain or empower victims, how they make sense of their assaults, and the resources from which they draw to make meanings of their assault and react affirmatively to them.[37] Such findings about the racialization of assault survivors begs for a complementary approach to how race dictates how male perpetrators and Black men overall make sense of assault. Historically, race and racism have inundated the context and view of rape for Black Americans, and it is undeniable that an extensive history of racist myths about Black male predation has been weaponized against Black communities. In the late nineteenth century, when white southerners and northerners alike sought to violently beat back the Black political and economic advancements of the Reconstruction era, Ida B. Wells exposed how falsified sexual transgression allegations against Black men were used by whites to justify widespread terrorism against Black political and economic competition.[38] Angela Davis explained how the stereotype of the Black male rapist was a touchstone of white racial domination.[39] Propagandized hysteria about both sexual and nonsexual Black male "predators" has been a go-to for galvanizing the policies and practices of anti-Black political and economic violence well into contemporary American politics.

The context of these weaponized myths about Black male sexuality is never distant from the lives of Black male collegians. Studies of Black men in college have long confirmed that they are highly aware of their race-gender subjectivity, are keenly attuned to the pernicious stereotypes associated with their group, and see problems targeting Black men writ large as shaping their college experiences.[40] Over a century before these works on contemporary Black college men appeared, Du Bois theorized that education itself obligated African Americans to reckon with their "two-ness." In *Dusk of Dawn* he claimed that the veil sent well-educated racialized subjects on two distinct trajectories. The man who took the first path "avoided every appearance of segregation" by divorcing himself from Black communities and attempting to blend into white worlds, while the man who took the second "prided himself on living with 'his people.'"[41]

Morehouse men, like the graduates of many HBCUs, present a

conundrum in this veil of education, for these men pride themselves on being trained up among their people in preparation for presentation to a white-collar mainstream. While the most socially marginalized Black men go about their lives under extreme state surveillance, it is those Black men with class mobility—who stand at the threshold of the veil—who are far more hyperconscious of how they are seen by the white gaze immediately facing them. I want to make clear that I flatly reject any claims that this veiled existence makes Black men who are more prone to perpetrating sexual assault or participating in rape culture than any other group of men on college campuses. To the contrary, I see Du Boisian theory as a means to recognizing how racialized rape culture is not unique to Black men. At historically white institutions nationwide, white men learn the purchase of their white male privilege and the lengths white administrators, donors, parents, law enforcement, and communities will go to immunize them from accountability for sexual crimes and misconduct, and thus rape culture too serves an essential role in how white campuses make and apply meanings to whiteness. I hope that Du Boisian theory provokes campus sexual assault researchers to make these overdue inquiries into how *racializing* subjects understand rape culture as informing whiteness of their white masculinity. But for Morehouse, students who are far from the invisible men "turned loose in society" to "remain absolutely unnoticed" embody the tension of deploying gender violence to vie for patriarchal power among men and over women while facing the racial penalties of those acts from which white college men are exempt.[42]

Given this context in which Black college men are prone to hyperconscious thinking about themselves and their behaviors, readers may be asking how I got men to talk to me about sex and sexual assault, particularly given that when I spoke to them I was a young woman just few years shy of all their ages with numerous mutual friends and overlapping networks between us. How to talk to men about sexual violence has been a challenge for researchers who have long struggled with how both men and women often see nonconsensual sex acts (including those in which they engage) as normal and engage in nonconsensual acts that they don't categorize as assault. Asking them directly about their experiences with *rape*, as psychologist Mary Koss noted in her seminal works on rape culture, would not yield much useful data about the prevalence of sexual assault if their personal comprehensions of rape are more narrowly drawn than an inclusion of all sexual acts without consent.[43] With this in mind, more recent studies have called for an approach to interviewing men that is more accurately aligned with how they actually talk about a range of acts that constitute and are related to sexual violence and that emphasize behaviorally oriented dialogues that limit men and women from imposing their selective personal definitions of assault.[44] Both old and new scholarly camps call for empirical approaches to expand past narrow methods of getting respondents to talk about sexual violence. It follows that studying rape culture requires inquiries that expand men's talk about their experiences beyond explicitly placing them in the mindset of describing gender violence.

In my early days of exploring this project in graduate school, I proposed it to my dissertation committee as a study mostly about how Morehouse provided a keen example of the ways that becoming middle class shaped Black men's understandings of masculinity and gender. At the time, sexual assault had long been a recurring problem on the campus, but the scope of my interview questions focused more on the relationship between class-driven respectability politics and the homophobic violence that had made headlines in the years I was an undergraduate. I did not intend to ask men directly about sexual assault and, yet, it came up for about a fourth of respondents in ways that were worthy of abductively revisiting in my analysis. This may be surprising to readers who would expect men to avoid such a topic with a female researcher, but what Koss and other researchers point out about talking about sexual assault proved true in my conversations with men. That Du Boisian double consciousness that men were experiencing didn't lead them to suppress discussions of gender violence, but, rather, their hyperconsciousness about how issues of assault specifically affected the images and reputations of Black men led them to bring the issue up. Because Black college men tend to be primed to discuss how race is present in their nearly every social and institutional interaction, racialized narratives about women, sex, and gender surfaced organically as men made meanings of race and racism. Essentially, they were talking to me about rape because it was pertinent, in many of their views, to myriad ways they wanted to talk about race, racism, and the undue challenges they faced as Black men. Race, I observed, was not only a way of seeing these issues but also men's ways of talking about them.

Issues of sexual violence and related discussions of gender dynamics surfaced where men understood them to be relevant.[45] How, when, and where they felt these issues were relevant is, in itself, a great wealth of information about how race organizes their thoughts about their experiences with these issues. Their talk about these topics, I realized, could be analyzed primarily across three levels: individual, group, and institutional. The call for more nuanced means of talking about sexual violence with men—and understanding where they are talking around and about issues related to sexual violence—should bear in mind for us that these levels are not discreet categories of men's understandings, but, rather, are interrelated. At the individual level, I examined how men see personal characteristics such as conduct and sexual propriety as a deterrent against their capacity to commit sexual assault. I then focus on how the college structurally undermines the rhetoric of sexual propriety by organizing coed interactions into settings where men feel pressured to sexualize women. At the group level, I then examine the contexts in which men see themselves as competing racially with other groups of men and competing within the race with Black women. Third, I use men's accounts of the aforementioned high-profile 1996 campus rape of a Spelman student to unpack how the repercussions of rape allegations position these men to think of themselves as at odds with institutions, including the penal system and their college administration. Finally, I return to my question of Morehouse's aggressively homophobic campus culture and situate men's accounts of their efforts to render student queerness invisible as a counterpart to the same Du Boisian double consciousness that fuels their rape culture.

Propriety as Prevention

Understanding the underbelly of gender violence in this environment is incomplete without first acknowledging the roles that men imagine Black women play in the development of their masculinity. Women—or perhaps more accurately the *idea* of women and their idealized femininity—served as a prop in narratives about Black men's presumed rightful gender roles and ideals for Black manhood. Whether it be scolding men for having children out of wedlock or espousing rhetoric about respect for women, the notion of Black femininity provides a foil to the construction of the ideal place and role of Black manhood.

"Morehouse, if you do it right, trains you to be a gentleman," Davis told me, while almost gloating about the college's laurels. While the pride in his voice might suggest that this was a rare distinction, lots of men's colleges and academies throw around the language of molding "gentlemen" as a benchmark behavioral expectation among their students. For the men of Cambridge there is the "Harvard Gentleman"; for the men of the all-male Wabash College there is the "Gentleman's Rule" that obligates student conduct and honor. The Naval Academy boasts that an officer is a "gentleman of liberal education, refined manners, and punctilious courtesy, and the nicest sense of personal honor."[46] These mottos, however, are mostly relics from a time when most colleges and universities were all male, and thus these schools stressed that their students behaved as young men who met the expectations for distinction among the well-heeled sets of white male elites. Crafting "gentlemen" was inarguably meant to signify class status for these schools, but nowadays the majority white men at these colleges barely nod at these old hat expectations as though they were unwanted hand-me-downs of school pride from an expired age in higher education. The emergence of women onto college campuses forced a cultural shift for many other colleges and a feminist critique of how these male-dominated cultures of chivalry limited a view of women as serious scholars and equals. At Morehouse, however, that cultural era of the "gentleman scholar," as the late great Morehouse president Benjamin Mays termed his students, still reigns. The value Morehouse places on the role of a gentleman still served a necessary cultural function for men like Tadd who felt it imbued students with an "understanding of how to carry yourself in all situations, how to be a gentleman, attend school and be able to speak. It's a reaffirmation of [a] middle class, upper middle-class value system," he explained.

Instructions about how to conduct oneself around women have always played a significant role in the training of Morehouse "gentlemen." In my early years at Spelman one of the most common experiences I remember when walking with male classmates was how much attention they spent on publicly chiding guys who forgot to walk on the outside (street side) of a woman while on a sidewalk with her. Some of these customs seemed hopelessly outmoded, like, for example, when groups of men would apologize profusely for using profane language in the presence of a passing woman. Hollow gestures toward respect for women were key to how students performed and policed each other about being chivalrous. Many of these same young men, however, made up lude nicknames to fit the sexual reputations they tagged on entire dorms or individual women.

What I observed firsthand as their classmate, however, was only their real-time interactions with women, however contradictory. It was only through talking to them that it became clear that their ideas about women and sex were far more actively reproduced in their rhetoric than their actions, and that sex plays a prominent part in their beliefs about Black men's individual responsibility to the race. Midway through listing the professional attributes he sees in a Morehouse Man, McCoy, for example, veered off to declare that "as a Morehouse man, you're not fathering out of wedlock children, right?" he said as though he were imagining me as an audience of freshman mentees. "You're doing something to give back to the community, helping someone at some point. And you're providing, you're setting an example to other kids who will see you and you're saying this is how life should be lived, none of that nonsense on TV." McCoy's father was a decorated military officer, and that upbringing, paired with his college experience, imparted him with rigid ideas about men's responsibility. He saw Morehouse men as particularly primed to defy the worst sexual stereotypes about Black men.

"We would debate until three in the morning about how do you change society and how do you make Black culture better," Fitzgerald reflected similarly to McCoy. Coleman echoed the sentiment in saying, "We talked about a lot of these issues—a lot of Black males don't have any positive role models. You can't be a positive role model if you're doing [out-of-wedlock fathering] that makes it worse," while adding that "you can't go tell someone else to change their life if you brought a kid into the world and [are] not being a positive influence to them. You have no credibility." McCoy agreed that Morehouse men were obligated to "be respectable in relationships with women and develop themselves as community leaders."

As a point of pride, he noted that none of his classmates had fathered out-of-wedlock children.

Black men can justifiably claim that their sexualities have been highly vilified historically, and that the myth of the Black male rapist is but one of the ways that Black men's sexuality has been assaulted by racialized state policies.[47] Rhetoric about the hypersexuality of Black men (and women) and widespread stereotypes of absentee fathers with multiple unplanned children with different women helped to fuel state-sanctioned class warfare against working Black families throughout the late twentieth century, even as studies show that 59.5 percent of Black fathers live with their children and that Black fathers are more likely than their white or Latino counterparts to have direct, hands-on involvement in childrearing.[48] The college experience is no refuge from this loaded racial history.

One can hardly imagine the men of Wabash, Harvard, and the Naval Academy spending the wee hours of their night in their dorm rooms debating about how their sex lives could improve the reputations of white men and better the conditions for white families. The hook-up culture and binge drinking that are commonplace on white campuses are not prominent in HBCU campus life, likely because these behaviors carry different stigmas and have lifelong reputational consequences in the close-knit networks of Black college alumni.[49] Fraternity houses where such parties occur are nonexistent at Morehouse. Casual sex still happens, but the meanings men make about sex reach far beyond the context of a coed romance. In the above narratives, men connect their personal sexual propriety to race-betterment, but this kind of talk about women and sexism was not limited to gatherings of students. Dewey recounted that convocations discussed "the degradation of women" and how "you shouldn't be treating women this way," before directly tying the treatment of Black women to widespread stereotypes about Black men by adding that "it's all tied to not being what the world tells you you are." Mort recalls, discussions of women took on a more paternalistic tone when male administrators spoke on the matter to audiences of students. "There were issues of sexism that [were] talked about," he began. "I remember this one Crown Forum, [the speaker] talked about sexuality, sexism, but he said something, and Spelman women just so happened to be there and they walked out on him. They were upset." When I probed for any details of what he guessed upset the women, he couldn't remember the specifics but made clear that "they were upset. He made a comment about protecting—Black men protecting Black women."

The construction of the iconic race man has been historically predicated on the assumption that Black men can rightfully hold racial leadership inasmuch as they protect Black women. Black feminists such as Farah Jasmine Griffin have critiqued how Du Bois, among other Black intellectuals and leaders, used highly paternalistic language to describe Black womanhood, even as he championed the importance of Black women's suffrage movements to overall racial equality.[50] Watching the Spelman students walk out on the speaker sparked Mort's awareness and later activist allyship about feminist issues, mostly because he struggled in that moment to understand what had upset them in a speech he felt at the time honored Black women. Until that moment of realization, however, Mort was like almost all of the respondents who, throughout their college years, viewed modeling normative masculine roles and sexual propriety as paths through which they imagined their individual lives improving the race. They were not only aware of how Black male sexuality is seen beyond he veil but also projected a gendered veil onto Black femininity where Black women are discussed primarily inasmuch as they reinforce and complement normative masculine roles. If Black men's path to restoring their masculine roles and images banked on performing normative roles as breadwinners, providers, and residential fathers, then Black women were key ingredients for making the families that would restore the image and traditional roles of Black men in the household. As Coleman railed, "The misogyny, the disrespect of women, Black women, other women, the disintegration of the Black family…Once you disrespect yourself, you disrespect the Black woman, you no longer have a Black family." Race betterment, in this view, is accomplished not by examining the conditions facing Black women and children, but, rather, by improving the status of Black men within the race, from which the whole of the race will subsequently benefit.

Personal behavior and propriety have deeply racialized meanings in the lives of Black men, particularly with regard to schooling. Schooling is an especially veiled experience for Black boys who become aware that they are hyperpunished in the K–12 years[51] and, if they are high achieving, often carefully navigate academic success for themselves by observing and (as best they can) avoiding behaviors for which they witness other Black boys being punished. Through this racial lens on punishment and propriety, sex is not only approached as a social expectation for college life but also carries meanings that men associated with risk, impropriety, punishment, and highly negative outcomes. Even as men discussed sex in the context of dating they also expressed anxieties about sexual behavior that "gets you in trouble," damage's one's reputation, or leads to highly undesirable life-altering consequences. College, then, is not so much seen as a time for free exploration with limited long-term consequences but, rather, as an experience riddled with risks to navigate for one's personal posterity and for the reputations of Black men. Being a "gentleman scholar" may have been a social contract for good behavior on campus, but their college years were also flooded with the awareness that Black men on college campuses to were also obliged to a contract with the race.[52] As one respondent stated firmly: "You cannot have an all-Black male school be known for sexual assault. It just did not work."

Projecting the veil onto personal sexual propriety continued even in their postgraduate careers. Many of the men explained how they intentionally talked about and displayed their (heteronormative) marriages and families in order to counter assumptions about Black male promiscuity from mostly white (mostly male) coworkers who at times made racist and unsolicited comments about their sex lives. In the professional world, they learned to use monogamy with Black women spouse and partners as strategies against sexualized racism in the white-dominated workplace, but in their college years sexual propriety was considered a safeguard against the two behaviors men distinguished as having the most life-altering consequences: unwanted pregnancies and rape accusations (sometimes generically referred to as "problems with women"). The normally reticent Fitzgerald didn't offer up much about his college friends, but when he did he told me somberly of how an unwanted pregnancy can drastically alter a young man's future. His friend dropped out of Morehouse to work a menial job after getting his girlfriend pregnant. "She finished [college] he didn't. All the rest of us finished, he didn't." Fitzgerald seemed to repeat himself out of sympathy for his friend. "He wears Morehouse attire all the time, talks about Morehouse, he said he's going to [finish]. It's ten years later." For Coleman and McCoy out-of-wedlock children disqualified Black men from moral leadership (and, thus, racial leadership), and for Fitzgerald, casual sex with women loomed as a cautionary tale about the potential pitfalls to a man's upward mobility.

This idea of "getting in trouble" was one of the most frequent contexts in which men discussed rape, most often in relationship to punishment. Six of the men (including the three aforementioned) claimed that even consensual sex (in their perception) "gone wrong"

Sexual Assault

What Every Morehouse College Student Should Know

Morehouse College does not tolerate sexual assault in any form. There are caring faculty and staff at Morehouse College to support you if have been sexually assaulted. While **sexual** assault is a <u>crime</u> with a legal definition, there are many **other** exploitative behaviors that may not be defined as assault, but which may result in disciplinary action. Sexual violence is a term that encapsulates many behaviors that could be sexually inappropriate, hurtful, and coercive or any sexual contact without consent. Report any suspected incident of **sexual assault** or **violence** to the **Title IX Coordinator Crystal Lucas located in Gloster Hall, Room 109, via email: crystal.lucas@morehouse.edu 404-215-6200** or the **Assistant Dean of the College for Student Conduct in the Office of Student Conduct (OSC) 404-215-2681.**

If you think you have been sexually assaulted, we encourage you to take the following steps:

- ✓ Get to safe place and call the police, EMS, and/or someone you trust, like a friend, Resident Dean (RD) or Resident Assistant (RA).
- ✓ Do not bathe, shower or change clothes. Doing so, you may destroy evidence that can be used to press charges if you choose to do so.
- ✓ Go to the hospital. It's important to get medical attention for any injuries, as well as address any possible sexually transmitted diseases. You can call **the Morehouse College Police Department, MCPD (404)215-2666.**
- ✓ Seek counseling. You don't have to cope with sexual assault alone. For advice and emotional support, you can call the **Morehouse College Counseling Resource Center (404)215-2636.**

Reporting Outside of Morehouse College

Call 911 or go to the police department that has jurisdiction over the area where the incident occurred. You can call **Morehouse College Police Department, MCPD (404)215-2666,** if you need help determining where to file your report or if you would like, for them to accompany you to that police agency.

Reporting Through Morehouse College

If the incident occurred on campus, you can file your report with MCPD, and if you have questions or a complaint about sexual harassment or sexual violence, you should report your concerns to the **Title IX Coordinator located in Gloster Hall, Room 109, Crystal Lucas, crystal.lucas@morehouse.edu, 404-215-6200.** Please note that all suspected cases of sexual violence or misconduct will be investigated by **Title IX** and adjudicated by the **Office of Student Conduct (OSC) 404-215-2681.** The Assistant Dean of the College for Student Conduct enforces the Student Code of Conduct and Policies that govern Morehouse College students.

For further information concerning sexual misconduct, please refer to the Morehouse College Student Handbook.

FIGURE 10. Morehouse sexual assault pamphlet.

held out the possibility for life-destroying consequences and severe sanctions. Horace pressed on me the seriousness with which both students and the administration took sexual assault allegations. "You were told this from Freshman Orientation. It was repeated. [Staff and administrators] were like *look if this happens all hell is going*

to break loose. We will have zero tolerance. We will not tolerate the as-
sault of women on our campus." I probed Horace for any concrete examples of sexual assault prevention efforts on campus (for example,
workshops, teach-ins, or campus services). He responded: "That's
interesting. That's a good question. But I don't know if they really
sat down and said *this constitutes sexual assault.* But you just knew.
Most of us kind of knew. But I would say the main rule is like if she
says '*no,' no means no.* You don't push. And if you get accused, that's
a problem." The murkiness in Horace's response should remind us
of why Koss argued that men's definitions of rape exclude an array
of nonconsensual sexual acts. This example suggests that sexual assault prevention at Morehouse relies on men to correctly fill in the
gaps of a very incomplete discussion about prevention. The college's Department of Student Conduct issues a two-page guideline
for "Etiquette and General Behavioral Expectations" on its official
website, but a one-page PDF with the heading "Sexual Assault: What
every Morehouse College student should know" points out the steps
to report an assault and contact the college's Title IX officer (it says
nothing of preventing assault). While the college temporarily authorized a campaign of campus signage where a banner read "Consent
is Sexy," there is no official college literature or programming about
consent or assault prevention, nor is there a rape crisis center or any
personnel who specialize in LGBTQIA counseling. With 2019's Title
IX ruling, the administrators have worked on introducing a com-
prehensive gender violence prevention training program for students and staff, but it is yet unclear if the training will be mandatory. Since the 1996 *Emerge* article, Morehouse administrators have
repeated their stance that "inappropriate sexual conduct has never
been acceptable on the Morehouse campus and it will not be tolerated now."[53] Which begs the question, are "conduct" and appropriateness stressed in campus responses because they have individualized behavioral connotations? Sexual assault was underscored by

administrators as a matter of personal conduct, in lieu of instructing students on fundamental definitions of consent, violence, coercion, or force.

Despite his claim that "most of us kind of knew," Horace, like nearly all of the men interviewed, did not seem to know what constitutes sexual assault. Sexual assault includes a range of behaviors including unwanted physical contact, stalking, harassment, fondling, attempted rape, and rape, which is a sex act that occurs without the affirmative consent (voluntary and active participation) of both parties. The masculinist law enforcement jargon of "zero tolerance" may be Horace's attempt to infer the seriousness with which the college took the issue, but the absence of any formal prevention policies or instruction suggests that the rhetoric of rape prevention was more memorable than any efforts behind it. This association of rape with Black male respectability is itself a double consciousness way of thinking. Where existing literature has defined rape culture as a means through which men trivialize rape, Horace's narrative suggests the exact opposite: men who see personal conduct and sexual propriety as yoked to the advancement of the race via the improvement of Black masculinity take sexual assault very seriously. This conceptualization of assault seems to exclude any contexts in which men don't see themselves as misbehaving or failing to meet respectable masculine ideals. The tacit message in this racialized rape culture is perhaps the loudest: individual sexual propriety is a sufficient form of rape prevention because *good* Black men don't rape.

That these messages about propriety-as-prevention are delivered in the absence of formal prevention efforts does not necessarily mean that prevention-oriented education wouldn't work. When Mort began his journey to feminist awareness he largely credited the narratives about women and gender violence that he learned in a class from women instructors and that directly countered what he had heard from male administrators in convocations. "We discussed how we treated women our age.... They showed us we have got to get beyond materializing women and that they are important to us in terms of our people succeeding." In a second instance he described a guest lecturer who challenged students to rethink the gender violence in their casual slang. "When you say terms like *I'm hitting it, I'm killing it, I beat the pussy up* they wanted us to think about those terms and what they meant and kind of check ourselves." He otherwise recalled having "learned nothing" about sexual assault through other institutional channels.

Undermining Propriety

Staff and administrators may rely on individual men to comport themselves properly in order to curb sexual misconduct, but the rigid culture of campus rules indicates that staff and administrators often assume the worst of students' abilities to conduct themselves. While eighteen of the thirty-three respondents griped about feeling regulated, rules and practices that dictated interactions with women were especially memorable. Unlike most single-sex institutions, Morehouse men regularly interact with women from neighboring campuses. An extracurricular scene mostly driven by coed events and off-campus parties converges the student life of Spelman and Morehouse. Outside of residence halls and predominantly single sex classrooms, interactions with women form such an integral part of the campus experience that several men mentioned that they applied to Morehouse, ironically, because of the abundance of women nearby. Formally, women and men can cross-register for select classes at the respective campuses and often share student clubs, organizations, and major events such as homecoming festivities.

Informally, a culture of male dominance dictates interactions in mixed social spaces both on and off campus. In these settings, "girl watching," a behavior described as men "sexually evaluating women, often in the company of other men"[54] positions entire groups of men in control of gender-mixed spaces. "It wasn't a whole lot of *I respect you, I'm serious about you,*" Ramsey recalled while seeming to regret his participation. "It was more, *we're gonna do what we want to do.*" Even women who must pass through groups of men as they walk to and from classes or meetings are subjected to a form of sexual harassment that can range from quiet stares and nonverbal gestures to catcalling and following. Four men explained that the specific social draw of these spaces was to "watch and meet girls" or joked about when they were "unsuccessful" with women and thus were losing this tacit competition with men. When going over my notes from Ramsey's interview, I recalled vividly that my reaction to catcalling and girl watching when I was a student was one of my first realizations about the control "the boys" held over common spaces—even spaces on Spelman's closed campus. My first act of college feminism occurred my first semester when I waged a cold war against the fraternity members who camped out on Spelman's benches to "holler" at passing women in our pavilion-like common spaces. It was a daily activity for them until my consistent calls to campus security helped me in daily escorting them off the premises (those guys are my friends now, but our introduction sealed my reputation with them).

Girl watching requires male complicity in a mutual pastime in which men are sizing each other up but are also group bonding around this shared intimidation of women. But the culture of girl watching carries over into how men think even in formal institutional rituals. Morehouse students are "brother-sister" paired with Spelmanites during a matching ceremony after the gender-segregated first week of New Student Orientation for both campuses, when, as Philly put it, "we had so much testosterone pent up that everyone's mom started looking good." Ostensibly, matching provides first-year students with friendship networks and builds camaraderie between the institutions, but under the gaze of their classmates and the build-up of the event, men eagerly display their "sisters" as opportunities for dating and ranking women's attractiveness. "Guys joke about the range of sister you can get" regarding sexual desirability, Tadd jested.

Outside of such formalities, the college provides few spaces to interact with women informally and platonically. Strict residence hall visitation policies forbade overnight female guests, imposed a curfew for all dorm residents, and required that women be signed into dorms (at front desks located in lobby lounges where other men hang out and watch). Rules about visitation forced coed interactions into intimate spaces like bedrooms. The college seems to impose its internalized anxieties about young Black men's sex lives (and the risks to reputation associated with Black men and sex) into its structure, but the rigidity of the rules invites breaking them—as men readily admitted to doing in order to maintain sex lives in their young adult years.

The college may attempt to turn a blind eye to sex on campus, but by forcing sex into the secrecy of rule-breaking and sneaking women in and out of dorms, what could otherwise be casual late-night interactions are forced into overnight stays. Female guests, for example, are often left alone or in pairs, hiding in bedrooms until visitation hours resume the next day. Having an active sex life, then, becomes a masculine status symbol not only of those who are actively dating, but who also who don't submit to authority when it comes to their sex lives. "I had so many [women's] phone numbers I never got a moment's peace in my room," laughed Dolphy.

In analyzing these memories of interactions with women, however, I noticed a startling absence of stories about platonic coed friendships. That made little sense to me. While at Spelman, I had multiple meaningful friendships with Morehouse men, as did every woman I knew. Missing accounts of nonsexualized encounters with women could not mean they did not occur. Rather, it confirmed what neuroscientists have established about episodic memory: it is organized spatially.[55] Neutral campus spaces like study halls, common lounges, and recreational facilities routinely prohibit women (either at specific or all hours) or require Morehouse IDs to enter (like the dining hall). Men were remembering women sexually due to the sexually charged spatial contexts in which they encountered them on campus. In those male-dominant and limiting spaces, men found themselves caught between the pressure to impress other men by sexualizing women or live up to the institution's "gentlemanly" image to evade punishment and risk being associated with these encounters. "You gotta realize there are going to be women who will want to come over, who will want to stay in the dorm," Horace told me sternly, as though cautioning current students or even his figurative former self. "You are an adult now. You need to make that decision. Understand there are grave consequences if something happens."

The structure of space and rules on campus places men's coed interactions on continuous display to other men in contexts where they sexualize women. Girl watching may turn women into objects of the male gaze, but it also places men within the male gaze as they watch and evaluate each other and create an expectation for each other that social interactions with women must have a sexual intention. The college may promote ideals of gentlemanly sexual propriety in its rhetoric, but its rules and physical structure promote pastimes of gender dominance and leave men with little to no common spaces to hang out with women casually or individually without performing to the expectations of group cultures of masculine dominance.

Rape culture is masculine culture, and how men use girl watching and sex to impress and size-up each other is part of how colleges organize men into hierarchies that are constituted by their intersecting lines of race, class, sexuality, and physical ability. The differences in status, power, and place in the pecking order that men ascribe to each other (either as individuals or as groups) is captured by a concept that gender theorists call *hegemonic masculinity*. Hegemonic masculinity explains these kinds of hierarchical relationships among men in different settings, where race (and class, and sexuality, and such) determine how the same men can have power and dominance in some settings but are rendered subordinate in others.[56] For example, on a predominantly white campus all Black men would be racially marginalized to white men, but in the almost racially homogenous setting of an HBCU, Black men have power over women and different degrees of power over each other. By situating rape culture in relation to how college men do hegemonic masculinity, it can be viewed as a substantial part of the process through which men negotiate and renegotiate their power across these different contexts. Gaining dominance over men (and other women) by sex or other ways is a means by which men vie for the resources they do and do not have in order to shore up their masculine pecking order—even if the goal is only to impress each other or conform to group expectations about how men should be and act. Michael Kimmel, a sociologist who studies the social worlds of (mostly white) college-aged men, pointed out this dynamic as a foundation of what he called "guy culture" by explaining that "men subscribe to [masculine] ideals not because they want to impress women, let alone any inner drive or desire to test themselves against some abstract standards. They do it because they want to be valued by other men."[57]

But those masculine ideals are themselves racialized and require understandings of how college men engage masculinity differently and thus perpetuate rape culture through a lens of racially specific meanings. Too often—even as campus sexual assault scholars acknowledge the masculine basis of rape culture—approaches to studying college men and rape assume a *one size fits all model* where the ways white men think about manhood and the masculine ideals they uphold are blanketed onto all other groups of college men. Overlooking racialized men in rape culture and sexual assault prevention scholarship isn't just a matter of missing an experience or acknowledging difference. Such an omission reproduces incomplete and inaccurate understandings of how rape culture benefits and is deployed by men. What I heard in the responses from my participants was that their construction of rape culture and views of rape weren't just different from the dominant narrative about rape culture but were actually contradictory. These men weren't participating in rape culture as a means of syphoning themselves off into a "guy culture" that insulated their college years from the responsibilities and consequences of the "real" world. To the contrary, rape culture was one of the ways they positioned themselves in relationship to the larger world and tethered their sense of their own masculinities to the burden of being seen by a world that racially marginalized them. Their concept of rape culture not only provided them with a sense of how to "do" gender for themselves, but also provided them a means of doing race. Through rape culture, they project a lens from the outside in—a way of seeing their masculinities through the eyes of others and of validating racism's veil on their manhood.

Competition as Compensation

Hegemonic masculinity invites us to consider race within examinations of college men, but it is not a sufficient theory of racialization unto itself. While it describes how men have or lack power in relationship to each other, it cannot account for how racialization from that power dynamic in the way that Du Boisian thought fully accommodates. Within double consciousness theory, the veil is constitutive. Its power organizes the lives, hierarchies, and dynamics among the racialized subjects behind it. For young Black men, the college experience is one of the sites in their lives where their immediate sense of hegemonic competition with other men converges with a double consciousness about how Black masculinity is also staked on their ability to maintain gender dominance within the race.

Masculinity is not static, but, rather, it is gained, lost, and reproduced on the contested grounds of the power relations that fuel male competition.[58] What resources and power men lack in hegemonic relationship to each other must be compensated elsewhere and through other means.[59] For racialized masculinities, college experiences are enmeshed with myriad attempts to navigate, strategize, and "bargain" not only within their immediate pecking order with each other but also for the racial power they do not have in the larger social and political masculine pecking order.[60] Rape culture and dominance over women—particularly women within their racial group—provides a means of doing that bargaining, but extant approaches to campus rape cultures have missed the dimension that race adds to college men's view of competition.

Competition surfaced as one of the three most frequent themes in the data and was particularly pronounced in peer dynamics. Masculinities scholars such as Sharon Bird and C. J. Pascoe have illuminated the principal role that competition plays in organizing men's lives within homosocial spaces, schools, organizations, and workplaces.[61] In a pool of over 2,000 Black males, comparisons are nearly inescapable, and Morehouse men size each other up as they compete for jobs, grades, scholarships, fraternities, and student leadership positions. Over two-thirds of the men described themselves in high school as being one of a handful of academically high performing Black males (if not the only). Arriving in an all-male setting where competition was spread across so many high performing Black men can be new, eye-opening, and anxiety provoking.

"Most of the competition, it started out freshman year because everybody wanted to be *King Ding-a-Ling* because everybody was that in [high] school. When they were in high school most everybody did something and they wanted to reestablish their dominance in a room full of dominant young men," McCoy spouted frankly. Fitzgerald voiced a similar experience when sharing that "for the first time, you're competing with Black men who you ain't never competed with in your life.... The environment of Morehouse in particular, it's a bit problematic." From the day they arrive on campus, men spoke about competition as coloring most of their interactions with other men. "The pressure is definitely who's going to be the hot shot," Fitzgerald added. "Who's going to be the catch, if you will, later down the line." For Yusef, establishing himself in the male hierarchy was a core motivation. "When I decided to go to Morehouse I said the only way I'm going to Morehouse is if I'm at the top of Morehouse."

But "later down the line" for these men can mean crossing over to a world dominated by white men and white masculine standards, against which they will always be judged. Even in the almost entirely all-Black space of Morehouse, men spend their college years having their anxieties stoked about proving their fitness for professional competition with white men. The ways they talked about white masculinity—most often in the context of graduate school, career competition, or simply universal white male dominance—were nearly always colored by a need to compensate for being judged unfairly in a mainstream where whites had numerous advantages. "Life is not fair and to get the same thing I would have to work twice as hard," Roy sighed. "If I can tell myself I worked just as hard as that white guy, well, I didn't work hard enough." But the white men with whom they are competing also set the rules of the game, and Morehouse men's college years are spent adopting that Du Boisian "two-ness" where white masculinity is dually upheld as the standard of success they must appease and the rivals against whom they are perpetually disadvantaged. The formidable task is commended with racial pep talks from faculty and administrators. "We were told that in any [career] you go into that there's no one better, and that's Black, white, anybody," Ornette said, reassuring himself that Morehouse had prepared its men for white dominated professions. "You can contend with the guys at Duke and Princeton."

The peer-to-peer pecking order is also bargained on the dating scene. Spelman and Morehouse belong to a consortium of six historically Black neighboring member institutions. The two single-sex institutions have a long-held reputation for attracting more affluent African Americans than adjacent schools like the coed Clark Atlanta University. The ranking of women's desirability organizes the hierarchies of the men who date them, where social class largely determines a woman's "rank." McCoy explained this dating hierarchy to me: "The top of the heap is if you had a nice-looking girl at Spelman. If you had a nice-looking girl at Spelman you were winning. If you had a nice-looking girl at Clark [Atlanta University] you were still winning, but it was like a 10 at Clark is a 7 at Spelman. Because she might give you some nice-looking kids but they might not be that smart. I'm not trying to say people who go to Clark are stupid, but it is what it is." The ranking of female coeds is a crude system, but the complexities of intergroup gender dynamics for Black collegians are far thornier than can be observed on the dating scene or even on campus. In Kimmel's *Guyland* or the alcohol-laden party scenes and "hook-up culture"[62] that depict campus casual sex and that have grabbed sociological attention of late, men's sexualized dynamics with women are primarily oriented toward the sexual consumption of women. These race-muted analyses miss a key dynamic that Du Boisian theory centers and enriches: Black male collegians are immersed in a campus context in which Black women are not simply tools in a male competition for resources but can also be viewed by Black men *as* competition themselves.

By the time they reach college, most Black male collegians are drenched in a rhetoric of "Black male exceptionalism"—the belief that Black men and boys fare more poorly than any other group and that racism disproportionately penalizes Black males.[63] All of the respondents referenced the challenges facing young Black men nationally, but Tadd specifically saw Morehouse as having a direct role in "creating leaders out of Black males, males who are by definition at risk, as some would say, starting at a lower point than other males." Proponents looking to drum the rhetoric of Black male exceptionalism have often looked to higher education as proof that Black men are losing out to Black women. Minister Louis Farrakhan, the firebrand leader of the Nation of Islam and organizer of the Million Man March, was highly vocal about casting the higher ed gender disparity as a sexual crisis for Black men and a rationalization for assaults on Black women. In a 1994 speech, he upbraided an all-female crowd of over 10,000 attendees to: "Look at all these young women going to college.[64] When you [Black women] come with your degree, he [the Black man] is already behind. The only thing he has is his physical strength and his sex.... To have power, the white male broke the black male. Once your male is broken, you [Black women] are fair game for being the victim."

While Black women earn nearly two-thirds of all bachelor's degrees for African Americans, 70 percent of master's degrees and 60 percent of doctorates,[65] the reality of higher education is that both Black and white women outperform boys in high school grade point averages and out enroll men on campus.[66] While Black male college enrollments have doubled since the 1970s,[67] the rhetoric that Black women are outpacing Black men in education and careers has colored intraracial gender dynamics and institutional responses for African Americans across US campuses.[68] Morehouse's enrollment consistently outnumbers Spelman, but since the 1990s the endowment gap between the two colleges has widened, and Spelman's national rankings have climbed well past those of Morehouse.[69] The status of Spelman and its women can pose a threat to those men whose expectations for Black masculinity come with a sense that masculine dominance on campus should mirror masculine dominance within the race.

My conversation with Shadow reflected much of this uneasiness. Shadow was deeply involved in student activities that put him in regular dealings with Spelman's student leaders. I was caught off guard by how seamlessly he transitioned from thinking about his status among his male peers to thinking about sex as a tool of social dominance. I asked him who he saw as his contenders when he was at Morehouse: "Everybody... I think there's a healthy sense of competition with all my Morehouse brothers, and, for that matter, you know, with other colleges. With Howard, with Hampton, with Clark.[70] With Spelman in a very weird Freudian sexual way." Intrigued, I asked him to explain what he meant. He replied: "Well, okay, if your school has more money and it's ranked better, that's great. But then you can conquer her by having sex with her."

Competition with Black women is the lone arena where race is not Black men's shortcoming and patriarchy is their foreseeable advantage. For many college-educated Black men, that patriarchy is largely maintained by staying "ahead" of Black women's accomplishments. Shadow could not be blunter in viewing sexual dominance as a means of compensation, within intraracial gender dynamics but also in relationship to the competition men experience elsewhere with their classmates and with groups at other institutions. It is only by conjoining the Du Boisian and hegemonic masculinity frameworks that we can cast the meanings Shadow and other men use to make sense of competition across different contexts where they have varying levels of resources available to them. With white men, the strategy to compete professionally was work ethic, while sexual dominance was the available resource for competition with Black women's impending educational and professional advancement. Extant literature on college masculinities mostly cap-

tures the immediate peer-to-peer scope of competition with surrounding men, and yet college masculinity for Black men isn't just a
matter of gender-bargaining within their immediate campus pecking order. The act of being in college itself carries with it contexts
that trap Black men between the anxiety of racial disadvantages
ahead of them and the mindset of competing with the Black women
next to them.

The Veiled Threat

I would be dissatisfied with this book and myself as its author if I did
not address the original question that spurned my pursuit of this research so many years ago in my senior thesis at Spelman. My question then, as it is now, is a culture of antiqueerness and homophobic
violence at Morehouse fastened to how men framed race and racism
in their lives? Thinking through double consciousness allowed me to
realize how the veil adheres homophobic culture to the other side of
the coin of rape culture. Throughout the 1990s, the *Princeton Review*
consistently ranked Morehouse among the most homophobic campuses in America.[71] Yet there is a disturbing amount of disagree-
ment among graduates of that era about whether this is even a problem. As alumnus and campus LGBTQ activist Michael Brewer put it,
"Morehouse is like this enclave where Stonewall never happened."[72]

This homophobic culture is provoked and intensified by a self-
consciousness among the student body of Morehouse's well-known
reputation for its disproportionately queer student body. Throughout
my interviews, the majority of the respondents—with the exception
of a small number of men who consider themselves queer allies—
expressed discomfort with the college attracting, if not incubating,
both closeted and "out" gay men as well as a small number of nonbinary students. Gay jokes about the college from outsiders annoyed
Elvin and Yusef. Even for Archie, the six foot five inch athlete who

physically intimidated his way out of submitting to NSO leaders who "couldn't get more girls" than he, there was no denying that a large part of campus life is organized around the closet. "The college is in the closet about how many students are in the closet," he deadpanned. The closet actively organizes student life and even physical spaces. Entire dorms are loudly rumored to "be gay," as are student organizations like the Glee Club.

The existence of gay students and spaces, however, relies on rendering them invisible to the outside gaze on the college. Much like the rhetoric of women and families in previous narratives propped up some respondent's notions of valid and rightful forms of manhood, so did men like Bird use the same rhetoric of families and the Black men who lead them to disqualify queer Black men from having a visible role in the race. Bird was one of the respondents who was the most consistently forthcoming about his strong opinions, and by the time he was telling me firmly of his views on sexuality, we had been on the phone for hours. "If [faculty and staff] are trying to teach us how to build strong Black families, I think all these gay cats, kind of, it's a dual message," he said with a slightly hesitant tone as though aware of how his thoughts might offend me. He picked up the pause in his sentence by saying: "To the extent that I don't necessarily believe a gay man can raise a strong Black family. So that can be a difference of opinion, there can be statistics to prove me wrong, but that's the belief I have. So that means they want to have families. So given that we're the Talented Tenth, we're supposed to lead Black families. I don't see how that's a productive endeavor." Confused by who he referred to in his last statement, I asked him to elaborate. "To be welcoming and accepting of a blatantly gay lifestyle," he again searched carefully for his words, "you can be gay all you want, but the lisp, the being feminine, this that and the third? I don't know if that raises a strong, productive family."

Bird's-eye views were not shared by all of the men. To the contrary, many of the respondents had evolved their stances on sexuality since their years on campus. Ornette advocated that the image of Morehouse manhood be expanded to include gay men, although he did not explain the extent to which these students could be femme or non-gender-conforming. Monk criticized the homophobic culture of the school, and he was among the minority of men who appeared to have no interest in ostracizing gay students. Mort prided himself on having stood up for rights of gay student organizations as his schoolmates loudly jeered him during a campus town hall. But Bird communicates something more complex in how he feels about queerness. Like Archie, Bird is well aware of the considerable number of queer students who operate both within and outside the closet. It's the *visibility* of queerness that's the problem. He says as much: *you can be gay all you want*. Bird is not committed to getting rid of queerness, but simply to hiding it from view.

Visibility is a finite resource for the racialized subject. For Black men who have historically grounded their claims to citizenship on morality and who have had racist views of Black male sexuality weaponized against that morality, deviations from that expectation of heteronormativity can be met with aggression. When queer students organize for safety, recognition, or resources, backlash can swiftly ensue. Negotiating for finite resources may be one tactic of hegemonic masculinity, but those who possess the means and power will simply eliminate competition where it threatens their share of resources.

This was poignantly evident in the reflections Mingus had on his days as a Student Government Association officer. Several others mentioned Mingus as the classmate they felt epitomized success. Yet his experiences led him to reevaluate the messages about masculinity he received at Morehouse. "For me, college was business," he announced, with more creed than ego in his tone. He recalled an incident in high school where he found himself embarrassingly distracted from a chemistry teacher who had called on him because he was flirting with a girl he liked. The incident had made him think that it would be difficult to be academically serious in the presence of women, and he had seriously considered Wabash and West Point for this reason. "If college is a business then I need to be in an environment where I'm going to maximize my business. So, I decided that what's best for me would be a predominantly male environment."

At Morehouse, Mingus had excelled in high profile student leadership positions and quickly gained the respect of his peers. "I was uber aggressive," he admits. "I [was] very bent on leadership and being in charge." He had chartered his own student group with the express aim of gaining a senate seat in the Student Government Association. "Leadership to us was student government. That Morehouse Man image looked like student government. So in my effort to maximize that Morehouse image, I did student government. Being in charge meant you got respect." After graduation, he went to work on Wall Street in a high-powered corporate environment for which he was at once overly prepared and woefully underprepared. He had interned with a prestigious brokerage group his senior year. His handshake was firm, his ties straight, and each morning he arrived in the office well before his colleagues and waved them good night as he stayed late.

But he was no longer in charge. His first boss, an out gay white male executive, defied the cartoonish image of Gordon Gekko-style corporate hypermasculinity he had expected.[73] "He was six feet six, the prettiest white boy I'd ever seen in my life. And he was gaaaaaay," he said, drawing out the word for emphasis. "This was the guy you'd see in the village with the Latin boy with a baby t-shirt. But they were in charge and they made millions." He was working alongside women who were mostly white and found himself competing with their relentless ambition instead of being distracted by their presence. College classes on professionalism had groomed him to be impeccably tailored in Oxford shirts and power ties, but as his career accelerated and remote-working technology improved, he found himself increasingly working from home in jeans and sneakers. Out in the world, he found himself rethinking, if not *unlearning*, the Morehouse message. "I didn't know how I was going to be able to cope," he admitted, describing the consternation he felt in his first steps beyond the boys' club of college. As we talked, he actively reevaluated how his young adulthood had been staked on impressing other men and retaining power over them. It gave him pause when he recalled times he had used his narrow ideas about masculinity to exploit that power.

"I'm not very proud of this moment, but if we're being honest about it, I was pretty homophobic in college," he acknowledged. At Morehouse, he explained, queerness "was very open." He continued: "When I was there they tried to start the first gay club. All the clubs had to be approved by the student senate. At that time I was secretary of the senate and of course the VP [vice president] is the president [of the senate]. The VP was on a witch hunt to keep them off campus, and while publicly he was the one who voiced all the concern, made a grandiose speech about it, we effectively orchestrated this coup to make sure they couldn't get chartered on campus."

It was readily apparent that Mingus was thinking back on his remorse about this experience for the first time, and I treated his vulnerability with kid gloves as I invited him to tell me more about the incident. He told me that nearly the entire student body had backed student government's homophobic stance, and a campus-wide town hall was held. He explained the reasoning behind this hostility toward the queer students. "It was pure…" he hesitated, catching thoughts he had never before been asked to order. "It's not what Morehouse is about. Like it doesn't say gay Black man, right? That was my concern at the time." I replied by pointing out that nowhere does it say *straight Black man* either. "Yep! You're very right," he chirped, as he continued to explain the behaviors that he now regretted:

> For me at the time, it was probably pure fear. Pure fear…I think it was generic homophobia couched in what would deteriorate the Morehouse brand. I'm pretty sure we said all that BS. It came down to pure irrational fear that somehow allowing them on campus said something about my own manhood. That's what it came down to. If anybody's being honest, and I think most people won't say that, but that's what it came down to: irrational fear that them being gay on campus said something about my own manhood. When actually it had nothing to do with me….Honestly, I associated the Morehouse brand with masculinity. That meant heterosexual to me. And I thought that's what we were protecting. Honestly it's hard for me to talk about it now because it's one of the dumber things I've ever done in my life.

Mingus and his allies were not sniffing out queer students. He had worked alongside several student government leaders who were rumored to be gay and some whose closet doors were more frosted glass than opaque. "There were other gay people in our administration that have come out to be gay now. That I knew were gay. That I've been on trips with, been in dorm rooms with." "One on one," gay students, he insisted, "never bothered me." But Mingus's homophobia, like Bird's, was set to the veiled dial of how Morehouse men were viewed from the outside gaze. He bristled at jokes made by a male cousin at another HBCU about Morehouse's gay reputation. "I've been conscious about that joke since elementary school," he explained, adding that it reverberated through films like *School Daze* where he knew the homophobic jokes were not-so-quiet digs at his school. "I probably still bristle to some degree," he admitted. But it was the "open display of it" that had driven Mingus and his student government co-conspirators to the point where in-house legal counsel had to intervene. "I'm still big on that image that Morehouse portrays. It is an institution for educating Black men, and in my mind that pertains to a certain box, whether you agree with that box or not, I still believe that." That box, however, was like a window dressing placing Morehouse manhood on constant display to view from beyond the veil. He seemed to be trying to reconcile his actions with his beliefs about his own character. "The reason I'm so disgusted by the experience was that my entire life I've been a proponent of fighting bullies.... My most disgusting moment was when I became the bully."

Racializing the Repercussions of Campus Sexual Assault

Organizing to block a queer student group's charter would prove to be the second largest controversy in which Mingus got involved. He was among roughly a fifth of all the respondents who were students during the time of the college's most high-profile rape case to date, the previously noted 1996 rape of a Spelman coed that made cover stories and headlines across various outlets. For those who were students at the time, it was a landmark controversy. Davis recalled, when telling me of some of his most indelible memories of campus news, that "four or five of my Morehouse brothers were brought up on charges of rape" of a Spelman freshman. The incident sparked immediate outrage and calls for legal recourse from Spelman student activists and administrators. Davis had been close friends with one of the accused and had expected administrators to fully come to his friend's defense.[74] He continued: "[Then Morehouse president] Dr. Massey felt that it was better to let the justice system do what it was going to do and that the college would just wait to see how the whole police investigation went, when it was really some hearsay type stuff. And Johnetta Cole at the time was the president of Spelman and she was lock stock and barrel behind the Spelman student. Who turned out to be lying." That the victim was "lying" is unsubstantiated, but charges were later dropped against the accused. As a student government leader, Roy boldly voiced his disappointment with the administration's lack of support for the accused directly to deans. "I was led to believe this was a brotherhood and brothers stick together." He consistently framed the accused men as the injured parties whose characters were under assault by Spelman women. Similarly, Davis firmly voiced in regard to one of the accused: "This was a young man, college student, never been in trouble a day in his life and now he sits in jail accused of rape and at the bail hearing [President Cole] spoke at length about how my brothers were monsters and that you cannot release them off into the streets. And Dr. Massey, who I have a great deal of respect for till this day and I was very close to him, did not do anything." Mentioning jail seemed to particularly pique the emotion in Roy's tone. The relevance of thinking about incarceration cannot be understated in the lives of young Black men, even those whose everyday lives are otherwise distant from the realities of incarcerated Black men.

Given the racial discrimination against African Americans that pervades the penal system, Morehouse men, like many Black male collegians, talk about themselves as men who avoided an "alternate fate" of being criminalized. The sentiment about the unfortunate outcomes of other Black men frames their reverence for their college. Percy remarked, "This is Morehouse. This is 3,000 Black men. You will never see a collection of Black men like this anywhere outside of prison." Clifford explained that a common thread throughout student discussions was that "we could be part of the ones who were succeeding, not in jail." Sexual assaults are one of the most serious acts that can put Black college men within reach of the white carceral state, and, thus, the emphasis they place on the penal system in their understandings of campus sexual assault cannot be overstated.

Thoughts about incarceration within the racialized rape cultures of white male collegians may be absent from existing studies because colleges are institutions that have historically immunized white male students from the consequences of their most common criminal behaviors. But for Morehouse men, the context of incarceration was present overall in their thoughts about their roles in college and hyperpresent in their understandings of assault allegations. Where Black women collegians are already presumed to be competition within the race, the most vocal respondent reactions to rape allegations largely cast Black women victims and their supporters as out to get Black men. Perhaps because they viewed campus rape allegations as one of the most divisive issues of their college years, Davis, Mingus, and Roy had emotionally charged memories of how the high-profile assault implicated their classmates. Woven together, their narratives walk us through how men's understandings of assaults with Black male perpetrators constitute a race *and* gender-making experience that placed Black males at odds with institutional forces for which the penal state and their college are the institutions at play.

Mort, the consistently lone voice of dissent, broke ranks with his classmates and sympathized with Spelman activists. He contextualized the 1996 rape within the growing national Black feminist backlash to Freaknik,[75] a city-wide Atlanta street party that, by the mid-1990s, drew 200,000 Black college revelers and became notorious for its wanton sexual harassment of women.[76] "The group of guys I was with,[77] we were like, this is not cool. We, in solidarity, were with Spelmanites. We would wear buttons [that read] *I Am Not a Freak*." The rest of his classmates, however, by and large closed ranks against any supporters of the victim, who were overwhelmingly Spelman women and administrators. Male solidarity in the face of women's accusations of sexual misconduct and assault is a consistent feature of institutions with pronounced rape cultures and commonplace in the literature on masculinities,[78] but at Morehouse this solidarity was intensified by a belief that the accused (who seemed to symbolically represent the vulnerabilities of Black manhood for their defenders) and the larger student body were closing ranks not just against women, but Black women who were cooperating with law enforcement. Both Davis and Roy hold the view that Black women are manipulative "lying" agents who are willingly complicit in the penal system's criminalization of Black men. Deprived of the privilege of white men, whose colleges shelter them from law enforcement (or whose campus law enforcement agencies largely contribute to the institutional structure of rape culture),[79] Roy and Davis frame accountability as persecution and betrayal of male solidarity.

Just minutes before in our interview, Davis had extolled his "brothers" for how their respect for women demonstrated the virtues of Morehouse manhood. "The speech that a lot of young men are given, that 'no means no' speech. Of course, we were given that," he reported proudly. "We respected our sisters, we love our sisters, and we treat them a certain way, and diversions from that weren't tolerated because when I was in school you took the Spelman sister thing really seriously." When real allegations thrust Black men into the spotlight, however, the anxieties about the public criminalization of a "college student" who had "never been in trouble a day in his life" contort the veil. This distortion of campus sexual assault positions Black women as being on the offensive, racist law enforcement as primed to pounce, and situates Morehouse—the institution that Roy, Davis, and Mingus looked toward to safeguard Black men from those alternative criminal fates—as violating bonds of Black male patriarchy by offering their own up for prosecution. This campus rape incident was the first and only time I heard Roy, Davis, and Mingus, who were otherwise dyed in the cloth cheerleaders of their alma mater, speak negatively about administrators who they viewed as failing to shield the accused from the reach of the carceral state into Black men's lives.

This conviction about Black male solidarity translated into student action. Mingus and others organized student support for the accused including attending courthouse proceedings. "We were advocates for them, talking and arguing with the president about [whether] they should be expelled, trying to keep them in school," he said in a tone calm but deliberate. "We were quite adamantly fighting for their college lives because nobody else was." Elsewhere in other interviews, men such as Clifford, Shadow, and Mort complained that Morehouse students were politically inactive and rarely engaged in larger Black political causes. It is remarkable, then, that solidarity with accused rapists was a peak galvanizing point for politically organizing the student body.

Roy's stance was prominent in this organized front but was less calm when describing where his loyalties fell. "Oh, it was no support for the victim!" he exclaimed after I asked if he recalled if any Morehouse students stood with Spelman activists. "The victim was looked at as making a false call." When I asked Roy why he felt so sure that the victim was lying, his tone tempered. He paused pensively before conceding a point: "Although we knew something happened that might have been inappropriate, she wasn't raped as she had accused her accusers. So for us, we looked at it as *you messed up these brothers' lives*. They had to go through immense media scrutiny. They'd been kicked out of school. Two of them weren't able to come back. [The accused were] popular guys that we thought were reputable. We were shocked to hear the allegations. It tarnished the relationship [between the two colleges] for a minute."[80]

Roy's description of the incident as simply "inappropriate" reframes the men it implicates as nonviolent passive actors. Besides the obvious ambiguity it leaves around nonconsensual acts, his retelling of the account distances them from the stereotypes of Black male predators. In contrast, Roy and Mingus presume the victim ruined the lives of otherwise upstanding men, and that these men and their reputations paid the greatest cost in these incidents. This rhetoric that positions Black male perpetrators as targets of the racist state belongs to a larger racial context that looms over Black men in college. Legal scholar Devon Carbado called this way of thinking "Black male victimization," and noted that Black communities and organizations are complicit in helping Black men "occupy a privileged victim status in antiracist discourse."[81] These assault cases provided the opportunity to frame a defense of Black male perpetrators as antiracist work that unmasks the extent to which the criminal justice system victimizes Black men. As feminist philosopher bell hooks explained, ideas about the exceptional racism and societal pressures Black men face in relation to Black women are often presented as justification for their displays of anger and violence against women. "Many of us were raised in homes where black mothers excused and explained male anger, irritability, and violence by calling attention to the pressures black men face in a racist society....Assumptions that racism is more oppressive to black men than black women, then and now, are fundamentally based on acceptance of patriarchal notions of masculinity."[82]

As a point of clarity, few people, least among them college coeds, understand the legal apparatus of Title IX, which governs university sex-based discrimination and responses to sexual misconduct allegations, operates on what the law calls a "51% standard," meaning that Title IX cases must present a preponderance of evidence that shows that misconduct occurred more likely than not. This is quite dissimilar from the criminal court's much higher burden of proof of "beyond a reasonable doubt." The frustrations I heard from Roy, Davis, and Mingus may be due to the fact that they were not making a distinction between a criminal burden of proof, which may have failed to convict their friends, and the Title IX preponderance standard on which college administrators acted to expel the students. On Title IX grounds, the students were not necessarily innocent, and their criminal case dismissal says little for how that should bear on the college's internal Title IX investigation. What these three framed as a grave injustice against "good" brothers was, juridically and technically, the justice system working to a standard, just not with their understanding of it. We should consider the possibility, perhaps, that a feature of racialized rape culture involves how Black men's veiled hyperawareness about the racist criminalization of Black men by the penal system strongly influences if not warps their view of Title IX's sex-based legal apparatus.

It may be striking that Davis, Roy, and Mingus framed the injustice in this incident on the possibility of a Black man being put out of school as opposed to the lifelong emotional and physical trauma inflicted on Black women victims. Any rape culture is sustained in part by rape *myths*: narratives about the nature of men, women, and sex, such as "women ask for it" or "men are naturally sexually aggressive," that shift blame onto victims. In racialized rape myths, both men and women within a racial group construct baseless narratives about gender, sexuality, and violence that are aligned with their own racial self-interests. A belief in Black male victimization takes a racial truth about the racist criminal justice system and twists it into a misogynistic claim that any allegations against Black men are motivated by a selective disdain for them. When used to protect perpetrators, sentiments such as *they're just trying to bring a good brother down* or Roy's claim that Spelman students "messed up these brothers' lives" trivialize the legitimacy of valid critiques of systemic racial violence and injustice. In Roy's account, for example, a discernable racialized rape myth can be heard in the presumption that both the media and law enforcement are prone to believe lies about Black men's violence. Such a myth requires us to accept that a racist system believes and supports the accounts of Black women and selectively reserves its racism for wrongfully criminalizing Black men.

An ardent belief that female accusers are lying may be related contextually to how rape was historically weaponized by white women accusers. Feminist legal scholar Janet Halley writes that "from Emmett Till to the Central Park Five, American racial history is laced with vendetta-like scandals in which black men are accused of sexually assaulting white women that become reverse scandals when it is revealed that the accused men were not wrongdoers at all."[83] The racial meanings Davis, Roy, and Mingus made about this incident were likely colored by the penal system's violent history of backing white women in their accusations against Black men. In both high-profile and obscure cases, Beverly Guy-Sheftall (a noted feminist scholar and Spelman professor) observes that Black women are placed in the same category as white women accusers.[84] But sexual assault, like nearly all violent crime, overwhelmingly happens *within* a racial group.[85] A belief in Black male victimization assumes that a racist penal system is committed to seeking justice for Black women victims, and that Black men are the rightful lone beneficiaries of antiracist community efforts. In this way of thinking, rape culture racializes Black men but *de*racializes Black women and girls.[86]

Rape begins and ends in the minds of men, but rape cultures are enabled by the environments that do not hold them accountable. The field's currently narrow one-size-fits-all approach to analyzing the direct relationship between masculine culture and rape culture fails to take into account that college men have vastly different ideals of masculinity based on race. In expanding the lens on campus sexual assault by bridging the Du Boisian double consciousness phenomenology to hegemonic masculinity theories, the narratives of Morehouse men have shown us that rape culture is not only a means through which these men are doing gender, but also, and just as importantly, it is a means through which they are doing race and racialization. The lack of Du Boisian theory in existing college masculinities and rape culture literature has failed to account for this, and, conversely, has failed to account for how that Du Boisian interplay between the college man and his understanding of himself in the larger world has kept us from acknowledging that college is a dress rehearsal for manhood throughout the life course. Learning to negotiate gender dominance through rape culture teaches Black college men the resources they do and do not have in comparison to white men, but it also teaches white men the purchase of white masculinity and the relative impunity they can come to expect throughout their lives. College masculinity is masculinity, and a Du Boisian framework holds great theoretical promise for eroding the narrow scope with which we have studied and understood college men to date.

4 *Who among You Will Lead?*

Despite his vast wealth, Robert F. Smith had enjoyed relative obscurity among Black communities for most of his life. The son of schoolteachers who both held PhDs, Smith was a rare fourth generation Black Coloradan raised in a middle-class Denver neighborhood. He displayed an early aptitude for engineering that took him to Cornell University, where he bonded with his fraternity brothers in Cornell's founding chapter of Alpha Phi Alpha, the first Black Greek letter organization in the country. After graduation, Smith combined his undergraduate training in chemical engineering and keen interest in computers with his budding business acumen. After Columbia Business School his career took him from Kraft General Foods to Goldman Sachs, after which he then founded Vista Equity Partners, a private equity firm that invested in technology companies. He quickly amassed what *Forbes* magazine estimates as a five-billion-dollar net worth.[1]

Despite being *the* wealthiest African American, Smith was mostly known only within investment sectors as one of only three Black billionaires. In public he was overshadowed by the ubiquitous celebrity of Oprah Winfrey and Michael Jordan.[2] That changed on May 19, 2019, as he stood facing a crowd of Morehouse graduates, families, and alumni. The sun basked over the rows of graduates sitting in

FIGURE 11. Robert Smith addressing 2018 Morehouse Commencement.

white lawn chairs, many of whom wore sunglasses and shielded their eyes to look up toward Smith and the dark velveted robes of faculty who flanked the stage behind him. Someone in production had an eye to place a wooden African sculpture immediately behind Smith, and the visual effect almost literally framed him in Black authenticity while he referenced such timely race issues as Black Lives Matter and the Me Too movement. Speaking comfortably to the crowd and rarely looking directly into the teleprompter, he reflected on the nine generations of his family on American soil, carefully walking his audience through the policies and laws that had denied them opportunity, even as they "nourished the soil with their blood." The repeals to those laws had made his life possible by the 1965 Voter Rights Act. As a child, he was among the first cohort of Denver's Black pupils to desegregate a high-performing white elementary school on the other side of town through a busing program. "Bus Number 13, I'll never forget it.... That policy of busing only lasted to my fifth-grade year when intense protests and political pressure brought the end to forced busing," he said with a hint of a prideful smile. "But those five years dramatically changed my life. Amazingly almost every single student on Bus Number 13 went on to become a professional," he boasted of his classmates. "Yet when I look at the extended community...those kids who didn't get a spot on Bus Number 13, their success rate was far lower.... Everything about my life changed because of those few short years, but the window closed for others just as fast as it opened for me. That's the story of the Black experience in America.[3]

His speech lasted thirty-five minutes but was almost immediately eclipsed by the announcement he made next. Smith affectionately chided the alumni reunion classes in the audience that, on behalf of the eight generations of his family who had lived in America, this graduating class was being adopted as "My class, 2019. And my family is making a grant to eliminate their student loans." A moment of shocked disbelief preceded uproarious cheers from the young men who, flanked by their families, rose to their feet to clap and wave their caps vigorously in the air. The gift, estimated to be worth $40 million, immediately sparked international coverage, heightening Smith's public profile and sparking comparisons to Bill and Melinda Gates and Warren Buffet.[4] Indeed, Smith was the first African American to join them in signing "The Giving Pledge," a promise to donate most of their wealth to philanthropy during their lifetimes.[5]

For Morehouse, the flurry of headlines generated by the announcement was a welcome change from the previous year of brand-bruising sexual assault coverage. The very image of an entirely self-made Black American tycoon benevolently devoting his private fortune to spare deserving young men from the burden of a national student loan crisis (that was driven in part by government rollbacks on higher education subsidies) crystallized one of the college's most quintessential ideas: that Black communities and institutions are best served by the philanthropy of their own exceptional members, instead of patiently awaiting justice or equity from changes in legal and governmental policies. If enough of us could become as rich and powerful as the white men who dominate the elites, then Black America could tend to its own problems. This vision was a sort of

Talented Tenth tuned to the intraracial wealth gap: A Talented One Percent. Just as importantly, Smith embodied the virtues of Black male leadership that the college consistently propagates among its men by dangling the hope that their predestined racial leadership can be rightfully attained through rugged capitalism. The virtues of corporatism and a narrow framing of success—in which community altruism is desired, but personal upward mobility is required—cast Black men's individual professional and economic gains as the fountainhead of trickle-down racial advancement.

In Smith's narrative of his own life the turning points of his early success were brought about by desegregationist policies, not philanthropy. Viral videos of the commencement address instantly made Smith an icon of Black philanthropy, but the soundbite allowed all who praised him to the ignore the irony that no corporate collaboration or donor generosity could account for how all of his classmates went on to professional success after they briefly benefited from a white school district's resource allocation. It was legislative justice that had made the difference in Smith's childhood, but the fairy-tale appeal of his philanthropy had already taken hold on the graduates and their families and Black communities throughout the country. That a Black billionaire had shown up and done right by his people was the only story told of that day, and Black capitalism was the savior.

This chapter examines the culture of community leadership and corporate influence at Morehouse to analyze the political alchemy that has forged preeminent ideologies about Black male success and achievement. Previous chapters have argued that ideas defying stereotypes about Black male deviance and predation maneuver within notions that Black males are more punished and burdened with stereotypes than any other group, including Black women—a phenomena termed *Black male exceptionalism*.[6] This chapter scrutinizes the other meaning that can be applied to Black male exceptionalism—one that traffics in the belief that Black males, especially those who are college bound and college educated, should receive resources and community investment ahead of other groups of African Americans. In this view, the advancement of the race—including its women—is harnessed first and foremost to the advancement of Black men, and what is best for the race follows from prioritizing what is best for its most promising men.

In addressing how Morehouse men are groomed to infuse ideas about racial leadership and advancement with neoliberal ideas about individualism, personal wealth, and corporate ambition, this chapter looks at the larger political undertaking that vested neoliberal and conservative ideologies within Black male achievement initiatives nationally. Institutions like Morehouse pride themselves on producing the vanguard of highly prepared Black men, whose Windsor knots, firm handshakes, and polished résumés continue to entice professional recruiters and propel them onto executive tracks. Both the college and its graduates are reluctant to acknowledge what lies behind its grooming of ideal corporate candidates; incubating high achieving Black masculinity has become a laboratory for ideological experimentation by public and private interest groups.

Assumed Leadership and an Imagined Community

To return to that moment of Smith's valorous display of philanthropic wealth is to be reminded of the ambidexterity of capitalism and racial consciousness within the hands that mold the college's ideals. In that act of racial altruism, Smith as a man, as a story, and as an incessantly repeated number with his net worth suffixed to any mention of his name, became the ideal bookend to Obama's "no excuses" rhetoric of race betterment via personal responsibility, which he had articulated only six years earlier. We can imagine the continuity of messaging and imagery from a presidential speech that called for abandoning the "excuses" of racial hardship to a titan of individual success who claimed to have amassed great wealth without any excuses about his racial disadvantage. His story affirmed a belief held by many Blacks and whites alike that educated Black men are the most likely African Americans to reach the heights of power, influence, and wealth that can seat African Americans at the table with white elites.

Throughout his life, however, Smith had held none of the traditional roles associated with Black leadership within social and political movements. While he had given heaps of money to education, health care, and cultural and historical institutions for African Americans, he had never been elected office, had been fairly detached from Black political organizations, and had not spoken out on any social justice or racial disparity issue of note. Yet he was accorded the reverence due to race leaders automatically due to his business preeminence and his decision to burnish his legacy by making a massive gift to a Black college. His financial support was solicited by the development staff and trustees of major Black-led institutions, who themselves adopted and popularized a message that participation in Black political organizations and speaking out on racial justice did not make as big an impact to Black progress as philanthropic gestures to Black institutions.

Plenty of universities nod at the laurels of leadership when advertising the academics and character instilled into their students, but the men I interviewed spoke about the inescapable rhetoric of racial leadership that is deeply ingrained into the ideals and imagery of Morehouse manhood in a way that overwhelmed their talk about the college's expectations. The college's messages about leadership are not simply empty rhetoric, and in the years since my respondents graduated, have been formalized within donor-backed institutional initiatives. The Leadership Center, a stand-alone building and academic center, offers programs that purport equipping men with the "knowledge, skills and character needed for a future civil society."[7] The Andrew Young Center for Global Leadership encourages interests in international diplomacy and is named for the civil rights activist, former Atlanta mayor and former US ambassador to the United Nations who, in later life, served as a spokesman for the Walmart Corporation.[8] In addition, the Leadership Studies Program claims to promote "both academic excellence and ethical integrity."[9]

The theme of leadership pervades the college's public informational and promotional literature and inundates student handbooks and curricular guides. As the college puts it: "Leaders, we believe, are made, not born. Since 1867, Morehouse College has been producing world-class leaders—men who are intellectually, socially and morally equipped to meet the challenges and opportunities of their communities and professions."[10] As an underpinning of the Morehouse Brand, the rhetoric and imagination of leadership, drenched in both masculine and racial ideals, heavily colored the tone of my talks with respondents as they considered the relevance of Morehouse men to Black communities. This relationship between Morehouse alumni and leadership was understood so axiomatically that it was often pithily interspersed within conversations about an array of other topics. The default way to refer to Morehouse men, it appeared, was as leaders. Ornette bragged that "we were well regarded in Black communities and looked to for leadership," while Blakey bemoaned how "people who didn't go to Morehouse don't have the extra burden of leadership." For Mort, the college's appeal to prospective students was built on "a chance to be a leader in a larger community," and Yusuf similarly articulated that "part of Morehouse's allure is that you're supposed to be a leader, and so how do you lead across all of those things. I think something that's definitely talked about in different ways, both in class and out." For Milt, leadership was hinged to the benefit of Black communities, and in his view "Morehouse men position themselves to contribute to a broader sense of Black community, to African Americans in general."

Still, others unpacked a deeper sense of the regard with which leadership is held, even as they were somewhat critical of the how leadership feels like a compulsory undertaking for many students. Wes, who was otherwise fairly critical of his experience and who, as an artist and hip-hop musician, had defied many of the expectations of his college and his upper-middle-class parents, told me how the expectation of leadership was pushed in a way that students often lacked a choice about their paths. "You go to Morehouse so that practically makes you a leader," he said, straight-faced. "You're gonna be put on the spot as a Morehouse man. Whether you want to be a leader or not, you're a leader. Contrastingly, Roy didn't see leadership as limiting. "Morehouse doesn't dictate the type of leader you have to be, you just have to be a leader," he told me. "I just learned there were so many great men who came before me who paved the road and made this and gave this institution a reputation that's unlike any other. And so, it's your obligation to your community and to yourself to go out and be the change that you want to see in the world. So, you have to be a leader."

For other men, a sense of class obligation permeated their call to leadership. Dolphy and McCoy invoked the Du Boisian notion of the Talented Tenth to signal the virtues of racial leadership and individual achievement. "They did us pretty much the same way that they did you all [at Spelman], that you are the Talented Tenth," Dolphy said while appealing to the social class commonality of our experience. The message he received from both student leaders and administrators was that "there's no group of African American people on the planet that are as smart, as talented, as capable, or who are going to be as, as successful as you guys and as a whole," and he had no objection to it. "That is the truth." McCoy came off as almost preoccupied with a belief in class exceptionalism. Out of all the men, he made reference to "the talented tenth" the most. "We are the talented tenth. We're claiming this," he boasted proudly. "We are going to instill [it] in our children like a noblesse oblige." His sense of racial leadership, I quickly realized, was not due as much to arrogance as it was to his belief that there was a binding tie (i.e., that *linked fate* belief in racial interdependency that Michael Dawson theorized) that obligated Morehouse's privileged class of graduates to lead the less fortunate of the race. "We take care of our people. Not to just live off the fact and be like I'm smarter than everybody, but to live off of the, much was given to you, so we expect lot. You have to hold up the race," he preached. For McCoy, It wasn't simply the education that entitled Morehouse men to this position, it was the class obligation that leased Morehouse leadership its moral grounds.

It was hard for me not to notice, however, that these lofty expectations of community leadership came from within the college, not *from* these assumedly downtrodden Black communities themselves. The idea that an imagined larger Black community desires, or even demands racial leadership from Morehouse men ironically mutes these communities' voices about the kinds of leadership they do and do not want. Further, the definitive qualities of leadership remain murky and detached from a clear aim regarding what a Black man should become and do, and the goals toward which he should lead the masses. Roy, while speaking excitedly about Morehouse men embodying leadership, made a declaration about the college's leadership goals that struck me as ambivalent about any definitive political or social grounds on which leadership should stand. "Leadership is making an impact on your immediate community," he said with an unwavering confidence, as though sales pitching me on a product that he himself proudly owned. "That can be the Repubs, that can be the Democratic Party, it could be Black people or white. You should be able to stand out in your community and be able to make some change in their best interest."

This assessment prioritizes leadership as a virtue in and of itself but says nothing about the principles or politics that urge one to lead. While Roy tried to unpack this idea of leadership to me, I thought of how the inundation of speechifying about leadership from convocations, faculty, administrators, and image-crafting promotional campaigns had left many Morehouse men with an impression that leadership in and of itself has a moral quality, if not a moral imperative. The conclusion that, "You go to Morehouse so that practically makes you a leader," or that graduates are "supposed to be leaders," situates leadership as a default status in the life of the Morehouse Man. These testaments that men must "hold up the race" and "take care of our people" suggest a one-way conversation that men were having about their life trajectories with an imagined Black collective. Being the lone interlocutor of their role in "the community" lends itself to framing racial leadership as an individualistic endeavor established by self-assessment. Even as the institution insists that its model of leadership "is less about self-preservation than other-preservation, a value system preoccupied less with I than Thou,"[11] its graduates construct leadership as a solely personal trait that, once accomplished, promotes men to a class of those with similarly exceptional qualities.

Cloaking neoliberal ideologies with this self-serving notion of leadership leads to prioritizing individual pathways to upward mobility. The references Roy and McCoy made to the Talented Tenth rationalize and tether the virtues of community uplift to the practice of individualism: that is, what is good for individual success expands the ranks of those who are Black and successful, and thus pulls up on the bulk condition of the race. Du Bois termed it the "Talented Tenth" not because of some innate elite exceptionalism, but because 90 percent of post–Civil War African Americans could not read or write. His original intention to hold the feet of literate African Americans to the fire for shirking the plight of the Black poor has here been turned into a trickle-down rather than bottom-up theory of racial uplift. Individualism is fundamental not only to the belief that personal responsibility paves each man's path to leadership, but it also closes an ideological feedback loop in which leaders serve their communities and communities are sufficiently or even best-served by the examples of attainment set by individual African Americans. The proud belief that Morehouse men provided "examples" of success to Black communities was replete across my interviews. When I asked Ornette what role he surmised Morehouse men play in improving conditions for Black men on the whole, he responded cuttingly that "the beginning is not to be a Black man whose condition need be improved. Our broader responsibility is to not only be examples to the community but to empower people to do and be that in communities."

"The Black community" can only be understood as figurative; these men did not actually mention any particular Black neighborhood, organization, or persons. But the individual successes they felt entitled them to racial leadership were both real and ostensible, most often expressed in their high regard for personal ambition, postbaccalaureate degrees, career attainment, and heterotraditional nuclear families. Undergirding all of these laurels and accomplishments was a founding belief that personal wealth is the bedrock of any claims of success in life. Ibrahim spoke with an uneasiness about how true this had been for the college's measure of success and, subsequently, his own: "Morehouse really showed me that it's not as important I guess from a day to day, [that] the people you meet and surround yourself with don't even have money because they're going to be loving, caring people, but..." He paused, slowly turning his thoughts toward disclosing a truth he had reluctantly learned during his college years:

> Successful people have money. I don't know where the dichotomy of that comes from. There's a certain success, you know, money comes with success. If you want to be successful you've got to end up having money, but you shouldn't judge people who make money. I don't know, it's a weird type of situation where I would never judge anybody for what they don't have, but at the same time it's like you want to push yourself to—I don't know, maybe just push yourself. I don't know, maybe it's the field I'm in because I'm in business and finance and maybe that's the career I chose. But the parameters are, the rule...[*he hesitated before continuing*] Success is measured monetarily.

I could sense Ibrahim was uneasy in assessing success this way. As the son of humble immigrants, he had looked with an outsider's eyes on the path he took through Morehouse and his subsequent career in financial services. He spoke about this narrow notion of success as though it was an externally imposed rule by which he did not want to abide or endorse. He was careful not to belittle the successes of those who had little to show financially for their accomplishments or whose achievements could not be measured financially. The way of the world, as he saw it, lay outside his own values: Money was the form of success that could be quantified and confirmed by society, just as the Morehouse Brand had taught so many men to affirm their masculinity through the eyes of others.

The equivalency of success with financial rewards and wealth accumulation is understood far beyond Morehouse, and as decades of masculinities studies have observed, the acquisition of money is central to the achievement of masculinity as a performance. Performances of masculinity are nearly synonymous with displays of wealth in any capitalist society, so it did not surprise me to hear men who were institutionally groomed to achieve masculinity would think of money as inextricably linked to that accomplishment. Moreover, for racially marginalized men, wealth is a gender strategy, a market exchange that compensates for the dominant forms of masculinity denied them by racism. For example, sociologist Anthony Chen found that Asian American men used wealth to "bargain" for manhood. As one of his respondents explained, "Even though I am a Chinese American man, and Chinese American men are seen as inadequate or incomplete men, I am rich. Therefore, I am a real man."[12]

The confluence of wealth, success, and leadership as a means to expressly antiracist ends is a slightly different, although related, construction than the gender bargaining strategy across race, masculinity, and money. Understanding wealth attainment as a pro-Black endeavor is situated within the forms of individual financial success that Ibrahim described but also speaks more broadly to the ways many African Americans embrace capitalism as beneficial to our condition. The idea that capitalism lies at the intersection of race and social justice has a storied history in both the practices and ideologies of Black politics. As political historian Leah Wright Rigueur argues, a shared belief in capitalism, rather than radicalism, underlies the liberal ideas espoused by revered and mostly male Black leaders. "Historically, black people have long viewed the upward redistribution of wealth via individual success in the free market as a solution in the broader black freedom struggle."[13] As political scientists Megan Ming Francis and Michael Dawson point out, this view is critical to understanding the Black neoliberal order. Across class markers, a belief in the virtues of Black neoliberalism emphasizes individual success while neglecting more traditionally liberal notions about the responsibility of the state to right injustices against African

Americans. The Black neoliberal order continues to acknowledge the state's role in the marginalization of Black people, if only as a celebratory nod to progressive ideals, but free-market solutions continue to be upheld as the most effectual means through which Black communities can address inequality.[14] Antiracism, as Lester K. Spence contends, provides the outwardly facing public principle of this belief, while neoliberalism (even though its flaws are acknowledged) consistently touts the pro-Blackness of entrepreneurial and enterprising capacities within institutions, communities, individuals, and spaces deemed "non-white."[15]

If social justice capitalism traffics so heavily in the narrative of pro-Black individual exceptionalism, then what we further learn about those individuals should also raise questions about the aims and goals of corporations and business leaders who claim to be helping Black institutions and communities. After nearly a decade of researching for this book, I completed the first draft right around the time of Smith's commencement speech. The atmosphere among SpelHouse alumni online and elsewhere was an effusive celebration. The news coverage plastered my social media feeds. Countless friends from outside of the Spelman-Morehouse alumni network sent me links to write-ups in what seemed to be every major media outlet. Even as I pride myself on my skepticism—particularly when it comes to capitalists and philanthropy—it was nearly impossible not to be happy for those families, who saw Smith's promise as life-altering for their sons' futures. Smith was smothered in praises and elevated to heroic status in the eyes of many African Americans. He had epitomized what Black evangelists of social justice capitalism wanted us all to believe: that there was a moral quality to "not forgetting where you came from," and that when given the chance to reach the heights of riches, the wealthiest African Americans would even the playing field by taking care of us the way the white donor class had predominantly white institutions covered.

The aura around Smith lasted a year and five months. In November 2020, when I was nearly done revising the first draft of this book, a flurry of texts and emails from friends was again coming my way, and this time Smith had made a historic first once again: he was at the helm of the largest tax-evasion scheme in US history, to the tune of $2 billion in offshore assets. Smith's philanthropic record pre-Morehouse visit had been fairly race neutral. Outside of supporting the Smithsonian Museum for African American History and Culture he had donated tens of millions to national parks and breast cancer research. Following his commencement speech, however, Smith's efforts took a decided turn toward race-specific advocacy. He lobbied the Trump administration to allocate $10 billion in aid for small minority-owned businesses hit hard by the 2020 health and economic crisis and told reporters that he saw Black owned businesses as "a bunch of canaries in a bunch of coal mines" when it came to predicting the global financial fallout of the COVID-19 crisis.[16] What seemed in headlines like race-conscious generosity was directly spurned by his tax scheme. Smith's charitable trusts were his go-to channels for the de facto laundering of the $200 million he attempted to "willfully conceal" from the Internal Revenue Service's probes into his offshore accounts.[17] Morehouse, and many of his other contributions that year, were part of his frantic attempt to offload the earnings he would then not have to disclose.

As of this writing, Smith faces no criminal charges after entering a plea deal and disclosing the role his older white mentor and business partner played in operating the offshore accounts and devising the scheme that became his tax scam. His fall from grace, however, points more largely to how the seductive narrative of the noble billionaire is intensified by a belief in racial obligation. The narrative that Smith was being generous due to racial stewardship obscured the truth of his self-interest. Since its origins in the Gilded Age, philanthropy has been widely critiqued as a tax-sheltered means for the wealthy to garner influence and power over private institutions and government.[18] If Smith and his ilk paid the same tax rate as did many of the men in my study, US higher education could effectively be tuition free and HBCUs (whose students graduate with 32 percent more student debt on average than their PWI counterparts)[19] could be adequately funded with government subsidies. A one-off act of philanthropy not only offered him tax shelter, but it also racialized him by marking his debut as the type of Black industrialist who was looking out for "his" community. Social justice capitalism frequently involves corporate entities in the lives of Black communities, but for Black elites, who are mostly male in the world of business and politics, social justice capitalism offers a mantle of racial authenticity that, in the eyes of many African Americans, frequently absolves them of conservative political leanings, histories of working to bring about policies that disproportionately injure Black Americans, or abhorrent acts and scandals in their personal lives. Most importantly however, the idea that there is something antiracist about their munificence distracts from a level of skepticism about their self-interest that Black communities should carefully consider. Smith's foundation did make good on its promise, although a gift toward one class at one small college is barely a Band-Aid on the crisis of student debt that can only be corrected with government policy. In the end, Smith got far more out of the deal than his beneficiaries. In the midst of a scandal that threatened to forever ruin his public image, he will still be widely revered and primarily remembered for record-setting giving to a Black college.

Black male elites like Smith, and the Black men who aspire to join them, have been some of the loudest drum majors for social justice capitalism and Black neoliberalism. Political differences within Black male leadership, however, correspond to clear class divides. While icons of radical working-class Black masculinity like Black Panther Party chairman Fred Hampton railed that, "We're not going to fight capitalism with Black capitalism,"[20] Black male elites in politics and business called for "pragmatic" positions on racial issues throughout the mid- and late twentieth century, including legislative solutions, Black entrepreneurship, public-private partnerships, and the elevation of individual Black success.[21] This perspective was "nearly indistinguishable from the views of black middle-class communities, moderate civil rights leaders, and black business and civic leaders" who saw a path for racial uplift through integration into the economic mainstream.[22]

Black nationalist, socialist, communist, and liberationist movements emerged from poor and working-class inner city and rural communities.[23] Organizations such as the Student Nonviolent Coordinating Committee (SNCC), the Nation of Islam, and the Black Panther Party mobilized those targeted by state violence, poverty, labor exploitation, and incarceration by rejecting the false promises of integrationist inclusion and modeling the types of economic development that replaced individualism with collective Black economic independence. Black Power scholars such as historian Ashley Farmer have analyzed the patriarchal ideologies promoted within Black liberation and emphasize that radical working-class Black women were often steering the political agendas and ground games of these organizations as well as trying to remedy the sexism of organizational structures and leadership.[24] While Black women were pulling many working-class Black male organizers back from a masculinist vision of nation-building that could ultimately be de-radicalized by their patriarchy, Black male elites were deciding the fate of the race in closed boardrooms with white men.

The lasting legacy of this political class divide has been the continued investment of Black male elites in the fruits of individualistic Black capitalism—the kinds of individualistic gains that are still being championed by those who aspire to the Morehouse Brand, or whose affluence earns them an invitation to deliver the commencement address. Unlike the "knowledge, skills, and character" that are made plain in the college's definition of leadership, the assumption that racial leadership requires individual financial success is not blatantly stated. If you have learned anything by now, Dear Reader, you have learned that Morehouse's unspoken messages are heard as loudly as anything else. Just as men could articulate the spoken and unspoken requirements of the Morehouse Brand, so too could they articulate the call to capitalism implied in the college's leadership tropes.

Implicit Messages of Market Value

As I listened to Mort, Wes, and Ramsey, I heard men rationalizing their ambivalent stance between acceptance and disapproval when explaining that the college placed a market value on alumni and the visibility of their individual career paths. These three shared a sense that while alumni may pursue "Morehouse excellence" in a wide range of fields, those who follow less lucrative pursuits, such as the arts or community organizing, would only be lauded by the college and fellow alumni if and when they achieved financial prominence. Wes pointed to Samuel L. Jackson who, when he was a struggling student artist, held the administration building hostage following the King assassination—a move that got him expelled for two years.[25] Decades later his acting career placed him prominently on both the Hollywood and Morehouse alumni A-lists, while a dozen of other professional actors, such as late Bill Nunn, are rarely mentioned among distinguished alumni. Mort and a few others pointed out that messages about the market value of careers are built into the structure of the curriculum.

Mort, Ornette, and Wes all entered college aiming for careers in K–12 education. Mort and Ornette majored in early childhood education, while Wes, who wanted to work with young people, focused on African American studies, in keeping with a growing racial consciousness that was seeded by his family's work in a large community-based nonprofit. Ornette remarked that education was not highly regarded at Morehouse or considered a challenging concentration. Men interested in teaching, as well as in dance and drama, are redirected toward Spelman to take their required courses, and the stigma that is attached to education for its supposed lack of rigor is outmatched by its association with feminized labor.[26] Ornette recalled classmates mocking his choice or cynically suggesting that he was really just doing it to meet girls.[27]

I asked Mort if he thought K–12 education majors were held in the same esteem as majors who prepared careers in business or medicine. "Absolutely not," he shot back. "And how did you get that sense?" I inquired. He replied promptly: "By the fact that there was no education department [at Morehouse]!" Mort and Wes had both observed the career hierarchies that pervaded the organization of the curriculum. Wes was put off: "I thought that African American studies was going to be incorporated within the overall curriculum a lot more," but "it wasn't."[28] So he had to look to the History Department and African American studies courses for the Black studies curricula he had assumed would be taught at an HBCU. "When I found out African-American Studies was just a program I saw that was like lessening the value of my degree," he said with dismay in his tone.[29]

These kinds of structural obstacles were common for men who pursued academic paths that were not prioritized. "I remember [the academic Dean] making us take extra coursework," Mort recalled. The small group of education majors at Morehouse confronted numerous logistical hurdles while navigating Spelman's incongruent credit system. He remembered thinking that Morehouse needed its own education program. Ironically, the rhetoric about improving the Black community that had drawn him to Morehouse, but the stigma of low-paying feminized professions pushed many of his classmates away from K–12 education and toward more lucrative careers. "I understood education because my mom was an educator," he explained. "It was very clear to me as an educator how I could make change. As an educator, I know that you can see results within a year. If you're an effective teacher, probably sooner than that." Mort, who went on to work as a community-based public health official, pointed out an interesting fact. "My closest friends to this day, from the Education Department, are not [K–12] educators." One had gone into law, and the other was a tenure-track professor.

A small liberal arts college cannot offer nearly the number of areas of study as large universities, but the twenty-six majors Morehouse does currently offer suggest that students are funneled into concentrations affiliated with high-earning-capacity careers (as opposed to majors that reflect a conventional array of liberal arts offerings). As Mort and Wes saw it, the earning potential of students was widely emphasized in the curriculum. Men get the message about the importance of accumulating wealth from this curricular steering just as clearly as they would had such messages been announced in convocations. Coleman and Yusuf, an attorney and a thriving entrepreneur, respectively, responded to instructions about wealth they received indirectly. Unforced by anything in my line of questioning, they self-consciously defended the capitalist emphasis in the college's ideals of community leadership and the consequent market-value assessment of alumni career paths.

> COLEMAN: I think [the college's leadership message] was the whole *as you rise take the community with you*. It was like, *as you climb, you pull up along the way*.[30] At least reach out and help somebody. To whom much is given, much is required. You know you can't really consider yourself to be successful if you have not in some way made your community, your immediate

community and the community at large, better. So yeah, you feel that. [Staff and administrators] stressed to us that it's not *just* about making money. I think that's what the institution did. It's not just about making money, it's about making the community better.

YUSUF: Making a lot of money and having power didn't mean that you didn't have a responsibility to your community. And it was a reminder of that, that resonated with me [and] around a bunch of people that I didn't think [it] would.

As one walks the campus grounds and halls of buildings, imposing depictions of race men from both the alumni community and beyond visually flood students with an imagination that they stand to inherit that legacy. None of these images openly declares that the road to racial leadership is best served through capitalist ambition, or even that wealth and leadership are correlated, nor do they note how men like Martin Luther King vehemently opposed capitalism and saw democratic socialism as vitally important to achieving Black economic justice. Like so many of Morehouse's messages about race and the obligations of manhood, latent instructions spoke the loudest. The sentiments Yusuf and Coleman articulated were similarly expressed by fourteen of the thirty-three men I interviewed. Rather than defending any assumption that money was emphasized in their college experience, they meandered around the presumption that acquiring money satisfies the requirements for leadership. Coleman did not deny that money is part of the college's message, but he justifies it by saying that it was not the *only* message and was accompanied by a belief that individual wealth should be used to advance the greater good. Here, the cultural logic that goes unstated is perhaps most important: associating individual wealth with racial progress attaches an intrinsic moral and political value to men who set out to make lots of money. It is a moral script for Black male capitalism, in which wealthy individual Black men benefit from the assumption that their road to personal fortune is guided by its potential for racial altruism.

In Corporation

The operations of social justice capitalism might take place in the conference rooms and think tanks where business personnel exchange handshakes with community leaders, but colleges are the breeding ground for the Black men who take seats at those corporate tables. "I think Morehouse pretty much revolved around the Business Department," Wes said unequivocally. A majority of his counterparts agreed. It is not all that uncommon for a small liberal arts college to confer bachelor's degrees in business or management, though small HBCUs are more likely to have business programs than similarly sized colleges.[31] What *is* unusual is the vastly disproportionate number of business majors at Morehouse. Ramsey's impression that two-thirds of the student body majored in business was an overestimate but suggests the Business Department's outsized presence on campus. As records indicate, the proportion of business majors was closer to thirty percent of students during the years respondents were enrolled.[32] Perennially, business is the most popular major on campus. Ornette, an attorney, said that it operates "nearly as the default major,"[33] while Tadd, a physician, quipped that "Morehouse is really a corporate indoctrination factory." Elvin, an engineer turned college administrator, was weary of the college's disproportionate number of business majors, noting that these skewed numbers had previously alarmed the college's independent accrediting body. Most notably, respondents discussed the business curriculum and majors more often than any other academic unit, and the culture of the Business Department, as nearly all the participants demonstrated with numerous references to it, influences the cultural temperature of campus in ways that far exceed academic instruction. Wes summed up this situation succinctly: "Primarily, at Morehouse, it's all about the Business Department."

Wes explained that business majors (like Student Government Association officers) wield a great bit of power and enjoy high status on campus. In contrast to concentrations in the natural sciences, which carry reputations for academic rigor and difficulty, respondents never mentioned that the business curriculum was hard or was known for attracting students who were at the top of their class in academic performance. Instead, the status and prestige of the Business Department is drawn almost entirely from the pipeline it provides to Fortune 500 internships and the dapper professionalism with which majors present themselves. "A lot of people from my class ended up becoming traders and stuff. Wall Street was the move," Wes said, listing Morgan Stanley, Countrywide, and JP Morgan Chase among their current employers (all companies, it should be noted, that played sizeable roles in the subprime loan crisis that resulted in the recession crisis of 2008). Mingus, who was regarded by his classmates as an exemplar of success in the financial services industry, matter-of-factly ranked himself as one of the top three students in his major and scored an internship with one of the most reputable and high-paying firms that recruited on campus. "I was being groomed to work on Wall Street. Period," he declared, and described the corporate climate that enveloped campus. "I think Morehouse has such a large corporate influence that the people who come back to speak present that corporate image," he said, referring to invited speakers at Crown Forum convocations and other special events. He continued:

> Whether it's from governmental context, political context, or a true business context. You just start seeing that. You see the seniors on

campus job interviewing, they look slick. That traditional corporate blue, gray suit. They're clean....So as you grow up in the environment you model after what you keep seeing. And all that's influenced by the heavy corporate influence on the college. Those in the Business Department mostly conformed to it because it's mostly the corporate uniform for business. Most students probably did not conform to it. All the student government stooges like myself did and everyone else did, but other than that you didn't have to.

According to Mingus, the business program impressed on students the importance of modeling themselves after the comportment of corporate executives, and the college placed nationally prominent business leaders on display to students with the intention that they aspire to that image.

Ramsey seemed to both emphasize and mock the performative dimension of majoring in business. In his description, this type of professionalism was "clean-cut, navy suit, walk, talk, pick up your fork, eat the salad with this fork...it was deep, man! You need to walk, talk, and behave this way." Clifford, who navigated his way into academia, regarded this preponderance of corporate influence as preempting other forms of career preparation the college should have been doing. "If you weren't going into those corporate environments, I felt like it left you totally naked," he complained. His words elicit a poignant contrast: on the one hand, this process adorned men in suits as though they were armored for a white-dominated world, and yet others were sent out bare in their endeavors, not nearly as prepared to forge paths of their own that were not in step with the capitalist order.

The process of "corporatizing" young men effectively functions as the capstone to the branding process—a bookend to the intake of New Student Orientation (NSO)—where the processed material of tailored young Black men is readied for consumption by an elite managerial labor market and the white (mostly male) personnel who dominate it. The ways men described the stringent rules and policing of corporatization are comparable to the rigidity and constriction they experienced during NSO. Here Erving Goffman's "tissues of constraint" again contract around a high-stakes point in the process necessary for conforming men to the institution's ideals. This is the last stop men experience before they are made visible to the white mainstream beyond the college's gates and the racial veil. The grooming Mingus recalled is strikingly similar to the centrality of dress in the imagery of the Morehouse brand. A "clean" and "slick" look can be accomplished with a suit that transforms young Black male bodies into would-be professionals, effectively accomplishing *realness*—to borrow a term from Black gay house-ballroom culture—for racialized men whose bodies might otherwise be seen as out of place in corporate settings.[34] Those on the queer Black ballroom scene would define realness as an accomplishment of passing every day, undetected, in a world where being outed has violent consequences for the communities that need to perfect this ruse.[35]

It's not drag. It's a survival technique wrapped in a political statement about what someone *could be* because they can pull off the look, if only the sobering realities of socioeconomic and racial barriers were removed. Entire categories of "Executive Realness" were prominent in the underground house-ballroom competitions of 1980s queer Black and Latinx New York. In its unyielding efforts to achieve its own executive realness, the Business Department functions as a brand within the Morehouse brand—a headstream of affluence-tinted gender performance that feeds the rest of the cultural currents on campus. The relationship between the Morehouse brand and corporate grooming went far beyond similarity for men who saw corporatization as overtaking the college's image. "The three-piece suit, cuff links, and all that was sort of the expectation that you could make it into the world, and that was discussed," said Clifford, a Detroit native who had felt the reach of the Business Department far into his social sciences curriculum. "What was maybe not discussed…was that it was always viewed as a transition into the *corporate* world."

"I still have a little book that business students get in business classes on how to tie a tie, what fork to use, utensils at diner, conversations to have. It's a physical book that I still refer to," Dexter reminisced fondly. A Detroit native from the high school that rivaled Clifford's, Dexter described his upbringing as inundated with religious services in a poverty-stricken but proud church community, which had accustomed him to dressing up and keeping his clothes presentable. "As a church kid I knew how to tie a tie," he explained, "but being poverty ridden I didn't have opportunities for dinners and things of that nature." In his junior year he was exposed to Leadership and Professional Development (LPD), the course that assigned the etiquette book and is required of all business majors. LPD is a nearly ubiquitous feature of campus culture and was mentioned by a third of the alumni I interviewed. Its requirements include mock interviews, simulated dinners, and planned business trips, with exhaustive instructions and guidelines for dress and decorum—techniques for fitting in, making small talk, and looking the part in elite settings. Nothing the etiquette course covers is academic, nor does the course funnel students into jobs by scheduling real interviews. Like NSO, LPD's personal grooming regimen can be drastic, and men with facial hair, braids, or locked hair could "actually lose grades if you didn't shave or tone down your hair," Ramsey remembered.

Ibrahim's recollections of LPD were more detailed than those of anyone else. His vivid memories included a mock dinner in which he learned which was his water glass or napkin at a formal dinner setting, which spoon was his soup spoon and how to move it away from himself and bring it back, how to make erudite banter about

Bach and Beethoven as well as what not to do, like "don't take the roll and cut it in half and make little butter sandwiches. I was like, *I like butter sandwiches!*" he chuckled airily. "We had a whole bunch of seating arrangements, and just the whole song and dance about how these work dinners and interviews are conducted." He then continued as though walking me through his user manual, "When you are supposed to sit, after you watch the lead, you want to watch the team leader, see when he sits, then you can sit." For Dexter, LPD was expressly an instruction in social class passing, but Ibrahim recalled LPD so vividly perhaps because, as a first-generation immigrant, he clung to what he saw as literal instructions for American assimilation. "Mind you, Sai, those are cultural things," he said soberly, "because I didn't grow up like that. Not in my household."

For Ibrahim, learning the LPD rulebook was not going to get the barrier of his Blackness out of the way, but it was going to minimize his foreignness. "I wanted the job so bad I just conformed to all of the Morehouse guidelines/rules. I didn't look at it as losing an identity," he said with a pleading tenor lingering in his voice. He repeatedly named LPD's sole instructor, the late Benjamin McLaurin, who taught the course for twenty-five years, directed the Career Counseling and Placement Center, and interfaced with nearly all business majors and most graduating seniors: "I think Mr. McLaurin did an excellent job phrasing it as, '*There's a game out there. There's rules to the game we didn't make up. We didn't make these rules.*' I won't necessarily say I agree with them or don't, but they're out there and people live by them and judge you on them. And the way he laid that out to me was in a way that was receptive to me because he was just telling you whether you agree with it or not, someone's going to judge you on that."

McLaurin's instruction taught Ibrahim a language through which his body could announce his place among elites and the cutthroat business world. I remember Mr. McLaurin fondly from my brief time in the Morehouse Business Association club (they always took enviable trips; my sophomore year it was a four-night Caribbean cruise). A bubbling and sardonically witty personality who took a liking to me during my year as campus queen, McLaurin, an alumnus himself, looked none of the part of the jet-setting executive lifestyle he taught. Day-to-day he mostly wore boxy pleated trousers and short sleeved, untucked button-down shirts over his portly frame. His voice was distinctly marked by a theatrical reverence for hitting every syllable in a word that matched the almost dramaturgical imagination of the upper-crust corporate world that he imprinted on his students. At the core of his teaching lay an observant cultural dramatist who did not need to embody the roles he directed in his actors because he understood performance—*realness*—to be as valuable as actuality.

Ibrahim was aware of the performative dimension of the demeanor he was being taught:

> I looked at it as "Yo, I want to play this game."…You kind of take that with you and you don't realize how much is ingrained in you by the time you leave. But when you get into the corporate world you just start to realize—first you start to realize you're as capable as anybody over there.…You know you're as tight[36] as anybody. If anything, Morehouse might, you might be overconfident by the time you leave Morehouse!…Our Business Department at that time definitely had people who taught us the game. People taught us the rules you need to succeed.

There is an irony to this idea that elitism can be taught as a performance or learned as a second language, given that one of the definitive properties of class performance is that it must go undetected. If anyone to whom this etiquette is second nature can tell that you are thinking about it consciously, then you've been outed. McLaurin ran Career Placement like a finishing school within a college, and Ibrahim's boast that "you might be overconfident by the time you leave Morehouse" made it clear that many others felt the same way. This nested charm school taught them to make small talk about European classical composers, to extend their comfort zone, and to conceal their backgrounds in the presence of white business elites.[37] In their minds, LPD inscribed their bodies and behavior with an air of success and smoothed over any rough edges that might announce to their future colleagues that they should not be in the room.

Curiously, which room and which elite culture the business program imagined is sociologically unclear, given the transformation that was beginning at this time among white American elites. In his study of St. Paul's School, one of the country's most venerable boarding academies and a perennial supplier of admits to Ivy League universities, Shamus Khan observed a tectonic cultural shift. The hyperprivileged, predominantly white teens of St Paul's are convinced that the American elite is meritocratic and that upper echelon status is granted not because of the family or wealth into which they are born and bred, but by the work they do. In reassuring themselves of this democratized version of affluence, the wealthiest St. Paul students had the most interaction with working-class staffers because they were "intentionally developing the capacity to interact with those 'below' them."[38] Without any threat to their solid social station, such interactions were intended as an effort to learn the social skills of inevitable future dealings with the middle and lower classes. The interactions also provide a means to feel better about their unearned privilege because students use them as proof that they *can* befriend those outside of their class, even though the relationships are mostly self-serving and shallow. This performance of democratic elitism invited the most privileged boarders to sample cultures beyond their bubble, thus recreating within their sheltered milieu an imagination of the diverse world beyond its environs. LPD may be preparing Morehouse men to break the ice with ham-fisted mentions of Brahms, but the dining hall loudspeakers at St. Paul's don't play Beethoven but Biggie—a.k.a. the hard-core Brooklyn-born rapper, the Notorious B.I.G.[39]

Whereas etiquette classes teach soon-to-be Morehouse graduates how mirror an almost cartoonish impersonation of how the rich and powerful behave, the truly privileged at St Paul's have already rebooted the culture of American elitism so as to be determined not by performance, but by practicing how to be multicultural dilettantes who can hold their own in any setting. The game that Ibrahim signed up to play, in which an ability to mimic high society unlocks the entryway to belonging among the privileged, was preparing him for rules that were expiring just as he was learning them. The idea that a white elite cultural playbook will stay fixed long enough for Black men to earn the opportunity to play the game—or even that the culture of wealth *can* be gamed by the underprivileged—seems to be a fallacy. The corporate cosplay of Leadership and Professional Development classes speaks to the gaping chasm between a *real* world of white elites beyond commencement and an *imagined* white gaze that is entirely made up behind Morehouse's racial veil.

Ibrahim clearly understands the process as racialized; he knows he was learning to play a white man's game to win in a white world. But his optimistic view of the upward mobility that could be made possible through LPD stood in jarring contrast to the perspective of men like Shadow, whose understanding of the racialization within this process was cause for much skepticism: "Morehouse, as much as it does engender a culture of leadership, I was personally at the time of the mind that also trains people just to be high paid corporate suits. And to me that didn't feel—that was the disconnect. It was like a factory in some sense, that they just kind of like had these stock courses that you needed to take so that you could play the game the way the white man plays it."

Shadow expounded on his belief that the college should be encouraging entrepreneurship and providing resources for students that opened paths toward Black economic independence. To him, the idea that a seat at the table with white elites would bring about any substantial racial equity seemed profoundly mistaken and flew in the face of the history. In his frame of mind, the critical question was why should any independent Black colleges be in the business of funneling graduates into corporations owned and operated by whites?

The answer to Shadow's question, I believe, lies in picking apart how social justice capitalism has drastically remodeled a belief for many Black elites about what antiracism requires in the post–civil rights era. An unsuspecting belief in social justice capitalism has a broader impact on Black masculinity than simply promoting the antiracist value of individually wealthy Black men with lucrative corporate careers. Neoliberalism's speciously commonsense practices have taken hold of US education systems from K–12 through higher education. Programs specifically targeting Black male "success" have become a foundry for melting together what are otherwise oppositional political groups with competing beliefs about Black males and their achievement. Corporations, civic and community groups, faith-based organizations, and elected officials compete for opportunities to "solve" the "problem" of Black boys and young men, often promoting politically conservative stances in the purported service of antiracist progress.[40]

For political scientist Keisha Lindsay, such exclusively Black male programs should point our attention to the ways that intersectionality can be repurposed to antifeminist ends. Responses to these male-only initiatives called attention not only to the exclusion of Black girls and young women from these programs but also to the ways such programs invited conservatives and business interest groups into the lives of Black youth when,[41] as Kimberlé Crenshaw notes, such groups had never before been interested in any other framing of Black student success.[42] Why, then, across national-, state-, city-, and community-level programs did the idea take hold that public-private partnerships, when matched with neoliberal cultural directives modeled at the boys and young men themselves, would dominate the institutional landscape in our approaches to Black male achievement?

The Strange Political Bedfellows of Black Male Success

In our search for an answer, we should return to where our question began: with Obama's commencement address. The president's visit to Morehouse was also a promotional stop. A year later his administration unveiled My Brother's Keeper (MBK), a 2014 initiative that specifically targeted young African American and Latino young men and boys. As the Obama White House's only initiative aimed at Black and Latinx communities, MBK represented both a culmination and an extension of local innovations, such as the Young Men's Initiative New York City's mayor, Michael Bloomberg, had authorized three years earlier.[43] This and similar programs elsewhere were now effectively franchised by the federal government. Just after announcing the name of the program at the inaugural press conference, Obama made unequivocal that "My Brother's Keeper is not some big, new government program,"[44] as though to assuage any critics of government social service earmarks. None of MBK's funding, however, is government provided. Instead, it subsists entirely on private-sector and philanthropic partners who raised $200 million for the program in its first five years.[45] The official literature issued by the White House describes the program as intended to address the "persistent opportunity gaps" facing this group by focusing on their college readiness and career preparation. Public critics of MBK included two hundred Black men who signed an open letter to the president stating that "in the absence of any comparable initiative for females," MBK "forces us to ask where the complex lives of Black women and girls fit into the White House's vision of racial justice?" "If the denunciation of male privilege, sexism and rape culture is not at the center of our quest for racial justice," they added, "then we have endorsed a position of benign neglect towards the challenges that girls and women face."[46]

Black feminists subsequently took the lead in publicly expressing concern about MBK. Over 1,600 Black women signed an open letter to Obama that went far beyond pointing out MBK's obvious exclusion of Black girls, arguing that even as Black women and girls are under-researched, glaring statistics continued to demonstrate that their disproportionately high rates of incarceration, wages, and unemployment persist. Most resoundingly, the June 2014 statement, which ran under the heading "Why We Can't Wait," pointed toward the logical fallacy promoted by the framers and proponents of Black male initiatives.[47]

> Those who have justified the exclusive gender focus of MBK often remind us that male youth of color are like the miner's canary: their plight warns us that something is wrong in the mine.[48] Indeed, something is desperately wrong when so many of our youth are falling victim to the consequences of punitive discipline, underfunded schools, poor job prospects, declining investments in public space, decreasing access to higher education, and worsening prospects on the job market.
>
> Clearly American society continues to be a toxic environment for many of our young people. Yet male-exclusive initiatives seem to lose sight of the implications of the canary's distress: it is not a signal that only male canaries are suffering. It makes no sense to equip the canary with a mentor, a gas mask and or some other individual-level support while leaving the mine as it is and expecting the females to

fend for themselves. If the air is toxic, it is toxic for everyone forced to breathe it.[49]

In mapping the origins of modern mass incarceration policies, historian Elizabeth Hinton stressed that there has been no more bipartisan effort in US politics than the political coalitions that formed to hypercriminalize Black communities.[50] I maintain that Black male achievement initiatives, of which MBK is a shining example and Morehouse is a long-standing laboratory, have long gone understudied as the bookend to mass incarceration's "tough on crime" bipartisanship in which mutually beneficial conservative and liberal interests similarly converged around beliefs about what is best for young Black men and boys. You may recall from chapter one that what fell below the radar of many of MBK's equity-minded and feminist detractors was the initiative's politically curious neoliberal origins within Eric Holder's vision for enhanced law enforcement that burdened young Black males with the responsibility of behaving better to get policed better. While the program was initially touted as an intervention by civic leaders into the lives of young men of color, its launch was attended and supported by such right-wing figures as Bill O'Reilly, who, during an interview with Obama, railed that Blacks' high poverty rate was being driven by the dissolution of Black families. "Seventy-two percent of babies in [the] African-American community are born out of wedlock," he chided. "Why isn't there a campaign by you and the first lady to address that problem very explicitly?"[51]

My Brother's Keeper is now sponsored by the Obama Foundation, where its advisory board is littered with private sector executives from NewsCorp and financial services conglomerates such as Prudential, Ariel Investments, and Deloitte. Even though MBK is the linchpin of the Obama Foundation's heavy dealings in the corporate sector, from which Obama himself drew over $400,000 in corporate conference speaking fees in his initial years out of office, responses to the corporatization of Black community-based initiatives have been mostly celebratory. The acceptance of MBK's neoliberalism within Black communities rests primarily on framing Black males and their low-income communities as in crisis and thus requiring paternalistic interventions from Black male elites and their private-sector backers.[52] It is not crisis that necessitates neoliberal paternalism, it is neoliberal paternalism that frames Black male youths as *in crisis* in ways their families and communities are incapable of handling. Community angst over what to do with Black boys has been handed over to corporate interests and undergone privatization. We may ask ourselves, then, what is the mutual benefit that leads otherwise disparate parties to conspire around the issue of Black boys? The answer is that the coalition around Black boys is a curious mix: community leadership holds to a belief that the expenditure of corporate funds in Black communities is a form of reparative economic justice, and both white and Black neoliberal conservatives hold fast to a congruent ideology that private-sector action is more effective and appropriate for African Americans than "big government" social programs.

MBK is an exemplar of "neoliberal governmentality," where big-business innovations are offered as a way to repair the character flaws of Black male youth.[53] MBK marked the neoliberal turn in antiracist politics, in which, "technical, entrepreneurial interventions replace political organization as the imagined solution to the social and economic inequalities" in Black communities.[54] Many of these corporate coalitions were formed around the founding of all-male, publicly funded but privately-operated charter schools targeting Black boys. When the city of Chicago rolled out its own MBK initiative in 2015, leading the way was Tim King, the CEO and founder of Urban Prep Academies, the best-known of these school chains. School privatization breathed new life into these academies by dangling them as an alternative to underfunded city-run schools available to Black families. Their proponents include the Open Society Foundation, which backs antiracist criminal justice reform.[55] Advocates have argued that the continuing Black-white achievement gap requires a radical intervention in the schooling of Black boys, often by placing them in single-sex schools, despite the fact that, as feminist researchers have shown, the academic performance gap between white and Black girls is actually wider than that between white and Black boys.[56] Like MBK, Black male academies have garnered support from conservative organizations such as the Walton Family Foundation by falling in step with foundational right-wing ideologies about ending state-run schools and abolishing teachers' unions.[57] In bringing together liberals and conservatives in these ways, schools for young Black males hit a "political sweet spot among populations that both love and fear them."[58]

Neoliberalism frames problems of racial injustice as though they are beyond the reach of political solutions. The state, in this belief, plays a minimal role except for facilitating the private sector's professional and managerial training of individuals in order to bring about individual changes to their condition.[59] In both contributing to and responding to a sea change in the education of young Black men, Morehouse occupies a premier space in the national imagination regarding Black male youth success. More specifically, Morehouse contributes to the neoliberal ideology that the "problem" of Black boys in schools is solved with professionalism and corporate alliances. "I believe that one of the good things about Morehouse is there is a consistency in their message," Davis explained. His adamant belief in the virtues of corporate partnerships and the obligation of Morehouse students to impress corporate partners was a consistent theme throughout our interviews. "To corporate America and the philanthropic community, we are the school for the better making of your African American men," he stated firmly. "But I think

FIGURE 12. Students assemble in King Chapel at Morehouse College.

the message always was about we are the premier training ground for young men."

Davis clearly understands Morehouse as a vanguard for Black male achievement and its appeal to the private sector, but the relationship between Morehouse and the national project of Black male achievement is actually reciprocal. As one of the most venerable and renowned producers of Black male baccalaureates and a bastion of rhetoric about the dress, behavior, and comportment that facilitates achievement, Morehouse has become a go-to template for the cultural curriculum of several Black male K–12 schools, including the Chicago-based Urban Prep Academies.[60] As a trendsetter for Black male schooling, Morehouse's influence is visible in the practice of uniforming students in striped ties and embossed blazers (see images). But its model extends further: the college serves as an organizational template for folding right-wing entities into Black

FIGURE 13. High school students assemble at Chicago's Urban Prep Academy.

institutions. The belief here—that Black male youth thrive in rigid environments of discipline and authority—has been a consistent conservative script since the time when Reagan-era films like *Lean on Me* heroized an image of Black inner city school administrators who intimidated students and ran their campuses like prison wardens.[61] Plans for creating well-behaved Black boys and young men formally invite strange conservative bedfellows into the administrations and private partnerships of schools for Black males.

Like all Historically Black Colleges and Universities, Morehouse has long had a relationship with Republicans that, while historically rooted in the "Party of Lincoln," dabbles in dealings with Black institutions as a matter of expediency and political football. The financial straits accumulated by Jim Crow segregation and ongoing resource deprivation forced many Black college administrators to accept aid from right-wing interest groups and elected officials. Overemphasizing that these alliances were made mostly from economic necessity, however, overshadows the undeniable ideologi-

FIGURE 14. President Donald Trump meets with leaders from historically black colleges and universities in the Oval Office, February 27, 2017. AP Photo/Pablo Martinez Monsivais.

cal concord that existed between Black college leadership, southern "Dixiecrats," and the Republican Party. For the last white southern Democrats (the staunch segregationists who were replanted into the Republican Party after the chiasmic shift caused by the Goldwater presidential campaign's opposition to the 1964 Civil Rights Act) support for Black colleges gilded the preservation of racial segregation in higher education.

For the new Republican southern strategy that followed that shift, kind gestures toward HBCUs played well for Black voters with whom their candidates routinely fared poorly. Those displays, of which some were purely symbolic and others substantive, served to "combat perceptions of their party's racial animus—particularly with institutions that don't disrupt conservative narratives. As it happens, historically black schools have a tradition of cultural conservatism, respectability politics and bootstrapping, all of which make them deeply attractive (and feasible) targets for Republican outreach."[62] Today, Republicans' interest and political maneuvering of HBCU alliances continue, ranging from the trivial, such as invitations to "listening sessions" turned empty photo opportunities in the former Trump Oval Office to the deeply offensive statement by former Secretary of Education Betsy DeVos who willfully ignored higher ed's history of racial exclusion and argued that HBCUs serve as "real pioneers when it comes to school choice."[63]

Colleges and political campaigns are the playpens of the donor class, and we can look much closer than Washington for the presence of Republicans; they are donors, administrators, and board members at Morehouse. As an HBCU for Black males, Morehouse occupies an even sweeter "sweet spot" (to borrow Crenshaw's phrase) for conservatives. While we cannot make a priori assumptions about how much influence donors have on the daily operations of the institution, we can safely assume that Morehouse Board of Trustees members have substantial power over the administration. At Morehouse, as at many other small institutions, wealthy board members and their private foundations and family trusts comprise most of the college's largest donors. At present, a seat on the board is held by Dan Cathy, CEO of fast-food chain Chick-fil-A, whose family has spent millions of dollars fighting marriage equality legislation and who has publicly supported gay "conversion therapy."[64] Among its corporate and private partners, the college lists Walmart Stores Inc.; the Bush Foundation; Goldman, Sachs and Company; Bank of America; and the Coca-Cola Company, which have all built strong reputations for supporting conservative social and economic policies. Corporate ties have provided much of the necessary cloak for conservatives' reach into Black male schools and historically Black colleges, but many of the private partnerships with white right-wingers that continue at Morehouse were ushered in by the Black conservative leadership that steered the college's institutional strategies in previous decades.

The Veil on Display

Maintaining these corporate ties requires more than good faith. Fundraising campaigns led by high-level administrators and trustees call on the Business Department and Student Government Association to identify the most polished students to place before potential donors, most of whom represented corporations. Both Davis and Mingus were selected as showcase students. Mingus was part of a group of eight students selected for this role: "They used to parade us around to fundraise....I went to LA, San Fran, New York, everything. We were massive ambassadors for the college, and so I was groomed to be a face of the college while I was there." While their audiences included an occasional Black celebrity (Mingus distinctly remembered Quincy Jones), both men made clear that donor audiences were overwhelmingly white, and thus their performance for them was tailored to white perceptions. "white folks like Black folks that they know and that they're comfortable with," Davis said as he tiptoed into a careful explanation of the college's fundraising strategy. He had watched and followed the lead of administrators who coached students and modeled a racially ingratiating behavior toward donors that "made folks incredibly comfortable. To the point where they were willing to write a check to a school that they would never send their own child [to]. Never. But they thought every Black child should go there.... The message was nuanced in that we are the school for the better making of men. Period. When there was money on the table, make them comfortable." Davis felt no need to be delicate about the obvious racial play in dressing up young Black men to white donors, but corporate fundraising is as much about which students are played up as it is who is hidden from view. "I remember when it came time for the white president of Pepsi to come to campus, or the white director of *this* or *that*, they didn't put us with them." "Us" was a reference to a minority of leftist student activists on campus. Mort laughed at the obvious reason why: "They didn't put us with the people who wrote checks [*laughs*] because we were probably too militant."

If all of Morehouse manhood exists within a veil that becomes visible to the gaze of the white mainstream after graduation, then business majors are pressed firmly against a glass in which the college manipulated how they would be seen above all others. In lieu of rankings and other markers of prestige that would be known to whites, graduates who journey into the bastions of capitalism validate the efficacy of the college's exhaustive grooming efforts. Mingus was particularly perceptive of the purpose business majors served in communicating the Morehouse Brand to these audiences. For "donors, potential employers of our students...it does well for the college when they're able to say we put more Black men on Wall Street than any other HBCU. It does well for the college to be able to say we have more Black men at Harvard Business School....Those are the types of positive statistics we seek to perpetuate." Always the professional communicator, Davis was even more succinct. He began by saying that business students "knew how to walk into predominantly white environments and make these white folks"—here he paused, taking a beat as though he were going to cut to the chase with me—"They might not love Black people, but they *love Morehouse men*."

Corporatization, if not the whole of Morehouse's grooming culture, is a process of racialization that measures Black male success by white approval. "Of course, it wasn't stated. I could be completely wrong, I might be kind of jaded on my own," Ramsey began tentatively. "But whenever they used the word 'corporate' it was *white* in my mind. We kind of make up our own mind about that. But it definitely wasn't trying to do much to associate with ourselves....Who else would we be trying to be pleasing, obviously?" Unlike Ramsey, Mingus and Davis were completely supportive of this approach. These contrasting viewpoints alert us to the dual functions of the college's corporate culture in the process of racialization. On the one hand, a fantasy of white elite spaces is simulated in the micro-finishing-school setting of LPD. It exaggerates elite refinement (and Black men's responsibility to mirror it) in ways that are out of sync with the real ways white elites are culturally shifting. Men switch from attempting to mirror white elites to performing model Black masculinity. However, the white gaze goes from being imagined to being actualized when students are selected to be put on literal display to corporate white donors. While being showcased to white elites, men must perform refinement, be impeccably presentable, and adapt to donors' ideas of worthy Black male beneficiaries. On this stage, the political docility of Morehouse graduates is showcased, while those with subversive racial politics are hidden from view. Far from challenging the Du Boisian veil, these institutional strategies to appease white funders take full advantage of it by offering whites a prearranged glimpse into the kind of Blackness they want to see at Black colleges, and perhaps the only kinds of Black male performances they will acknowledge with their financial support.

Voices of Dissent

That the college chooses to present its student body as politically nonthreatening to white donors is but an effort to conceal the realities of diverse and conflicting Black politics on campus. Morehouse's administration is exceptional, even among the field of culturally conservative HBCUs, for having a pronounced presence of Black Republicans in its leadership. A small handful of men I interviewed mentioned the Republican affiliation of Dr. Walter Massey, the renowned physicist and educator under whose presidency most of the respondents graduated. To the corporate sector he was well known as the former chairman of Bank of America. Objections to his conservatism were common in our conversations, and perhaps the most vocal was Shadow, an entertainment professional who had been raised in a decidedly pan-Africanist political environment by his father, an academic and West African immigrant. Massey's Republican loyalties were well known to students during the late 1980s and 1900s,[65] when the political climate among Black college students was shifting decidedly to the left. Black college campuses of that era were considered wellsprings for anti-Apartheid activism, protests related to the Rodney King rebellion, and a growing pan-African cultural and political consciousness.

Shadow, an LA native, was audibly still disturbed by the influence of Massey's right-wing politics on campus and passionately described an incident that he attributed to his influence. "When [Massey] got to campus he wanted there to be a Republican club. And the guy—Arthur *something*—he wrote an article in the paper laying out the fault of pan-Africanism." Shadow had submitted an opposing response to the paper, but it was passed over in lieu of a supportive reply from a faculty member. "I remember being fucking adamant that this guy should not have been validated by a professor!" he exclaimed. Shadow used this incident to point to the strings that conservative administrators pulled in creating a platform for voices within the student body that were opposed to Black liberationist or Afro-centric politics.

Which politics and practices are considered antiracist is widely contested within Black spaces and discourses. References to Morehouse's conservative campus tone and the center-right political leanings of many of its students and administrators were scattered throughout nearly a quarter of the men's descriptions of the overall atmosphere of the campus. The stalwart efforts by administrators and SGA leaders to present the student body as docile and culturally conservative to donors only seemed to mobilize the pockets of radically minded students and faculty who thrived in their shared Black nationalist leanings and radical student activism. Mort,

Clifford, and Wes, who were involved in progressive campus organizing were highly critical of the college's response to Black sociopolitical issues of the day. They often received backlash for their outspokenness, and their activism preoccupied administrators who sought to protect their alliances with right-leaning donors.

"Everything from the revitalization [of neighboring public housing tracts], to the college as a corporation, to the college as silent on social issues and social justice, it's sort of a conservative bent, I thought at the time," recalled Clifford. His reminiscences, like those of his two counterparts, revealed that some students experienced Morehouse as a Black institution that stood consistently at odds with progressive Black politics. In the criticisms they made then, and in retrospect, these men described their political leanings as Afrocentric (which some called "Afro-centrist" and Wes called African-centered).[66] They expressed dismay that the curriculum they learned at Morehouse mostly emphasized white Western standards. "I think the curriculum needs to be more African centered—Bach and Beethoven, alright, but give me some Stevie Wonder, give me some Herbie Hancock," Clifford advocated.

Many of the complaints men had about their overall experiences on campus were voiced softly, spliced in between other statements, and even made through humorous remarks about outdated facilities, administrative inefficiencies, and the hyperfraternal culture of brotherhood on campus. When it came to the curricular aversion to Black radical politics and the college's responses to racial issues, however, they expressed their criticisms more sharply, even sternly. Morehouse's administration "can sit in and say that somebody's trying to be Black and all this other type of stuff," Wes explained in one of his many riffs about how a profound disregard for Black radical politics echoed throughout course offerings, instruction, student groups, and the campus atmosphere. "We pretty much only celebrate our extension to the top of this European built hierarchy." Wes and like-minded others credited most of their awakened Afro-centrism to learning from subversive faculty members, whom Mort described as "very conscious," and who were solidly aligned with the Black radical and Pan-Africanist (albeit mostly masculinist) thought of that time. This dissenting and vocal minority of faculty members, however, only heightened their awareness that progressive politics were absent elsewhere on campus.

"The more racially conscious I became the more I felt the general campus wasn't that racially conscious at all," Clifford griped. He continued by narrating an experience that led him to that conclusion:

Particularly like I think it was my junior year where Amadou Diallo was shot like forty-one times in New York. And there were a couple of other incidents. I remember Imam Jamil Al-Ameen or H. Rap Brown, his incident went down at the time. Khalil Muhammad, he died around that time. Within a three to six-month time all these impactful events were occurring with black men. And I was distinctly struck by the lack of response from the school, the lack of response from my fellow students.... I think actually we held a protest after he was shot like that. We were trying to put pressure on the administration to say something about what happened, what it means for Black men, Black males. We thought that what happened to him was very central to the Black experience. And here we are at a Black institution, one would think that they would have this concern, or they would be in the vanguard about speaking to the issues related to young Black men. [But] the administration at the time was very conservative, so they didn't. To place Morehouse in a larger context, most HBCUs are very conservative, so we were probably under the mistaken notion that Morehouse could and would be a voice as it relates to that issue, especially under Walter Massey. There wasn't like a schoolwide discussion, to my knowledge, related to that sort of event.

Clifford, Mort, Shadow, and Wes had all been involved, to varying extents, with the major student protests of their day. Much of their activism was organized around the Million Man March, the death row case of journalist Mumia Abu Jamal, the city of Atlanta's proposals to "revitalize" its urban core by displacing low-income Black residents of public housing, and the swiftly changing environment in Black urban communities that was soon labeled the "War on Drugs." "In '96 the big issue of the day was crack being pumped into the Black community by the CIA," Mort recounted. "Morehouse didn't respond to that at all, and there was a collective of students that were bothered by that" lack of response. "Anything that had Morehouse in a positive or negative light? They dealt with *that*." As an example, he referenced the publicity around Oprah Winfrey's scholarship campaign, which the college promoted widely. "They pushed that, and they wanted communities to know that. That's not a bad thing," he interjected just before he described administrative efforts to keep sexual assault issues out of the limelight. "But that conversation superseded the conversations of bigger social issues."

Casting race betterment as a stand-alone antiracist endeavor has been widely critiqued by Black feminists for the perils that such a single-axis issue approach poses to Black politics and the injury it does to African Americans who are socially marginalized beyond race.[67] Without women in their classes, Mort and Clifford readily admit that masculinist claims by many radical faculty members went mostly unchecked. Mort recalls a lingering sentiment among even the most revered Black nationalist faculty who claimed that racism was an attack on Black male heteronormativity and that "sometimes Black mothers, or even Black fathers would raise their children—they raised Black men in such a way to be more effeminate."[68] This myopic view of antiracism has mostly been taken to task for the kinds of intersectional political movements it stifles, but rarely has it been scrutinized for the unanticipated political allegiances its fosters.

Single-axis racial politics make for strange bedfellows, as the presence of far-right corporate leaders on the college's board of trustees have already shown us. The question that Mort, Clifford, and others call to our attention goes a step further. Without tethering antiracism to other political axes, such as opposition to patriarchy or anticapitalism, race betterment wobbles across questions of what specific modes of racism it is opposing, and which Black people stand to benefit.

For Clifford, the college's private partnerships (forged in the name of Black male achievement) signaled its disengagement from issues that immediately affected low-income Black communities. In his last two years of college, Clifford became very involved in activism surrounding the police shootings of Atlanta residents, whose names he rattled off to me as though they were as fresh in his mind as Freddie Gray or Michael Brown. He thought that the administration and most of his classmates had swept these community issues under the rug. "You know," he said wryly, "if Morehouse came out and said *look, police brutality is at an all-time high in the Black community and these white police need to get their act together*, I figure that would jeopardize whatever corporate sponsorship they might be receiving. That part of it would jeopardize funding from philanthropists or donors." I interpreted Clifford's remarks as a way of sorting through his own drawn-out acceptance of the college's choice to weigh the political scales to serve its own interests. Rather than expressing angry disappointment, he explained Morehouse's racial politics in financial terms: "The college wants to avoid appearing radical in any sense, in a way that might threaten its financial sponsorship.... This institution in many ways was more like a business as opposed to what I thought a school should be." Clifford was neither resentful nor impassioned in assessing the college's position. Like several others, he realized that Morehouse's ideas of Black community improvement were starkly divorced from the low-income Black communities that neighbored the campus in southwest Atlanta—a neighborhood that, at its peak, was home to 40 percent of the city's Black residents.[69] The contradiction between the college's ideal of serving the "community" imagined in its rhetoric and its actual relations with its neighboring communities, however, was not lost on many students—particularly those like Clifford who came from neighborhoods that were their hometown's version of southwest Atlanta.

He blasted the college's unresponsiveness to local police murders and indicted its disconnect from issues affecting the city's Black poor. Other men similarly scorned what they saw as the college's at best ambivalent or at worst hostile stance toward adjacent Black neighborhoods. Through much of the time respondents were enrolled, the city of Atlanta and the AUC member institutions were in talks to raze University Homes, a housing enclave nested between the campuses of Morehouse, Spelman, and Clark Atlanta. Built as a Black counterpart to one of the city's other segregated public housing projects, University Homes was intentionally placed within the thriving collegiate center. As the childhood home of a number of AUC emeritus faculty, the development was as closely tied to Morehouse as any affluent Black organizations or civic leaders in Atlanta. It was one of the nation's oldest public housing developments, but its decline tarnished its reputation among the AUC member institutions. "I gave a speech that criticized what was going on with [the] revitalization program in Atlanta at the time. 'Cause they were tearing down these housing developments and displacing people without any real thought," Clifford recounted with the fervor of his activism still audible in his voice. "Brothers were excited, they were clapping, agreeing with what I was saying" about police violence. But "I think they got a little quieter when I started talking about revitalization."

With the tacit approval of AUC member institution administrations, the city demolished University Homes. The result was an increase in the homeless and vagrant population of the area, as the most destitute former residents' everyday networks were still tethered to the neighborhood. The surrounding colleges and their security forces reacted with hostility to street loitering. Wes took notice of the problem and the lack of a campus response. He began by describing "the lack of interaction with the surrounding community and some of the homeless people that be around there asking for change..." and then cut himself off. "For you to go out of your way to not be around them even say hello, it kinda says what you think about these kinds of people. Even though it was never discussed it's just the treatment. So, I don't have to say *I hate women* you know what I mean beating them down. It's obvious."

His analogy to the treatment of women is poignant. When a figurative imagination of Black community is belied by the realities of the college's relationship to Black neighborhoods within arm's reach, "community" serves as a mere rhetorical prop for Black male leadership, in much the same way that ideas about respecting and protecting Black women elevated Black male sexual propriety even as the men's interactions with real women undercut those claims. Lofty statements about obligations to "the Black community" morally validate the college's push toward Black male leadership attained through neoliberal channels of individual capitalistic ambition. "Revitalization" efforts, which displaced Black residents and buffered the campus from southwest Atlanta's poorest citizens, have increasingly relied on partnerships with private developers since the respondents graduated. Within the campus gates, business and capitalism are lauded as vehicles of race betterment, with Black captains of industry held up as blueprints for Black progress. But just a sidewalk beyond the gates, private enterprise preys on the Black poor, whose homes are located in places that are newly desirable, given their proximity to interstate highways, center-city commercial districts, and major event centers. Moreover, their appeal to developers also arises from the relatively affluent campuses they border—colleges they abut not by choice but because of Atlanta's violent history of residential segregation.

Morehouse's particular community contradiction is not unique. The interdependence between notions of community and notions of Black male achievement and leadership extends more broadly to the racialization of Black male success writ large. Anthropologist Aimee Meredith Cox, one of the original framers of the "Why We Can't Wait" open letter to Obama, notes that the term *community* masks differences in approaches when it comes to prioritizing initiatives focused on Black boys over those that benefit Black girls. In collecting community feedback on My Brother's Keeper, Cox observed that a commonly held belief when it comes to boys is that their success necessitates whole community investment and resources, and that their individual successes mark the shared success of a cooperative community. The success of Black girls, in contrast, is seen as a challenge they are able to meet on their own by gathering the resources they need without requiring community help.[70]

Cox's observation highlights the unidirectional construction of masculinity in the Morehouse ideology of leadership. The ways men conceptualized the ties between Black men's success and community improvement underline only the ways that communities benefit from Black men. They drastically downplay how much Black male success strategies disproportionately depend on the resources and attention of Black leadership and communities. Furthermore, a reverence for and emphasis on capitalist individualism may reinforce a narrative of social justice capitalism that valorizes wealthy Black men who use their means to pay off community challenges instead of seeking legislative efforts to right economic and social injustices against African Americans.

The private sector initiatives that have sent corporate recruiters to Morehouse's campus since the 1980s, however, and that established the college's reputation as a farm for Black male executives, can be attributed to antidiscriminatory federal legislation spurned by civil-rights-era activism. Across the Johnson and Nixon administrations, it was Title VII that shifted a fairly toothless policy of equal opportunity toward stronger mandates for preferential consideration of women and racial minorities.[71] In order to meet Title VII compliance, companies recruited directly from large pools of college-educated African Americans while being waved through by many Black business elites. Morehouse men may credit a narrative of cultural preparedness for their favored position with white elites, but it wasn't pinstripes and shrimp forks that enticed companies to initially establish hiring pipelines with the college. Rather, male-dominated industries looking to comply with federal mandates spurned from the civil rights movement that directed their recruitment efforts toward the country's largest pool of college-educated Black men.

A narrative of the antiracist capacity of capitalism, and an accompanying belief that Black male elites will help improve Black conditions, has established an incubator in many of our extant approaches to Black male schooling. Morehouse has both driven and been driven by this narrative and represents men who are products of initiatives around Black male success and men who sit at the tables where such initiatives are brokered with white private interest groups. I am sympathetic to the challenges facing Black males in higher education, particularly enrollment and completion rates, but narrowly framing success around which top students go on to reach heights within the business world or their individual careers draws attention away from the success of the student body on the whole, particularly men who aren't oriented toward corporate careers. I liken this corporate grooming and private interest dynamic to athletics. We would be reluctant to celebrate the "antiracism" of white interest groups if they funneled resources into athletic programs built around elite Black athletes. Elite Black athletes already receive an undue amount of attention and support when compared to other Black college students, and the industry of professional and college sports profits from grooming and training up their careers. With corporate interests in Black male success, however, we have taken a less cynical view, even as the men I interviewed made clear that white private interests focus on how the college crafts some students and not others. If programs for Black male success justify discrimination against women and girls, they should further admit that they are not inclusive of most Black men and boys.

Conclusion

The Journey Back

"Dear Dr. Grundy (Saida), I hope that this reaches you well," the email began. It was from a Morehouse faculty member I didn't know, a political scientist named Levar Smith, whose course on politics, protest, and social movements was part of a newly implemented campus-wide initiative to enhance the standard curriculum for first-year students. "As a pedagogical tool," he continued, "I often attempt to find scholarship which allows students at the college to situate themselves within the critical conversations they are having in class—and stumbled across your article 'An Air of Expectation' [*sic*] which you published a while ago....Your work spoke to the classroom personally. This has led to a deeper conversation among my students about where your work has grown in your examination of Morehouse as pertaining to race, class, and gender." He had found my contact information through R. L'Heureux Lewis, a close mutual colleague and fellow alumnus, and reached out "in the hopes that you would be willing to come and speak to the class and the broader Morehouse community about your work. At such a critical time in the life of the college your perspectives shed light on issues that our students are eager to learn about."

It had been years since I had been on the Morehouse campus, even as my research had kept the institution in the front of my mind every day for a decade. In that time, I had become known within Morehouse alumni communities as one of the college's most relentless feminist dissenters. I was even contacted by administrative representatives while a grad student due to their concerns about the effect my research might have on public relations and fundraising efforts. With that, I also knew well that there were threads of men within the institution's community who did not see Morehouse manhood as needing to be hostile to feminism or queerness, who were not overly invested in dressing up its respectability, and who even took issue with its conservative political leanings. Within me, a curiosity lingered about how the campus culture, or at least the minds of some students, had evolved.

I arrived at a classroom building that had remained unchanged since I last left it, though it was a bit surreal how much I had changed, standing now in a guest instructor role as nearly twenty-five warm-faced adolescent Black men awaited for me to lead a lecture and discussion about masculinities. Before arriving into the classroom, I stuck my head in the office suite of the chair of Political Science, an office now held by my longtime friend and occasional confidant Matthew Platt who delighted in the surprise visit as much as I delighted in his journey back to the place that had birthed his intellectualism. Joseph Carlos, a dear friend and former classmate who shot the cover image of this book and who now works in Alumni Affairs, got wind of my arrival and came to greet me. He took a seat among the students to hear my lecture and captured the moment in pictures. It was a small and welcome reunion I had not expected but reminded me why one of the unofficial slogans for Black college alumni is that we *can always come home.*

The students' questions were highly engaged, and they were already warmed up and in complete agreement with the understanding that men benefit from patriarchy (albeit differently) and were receptive to my explanation that patriarchy also arranges men's re-

FIGURE 15. The author addresses a class of first-year students at Morehouse, 2018.

lationships to each other and not only their relationships to women and nonbinary people. They asked thoughtful questions about consent and sexual harassment and "mansplaining" that seemed driven by an earnest desire to not do harm to women now that they were at the foothills of their journey through adult gendered interactions. More than anything, however, they seemed comfortable with the topics, and did not resort to posturing, antifeminist resistance, or performing for each other. Realizing that I was pleasantly surprised at this level of engagement, I had to admit to myself that I had anticipated that these students would remind me of the Morehouse students of twenty years ago, where, in my experience, discomfort and masculine grandstanding around these topics were the norm among my classmates. I also felt wholly respected, in that way that HBCU students seem innately deferential toward instructors and adult staff of all ranks, and the way that Black college faculty reinforce those boundaries. An eager and green student piped up to ask a question and called me "Ms. Grundy," to which I took no offense, but the male faculty members present did. "*Dr.* Grundy," they interjected in unison, whipping their heads toward him as if to put him on alert. The student seemed to take a humbling cue from how their tone matched the look on their faces. He corrected course instantly and sheepishly apologized. I can't imagine a scenario where my white colleagues would defend a Black woman's title and credentials so sternly.

After a few one-on-ones and group photos after class, I made my way out to take a glimpse at the grounds. My mind continued to replay how much this new crop of young men were open, curious, and seemed to reside in a world (be it online or on campus) where they didn't need convincing that some of the ways that Black men were learning manhood was a problem for which Black women could provide crucial insights. Just steps beyond the building's main exit, however, I stopped in my tracks. Facing me were looming flagpole-length banners hung from the sides of the buildings that lined the central promenade of campus. "Men of Morehouse Are Well Travelled" one banner read with a prominent group portrait of students in formal business attire standing below the seal of the president of the United States. "Men of Morehouse Are Well Balanced" announced another that depicted a collage of various students who were either immersed in engaging conversation, playing saxophone in a suit and tie, or working from a laptop against the backdrop of the campus's most photographed monuments. "Men of Morehouse are Well Read," was written atop a photographed student in a striped bowtie reading among the library stacks. Another, urging students to be "Well Spoken," attempted to capture the aptitude for oratory among student leaders. I rotated fully around to get the scope of all of them, only to find that draped over my head and behind me were side-by-side images of dapper young men posing in both black-tie formalwear and business suits, all of them looking directly and assertively into the camera. "Men of Morehouse Are Well Dressed," it

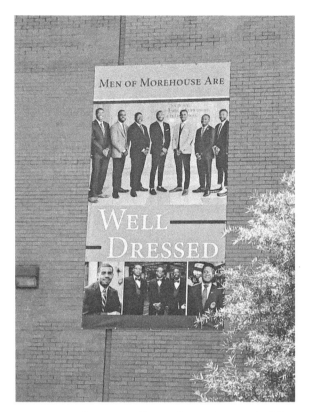

FIGURE 16. A banner outside Morehouse classroom building reads "Well Dressed."

read, and my mind went immediately back to how dress codes had been used to police and ostracize so many of the gender noncon-forming students who were the backbone of the explosive creativity and intellectualism that forms the quiddity of Black college cultures.

The slogans on these banners, which former president Robert M. Franklin dubbed the "five wells," originated alongside his 2009 decorum campaign that emphasized a type of Morehouse cultural education that extended far beyond academic instruction.[1] It was Franklin, in his campaign to cultivate "global" students, who imple-mented the "appropriate attire policy"[2] that banned "clothing asso-

FIGURE 17. A banner outside Morehouse classroom building reads "Well Travelled."

ciated with women's garb" and about which femme and trans students had spoken up so vocally when they endured disproportionate and direct targeting as a result of the policy's discriminatory structuring. Franklin's vision for globe-ready students was ironically quite parochial in comparison to the emphases on diverse student identities and unconventional postgraduate possibilities that were simultaneously emerging at other liberal arts colleges. When his tenure as president ended in 2012, a storm of media backlash to the appropriate attire policy resulted in a brief period of years in which strict enforcement of the dress code had eased. The banners before me, however, were recent readditions to the campus and revived the unapologetically constrictive cultural curriculum that harped all the way back to a Morehouse of over fifty years ago and Benjamin Mays's Jim Crow era idea of the "gentleman scholar." The contrast between the minds of the men I had just encountered and a college administration that was doubling down on outmoded cultural relics was glaring. The men of Morehouse were changing and adapting to a world that required them to have a social intelligence about difference, technology, gender identities, economic inequality, political dissent, and how to discern propagandized misinformation. Yet the institution charged with preparing them for that world continued to prioritize mastering necktie knots and the firming up their handshakes. Once again, small pockets of subversive faculty like Professor Smith picked up the slack of channeling students toward the curriculums that accurately captured the world of ideas that they were going to encounter upon graduation, while the college seemed to remain in denial that this world was rapidly changing.

Upon reading this book, one may conclude that my view of Morehouse is damning, but I simply have far too much respect and admiration for the Black men who helped shape the most seminal years of my life than to condemn them. To be clear, the college deserves every ounce of detraction it has amassed from feminist, queer, and politically radical advocates. Successive choices of administrative leadership have stayed true to the path of staking Morehouse's image and operations on patriarchal politics and methods that result in more pushouts than four-year graduates. Throughout this book I have threaded a theme of paradoxes—between the college's successes and failures, within the conundrum of producing "solutions" to a Black male "problem," and of grooming Black male respectability via means that produce and sustain abhorrent homophobic and sexual violence. To condemn Morehouse would be to dismiss it, and I have spent over a third of my life doing quite the opposite by dedicating my scholarship to the laborious and careful study of this institution because I am preoccupied with a paradox that looms over all of my questions in this work. While Morehouse alumni may pride themselves on representing ideal Black manhood, none of the college's problems are innate to or even characteristic of the kinds of changes and evolution that I consistently come across in Black men I know and love. In my extended family alone, I've witnessed the evolution of Black men whose formerly masculinist race politics were transformed by learning from Black women. In their conversations, social media posts, and our text exchanges over the years, many of the men with whom I graduated have come to think far differently about queerness now that social movements and Black queer visibility have put queer Black youth activists front and center in antiracist politics.[3]

As I write this conclusion, Morehouse recently announced that it will move to offer an online undergraduate degree program when online degree programs are still stigmatized by many four-year college administrators for their association with unaccredited schools, community colleges, and for-profit education. Colleges across the nation are financially and operationally straining to adapt to the social distancing guidelines of COVID-19, but this move was a long time coming for Morehouse administrators who struggled to expand the college's reach and stay fiscally afloat long before the global pandemic. As recently as 2012 the college was thought by many to be on the brink of solvency with budget cuts and faculty and staff furloughs spurned by a severe decline in enrollment, and the road to full recovery is still not clear.[4] Morehouse is facing serious challenges to stay afloat in the current and emerging climate of higher education. I would urge my readers not to take this book as a condemnation of Morehouse, but as a cautionary sign in the road, urging an institution to veer in its direction and away from a possible dead end. I have witnessed Black feminism improve the lives of too many Black men to believe that it can't also benefit the posterity of a Black men's institution.

At the same time, some of the trends that are observable at Morehouse point to some emerging trends that we should all find alarming among various populations of Black men. For example, Black men's support for Republicans has been rising in record numbers since the 2016 presidential campaign. Twenty-two percent of college-educated Black male voters and 20 percent of Black men with advanced degrees cast their votes for Trump (compared to 26 percent of those with a high school diploma or less).[5] While no single factor can be attributed to this shift, the contrast to over nine out of ten Black women's support for Hillary Clinton and Joe Biden point to gender disparities that must take into consideration how Trump's antifeminist and machismo rhetoric appeals to Black men willing whose politics are undergirded by conservative gender ideologies. Morehouse's patriarchal approach to Black male schooling also fits within growing critiques by feminist scholars of Black male schools who point to how Black male schooling is often predicated on patriarchal politics that come at the expense of Black women and girls.[6]

Such issues should point us to how decisions at Morehouse have a reach far beyond the campus, and that gender troubles at Morehouse give us keen insights into how patriarchy, misogyny, and homophobia contribute to other problems we can observe among Black men and boys. This book concludes that it is possible for Morehouse to improve on itself, to learn from feminist critiques how to create an enriching environment that develops all of its students, and to think about Black male education in ways that don't sustain patriarchal politics. I do this by first recapping the problems addressed in each chapter and theoretical implications for thinking about the interplay between the Du Boisian veil and the college's ideologies about Black masculinity. I continue with a discussion of practical steps the college can take to redress some of these problems, and I conclude with my reflection about how the Morehouse experience continues to affect the lives of former students long after they leave the college.

Theoretical Implications

Respectable has provided a way to understand how the theoretical underpinning that sustains so many of Morehouse's challenges is best explained by the Du Boisian veil. The veil is studied primarily for its capacity to structure the world into a one-way mirror in which the racialized subjects who live behind it can see out but racializing white subjects cannot see in.[7] This book has argued that studying processes of racialization that only occur between the Black and white worlds vastly overlooks the way the veil organizes Black life within Black spaces and institutions. In the introduction, I noted that Black political scientists have long studied the question of how and why collective racial agendas are set by African Americans. While the "linked fate" theory claims that Black Americans (as observed in bloc voting patterns) prioritize political agendas based on a view that their fates are codependent across class lines, political scientist Cathy Cohen challenged this theory by arguing that political exigencies like the HIV/AIDS crisis *should* have been at the forefront of Black community concerns but were politically marginalized by Black (mostly male, and mostly middle-class and elite) leadership because the disease was primarily associated with "hypermarginalized " queer and poor Black people. It is from Cohen that I took the idea that grounded my approach in this book: that if Black communities could be hypermarginalized by a crisis, then how could racial crises also inform us as to which African Americans were doing that manipulation and hypermarginalization within the race?

In the paradoxes and problems that continue to confront the men of Morehouse College, I saw this missing side of the story about the politics of Black crisis. Morehouse and its men are an observable case study for a far larger phenomenon in which a "crisis of the Black male" emerged as a gendered and classed redaction of what should have been a far more wholistic approach to the state of Black economics, schooling, and employment throughout the postindustrialization era of the 1980s and 1990s. While Black leadership responses to the HIV/AIDS crisis muted Black people whose visibility and concerns were already marginalized, the Black male crisis amplified attention to the kinds of cultural, neoliberal, and elitist campaigns that prioritized resource allocations for and dictated by the Black male bourgeoisie who historically held the power within the race.

Throughout post-Reconstruction history, educated Black male elites dictated racial agendas and consistently appointed themselves as representatives of the race. I argued in the introduction that middle-class and upwardly mobile Black men have historically responded to perceived crises within the race with cultural prescriptions about gender and manliness. In the post–civil rights era, a panic set in for much of Black civic, political, media, and corporate leadership when despite the era's antiracist legislative gains, African Americans fell victim to massive unemployment and neighborhood decline spurned by deindustrialization. Instead of reaping the opportunities promised by desegregation, the generation that came of age following the Civil Rights Act witnessed a surge in incarceration rates spawned by state economic warfare against low-income Black communities. Faced with these real crises that required more complicated solutions than much of what the existing antidiscrimination laws could provide, Black male leadership pivoted to a narrative that they drummed many times before in times of racial crisis: that these problems should best be met with a cultural and moral campaign of *reactive respectability*, that is, a cultural campaign of respectability politics that is formally deployed within institutions, propaganda, and strategies for racial agenda setting.

While all respectability politics are founded on a belief about performing gender role conventionality to prove a marginalized group's fitness for rights, Black male leadership in the post-civil-rights-era reactive respectability particularly prioritized college-educated and upwardly mobile Black men as the face of Black resistance to the new era's racial humiliations. Take, for example, that earlier in this book I referenced how Lerone Bennett, the editor in chief of *Ebony* magazine and a prominent Morehouse alum, used the August 1983 cover of his publication to reface and usurp the crisis. Through a visual language of a well-heeled Black businessman emerging from a yellow taxicab, Bennett repackaged the economic crisis narrative by switching out the face of Black unemployment to one that prioritized discriminations suffered by Black male executives who felt slighted by the everyday injustice of trying to hail cabs in American cities. In studying the politics of Black agenda setting and how crises emerge and arrange communities' resources, what we have missed—and what cases like Morehouse show us—is that reactive respectability can distort and manipulate which demographics these crises are disproportionately targeting within the race. Using reactive respectability to rebrand economic crisis into Black male crisis further disregarded the ways Black women took the brunt of deindustrialization when moves toward automation and globalization disproportionately eliminated women-dominated labor sectors. Economic warfare on Black inner cities didn't skip over the neighborhoods, families, schools, and resources that Black women shared with Black men.

In this book I have argued that the rationale for reactive respectability exceeds the mere self-interest of Black male elites. It is best explained, theoretically, by the Du Boisian concept of "the veil," which details how racialized subjects are made hyperconscious of how they are one-dimensionally viewed through the white world's racializing gaze. Du Bois's theory has mostly been used to discuss interracial dynamics for racialized subjects moving throughout white dominated spaces, but I've used the case of Morehouse to make the claim that this limited discussion of the veil ignores how it organizes life *behind* it in Black spaces as well. The veil invokes particular anxieties in spaces where African Americans must think of themselves as representing the race in order to be both "examples" to others within the race and to defy whites' racist stereotypes. The veil organizes Black life within Black spaces because it prioritizes expressions of gender, class, and sexuality based on what those who hold power *within* the race believe should be seen *about* the race.

Black life behind the veil at Morehouse is also a case for exemplifying two additional theories that accompany reactive respectability. First, I have shown that the deeply entrenched rape culture at Morehouse is a means for understanding how the national problem of campus sexual assault is sustained in part by *racialized rape culture* in which cultures that sustain, perpetuate, and keep men from being held accountable for sexual assault are not only a means through which to "do" gender, but also a means through which they are doing race. Rape culture extends the benefits of gender dominance to all men, but my conversations with respondents revealed how race dictates what those benefits are, how and when men can access them, and the resources they must negotiate or relinquish for them. Morehouse men do not control how they are seen by the world beyond the veil, but they use rape culture as a means of manipulating what view of themselves and intraracial gender troubles they project onto the veil.

Second, Morehouse is a site for an understudied empirical examination of the Black political economy where the neoliberal turn into Black politics is not only waged in the lives of Black males "in crisis" but also high achieving Black men who are groomed to be Black male elites. The belief that Black communities are best served by private-public partnerships in which Black male elites get a seat at the table of wealth and corporations is an ideology that I've repeatedly described as *social justice capitalism*. The term was first coined by political historian Leah Wright Rigeuer, but this work has made the empirical case for why this form of Black neoliberalism is particularly protracted through individualistic beliefs about leadership, paternalistic imaginations of Black communities, and the steering of Black politics away from the feminist leanings of Black radicalism. Social Justice Capitalism steers Black political economies away from MLK's calls for a bottom-up democratic socialist model of economic justice and toward a vision of top-down racial uplift that protracts the masculinist modalities of free-market economics into the grooming of Black male success in the managerial sectors of capitalist enterprise. The experiences that my respondents had at Morehouse—and the types of institutional ideologies that could still cling to cultural curriculum campaigns of "Well-Read" and "Well-Dressed"—posters, are outcomes of that veiled reactive respectability, racialized rape culture, and social justice capitalism and are wellsprings for how it is reproduced and sustained. The institution may see itself as solving the "problem" of how young Black males are seen by the white world, but the way the veil constructs hierarchies of visibility both within the race and on campus contributes to the problems that, in the end, undermine the possibilities for broader constructions of Black male success and understandings of Black masculinity that better serve Black men throughout their life course in a dynamic and shifting world.

Each chapter identified and explored one of the ways that the institution's ideologies about the veil and ability to suppress the visibility of men marginalized by class and sexuality manifests into urgent problems facing the campus. We began our look into the college experiences of men in this study by unfolding much of how the Morehouse brand organizes how men think about themselves in relationship to the institution's ideals. Chapter 2 situated the announcement of the trans student policy as an entrée into an institutional way of life where a cultural curriculum (about masculine ideals of decorum, dress, speech, and bodily comportment) is on par with academic learning. Men told us how the vast diversity with which they enter their first year is almost immediately met by the process of *branding* in which rituals, rules, practices, and peer policing mold and conform them to the college's ideals about how to behave, present, and comport themselves in preparation for scrutiny by the white world beyond graduation. While men overwhelmingly held a fondness for the brand and even accepted the daunting task of trying to live up to the lofty expectations of its fictitious "Morehouse Man" archetype, they were also aware that these branding mechanisms can be extreme, unfair, and unnecessary. This process of institutional branding is not fixed or even consistent, but rather its "tissues of constraint" expand and contract at various times in the process and around different men differently according to class backgrounds.

A rigid structure of rules, for example, highlighted vast differences between privileged men who had the means to abscond or negotiate rules (or who were unaffected by the rules because they already dressed, behaved, and talked in ways that were compliant) and those from marginalized backgrounds who found the rules overwhelming, infantilizing, confusing, or simply lacked the material resources to comply with them. Thus, while the branding process may aim to create a culture of brotherhood based on shared experience, branding itself exacerbates class differences. Ideas about which men do and do not deserve to become Morehouse Men based on how much they represent the brand serves as a justification to push out the large population of "riffraff" who don't graduate. While advocates of the brand defend it as making men, in reality most of the fraternity-like rituals such as the weeklong New Student Orientation put upperclassmen in the peer-to-peer position of hazing first year students and thus authorized a culture where teenagers and very young adults are deputized to intimidate and control their peers. Branding not only established a culture of rules that ostracizes and marginalizes low-income and/or gender-nonconforming students, but it also purports to be a rite of passage in a way it is not. Men from low-income backgrounds in particular, who were used to taking on adult responsibilities like income-earning and household-tending in their high school years, complained that the rules were infantilizing and treated them like boys. The culture of rigidity seems to assume the worst about young Black men's inclination toward delinquency instead of giving students freedom and choice to explore young adulthood within their college experience.

The prevalence of homophobia and gender violence is one of the most alarming outcomes of the way the veil organizes gender and sexuality dynamics on campus. As evidenced in the chapter on Morehouse's racialized rape culture, race coated the ways men talked about gender, sex, and women and understood campus sexual assault. Narratives about sex did not resemble the cavalier "hook-up" culture of extant campus sexual assault literature. Rather, across multiple narratives, men framed sex with women as a serious matter of personal conduct and obligations toward race betterment through Black male respectability. Women were dually and paradoxically framed as instruments for projecting Black male respectability onto the veil and as dangerous pitfalls that could ruin men's life chances.

My findings on group-level competition call attention to how race compounds masculine cultures of college competition for which sexual power over women is a tool in that competition. How men understood their race-gender subjectivity through the Du Boisian veil adds overlooked dimensions about who college Black men may view as competition and which resources they negotiate while vying for status compared to those groups. In competition with white men, respondents noted overcompensating for racial discrimination with work ethic, even as they were perennially disadvantaged by racism. Other men, however, are not who they see as their only competition. The propagandized belief that Black men are "losing ground" to Black women in education and employment stoked masculine anxieties about intraracial competition with Black women on college campuses. Sexual dominance over Black female coeds provided a means of compensating for the racial and masculine anxieties that are provoked by being bested by them.

Homophobia is the bookend to rape culture in this veiled way of seeing Black manhood. Visibility is the most precious and finite resource for men who see themselves as representing the race to an outside view, and competition for visibility extends group competition into how homophobic violence organizes student life. Morehouse has a wide reputation for its large culture of closeted and sometimes out queer students. As Mingus detailed in a remorseful reflection on his own homophobic actions, a belief that queer and gender nonconforming students "tarnish" Morehouse's brand triggered student leadership (of which Mingus and his cronies were members) to use their power to block organizations that would bring recognition and visibility to queer students. Mingus was not in denial that the student body contained many closeted students, and some were even counted among his friends. However, his veiled preoccupation with the image the college projected led him to believe that the threat queer students posed was a direct competition from a group of hypermarginalized Black men who aimed to also represent Morehouse to the outside world.

Morehouse's racialized rape culture is also bolstered by the ways that stereotypes of Black male criminalization loom in the minds of men who see their college years as defying the statistics about incarcerated Black men their age. Extant discussions of campus rape cultures often note that (white) college men are not made to take the consequences of sexual assault seriously, but within a racialized rape culture at Morehouse, respondents stressed how legally devastating and unjust rape allegations were for their accused classmates, to the extent that their understandings of rape mostly disregarded its consequences for the Black female victim of the high-profile assault that occurred while over a fourth of the respondents were students. In the climate around that high-profile assault, a campus that three men otherwise described as politically apathetic erupted with student activism in defense of the perpetrators. Black feminist scholars have noted how the defense of accused Black men in intraracial sexual assaults positions rape apologism as an antiracist act. The ways many Morehouse men understood and "did" race in that context allowed them to racialize themselves as victims of a racist penal system and white-dominated media, while deracializing Black women victims by effacing any role their race played in getting justice. While rape culture has long been understood by campus sexual assault researchers as a way that men "do" gender, the racialized rape culture evident at Morehouse points to an overlooked truth: rape culture is also a means through which college men are doing *race*.

Lastly, in the previous chapter I brought to bear the political consequences that neoliberalism and a belief in "social justice capitalism" have on the lives of young Black men when Black male elites and mostly white corporate interests conspire in their ideologies about how to manufacture and advertise Black male success. The driving principles of social justice capitalism emphasize individualism and personal gains, but the belief that these principles can be put to antiracist use through philanthropic and corporate engagement refaces that self-interest as a vehicle of racial uplift. The competition to "fix" the "problem" of young Black males who are on track for educational success makes political bedfellows out of antiracist advocates and conservative organizations who have otherwise shown little to no interest in improving outcomes for any other groups of Black youth. Morehouse is a testing ground for many of these Black leadership alliances with conservative-leaning corporate interests such as Walmart and Chick-fil-A, but it is also an incubator for ingraining masculinist traits into the concept of rightful racial leadership. In this way of thinking, race betterment is brought about not by improving the conditions of the Black poor, but by grooming more Black elites whose personal success and access to wealth trickle down to those African Americans for whom they provide an example of achievement. In male dominated elite spaces such as business and politics, advocates of social justice capitalism tend to view investments in the ascension of Black men as the most effective means of grooming influential Black figures. Such findings apply an additional meaning to *Black male exceptionalism* in the rhetoric around young Black males not only stresses how they fare worse than any other groups but also traffics in beliefs that high achieving Black males should be prioritized in the allocation of community and educational resources. In this version of Black male exceptionalism, what is best for the race flows from doing what is best for its most promising men.

Grooming Black men for influence in those elite spaces, however, also comes at a cost to Black men who would rather angle their lives toward community-based work or, simply, fields that are not known for high income earning. Training up future corporate executives isn't only encouraged through leadership rhetoric and notable campus speakers but is perhaps more effectively accomplished in the resources the college divests from fields and careers that don't fit its narrow masculinist notions of success. The small college of roughly three thousand students has three leadership centers and/ or programs, and yet men like Roy, when asked to explain what the college meant by leadership, expressed a sense of leadership that was divorced from any political groundings. For Mort and other students whose career interests were aimed toward education, social work, theater, or stereotypically feminized professions, the college provided few if any structural resources, and these men took their core major courses at Spelman.

Where students could find an overabundance of career resources, however, was in the business department, which is consistently the most popular concentration for Morehouse students and far outsizes the influence on campus culture that a such a program would expectedly have at a small liberal arts college. Within the business curriculum, a corporate etiquette course requires men to learn how to mimic white executives in social and professional settings, but what men are taught about discussing classical music and how to properly butter their dinner rolls is oddly out of touch with any real interactions with their affluent white counterparts. Etiquette classes may teach students how to imitate an outdated caricature-like idea of whiteness, but it hardly prepares them for the continually shifting culture of elite spaces. Black male elites may be organizing Black male success programs based on an idea of impressing whites on the other side of the veil, but the very belief that well-off whites *can* be impressed by performative affluent behavior is a distortion of how class authenticity is read in privileged circles.

The masculinist traits that inundate Morehouse's curricula and structure are not just an outcome of conservative and corporate political influences. Masculinist ideologies about race betterment also pull Morehouse's campus political culture to the right and cudgel the radical and Black nationalist politics to which a dissenting minority of students are drawn. This is no even fight between diverse student views as the conservatism that dominates the campuses is both backed and introduced by administrators and powerful donors. Gender maps the terrain of these racial politics. While there are masculinist veins within the ideologies of most substantial Black political movements, Black socialist, communist, and radical movements historically had substantial input from Black women organizers, who often saw Black women's interests as particularly aligned with combating labor exploitation and the economic oppressions suffered by working families. The masculinist angling of social justice capitalism may result in Black male leaders who pay lip service to Black families and communities, but when real crises such as police brutality occurred, men like Clifford, Mort, Shadow, and Wes were deeply disappointed by the political apathy of administrators and the student body. Worse, they deemed the administration complicit in supporting the forced displacement of low-income residents in surrounding West End Atlanta neighborhoods. Casting race-betterment as a stand-alone endeavor that hangs on the shoulders of individual male leaders allowed administrators, faculty, and student leaders to cast the uplift of Black communities as a "single axis issue" in which only racism is prioritized. As such, issues of class and economics that would be otherwise highlighted by perspectives that include Black women went grossly overlooked in the ways social and political issues were prioritized on campus. Without tethering antiracism to issues of patriarchy, capitalism, or homophobia, conservatism was presented as having as much antiracist potential as Black leftist politics by right-leaning college administrators.

The Way Forward

It is an uncomfortable conundrum for many of us to think that the men who have long been praised for uplifting the race have also used their power within those positions to cause problems for and harm to others within the race. The chapters of this book laid bare many several of these problems and how they occur due to a confluence of ideological stances about race and masculinity that are met by the everyday policies, lived practices, and real-life structural operations of the college. My approach to sociology has always been anchored by a belief that structures change behaviors and thinking more than our individual behaviors and thinking bring about structural and systemic change. In the previous sections of this chapter, I recapped the theoretical implications that resulted from how reactive respectability has guided policies and practices at Morehouse that have resulted in many of its challenges. Black male elites have long controlled Morehouse and have ingrained reactive respectability into its way of institutional life. But Morehouse also created successive generations of Black male elites, and a cycle of patriarchal, homophobic, and often misogynistic ways of doing campus life can be interrupted by changing many of the resources, rules, and protocols that usher Morehouse students into their adult lives. With that in mind, each chapter provided a generational backstory for problems that plague the college, but each chapter also provided an opportunity to take a wide-lens view of these institutional challenges and consider how practical steps and changes can begin to redress root issues.

One of the most consistent findings I encountered in the data gleaned across respondent narratives was that race, gender, and reactive respectability compound the politics of visibility. The promotion of image and reputation through the visibility of students far exceeds considerations of promotion, recruitment, and marketing. The Morehouse brand not only molds conformity to an institutional ideal of masculinity, but it also does so by masking and suppressing other expressions of dress and bodily comportment. The "hoe contract" stressed how rape allegations were a matter more important to Morehouse students' images than harm to victims. Mingus told us how student government officers organized a hegemony to suppress the visibility of a queer student group. Students who participated in radical and Black nationalist campus political movements were kept from the view of visiting donors. The politics of visibility are weaponized to ensure that students with certain expressions of gender, class, and leftist racial politics are not only shielded from outside view but are also invalidated from Morehouse Manhood because they are never associated with the idealized image. Therefore,

I recommend that administrators take immediate steps to reverse the course of queer erasure, not only superficially but also in, curriculum, student resources, and by repealing the current trans student policy.

Much of this erasure seems curiously contradictory at best and directly harmful to students at worst. As of 2016, African Americans made up 54 percent of new HIV/AIDS cases between ages thirteen and twenty-four, the majority of which were gay and bisexual men.[8] The college is situated at the intersection of an at-risk student population housed within in a city recently declared to have neighborhood rates on par with some of the most AIDS-stricken developing nations in the world.[9] Given the inevitability of HIV transmission within the student body, a women-led team of campus health officials moved to prioritize statistical reality over institutional image. For a college that so proudly celebrates its historical firsts, little attention has been paid to the Morehouse College Student Health Center being the first HBCU health service to administer the PrEP (pre-exposure prophylaxis) antiretroviral drug to students (with funding from an external grant).[10] The treatment suppressed the amount of HIV in an infected person's system to undetectable (and nontransmittable) levels and is considered critical to preventing the spread of the virus in both HIV positive and HIV negative people. But students don't know the drug is available on campus, and the refusal of administrators and many student body leaders alike to acknowledge that males who have sex with males are more than a small population of out queer students puts the entire student body and their partners throughout Atlanta at risk. What happens on campus is a microcosmic example of the hypermarginalization in Cathy Cohen's racial analysis of the HIV/AIDS crisis. A health crisis that puts the entire campus at risk should otherwise be a top priority for administrative allocation of student resources, but administrators have sidelined the crisis because of its association with gay and bisexual men and their partners.

Making queerness both visible and validating its place in the image of Morehouse manhood would make a sizeable impact toward redressing this problem. Invisibility and marginalization are among the most common experiences expressed by queer students at HBCUs, and LGBTQIA students consistently report suffering penalties from being "out" during their college years.[11] It is my informed belief, after having conducted this research, that part of the reason queer HBCU students have this marginalized experience is that they do not see themselves in their curriculum, their administrators, in student programming, or in types of alumni success stories their colleges promote. The banners that hung on the sides of those buildings stopped me in my tracks not only because they harked back to an oppressive dress code policy, but also because their heteronormativity buttresses the way heteronormative rituals (like the brother-sister matching ceremony) and rhetoric (across classes and convocations) is an assault on queer students that constructs closeted spaces around the lives of all students, even proudly out students who must navigate when and where they can be out across different social and professional contexts on campus. In the current age of social media and student activism, queer student clubs such as Morehouse Adodi organize pride events and programming for students, but these efforts are not matched with formal institutional resource allocations (the organization formerly went by SafeSpace but changed its name to acknowledge the original queer student advocacy group that formed in the 1990s and that Mingus's SGA administration organized to block). Morehouse has the choice to send the message that transphobia and homophobia are unacceptable and that queer students are integral to the institution, but instead the college delegates no LGBTQIA counseling services, the Title IX officer has no training in same-sex sexual assaults, and there are no classes that emphasize queer scholarship. When being able to openly discuss your sexuality is a matter of mental health, holding perpetrators of homophobic violence accountable, and keeping the student body healthy, the visibility of queerness and an attendant deemphasis on heteronormativity are matters of literal life and death.

A second matter that I find warrants immediate redress pertains to sexual assault and misconduct. Since the 2016 *Buzzfeed* investigative report, I have spent many of my academic lectures likening Morehouse's sexual assault problem to the Catholic Church's child sexual abuse scandal in that both are top-down systems of exploitation that are sustained by the complicity of their male-dominated highest ranked personnel.[12] The *Buzzfeed* article and follow-ups from the *Chronicle of Education* (2019) exposed years mishandling allegations and suggestions that campus police and administrators—either through deliberation or disregard—lost incident reports filed by victims. In 2014 a Morehouse dean helped muzzle victims' supporters by issuing a cease and desist order to a Spelman freshman who tweeted out that she already knew three classmates who had been assaulted by Morehouse students. Instead of being reprimanded for this malfeasance and negligence by top administrators, former Morehouse president John Silvanus Wilson was hesitant to hold perpetrators or personnel accountable and invoked common rape myths about "lying" female accusers.[13] This is not a one-off. Dating back decades, Morehouse administrators and leadership have consistently responded to assault allegations by perpetuating rape myths. For example, when Roy, Mingus, and Davis recounted how student reaction to the 1996 gang-rape case overwhelmingly supported the male perpetrators, administrators piled on to the victim-blaming. During a worship service in the campus chapel, a chaplain suggested that women's dress and attitudes brought sexual violence on themselves.[14] Like the Catholic Church, the college's institution-wide reaction to sexual assault is to deflect, deny, and to victim-blame. The Church was exposed for systemically moving around child abusing clergy from one parish to the next in an effort to protect them from prosecution, but Morehouse administrators simply wait out the graduation clock on perpetrator accountability (campus public safety officers told accuser Victoria Hall that her rapist was only two weeks away from graduating when she asked for follow-ups on her incident report).

Morehouse students deserve protection and transparent means of understanding the legal repercussions of assault and misconduct, but the women around them and the queer students who are most vulnerable to sexual assault within the student body also deserve protection from administrators, staff, fellow students, and the policies and procedures that sustain rape culture and homophobic violence on campus. Title IX is a federal law statute, and failure to comply with it not only placed the college under government investigation, but also the pattern of illegalities makes a definitive case for calling Morehouse a corrupt organization. Literature on organizational corruption and cultures of masculinity finds that they are highly correlated to organizations that lack women in leadership positions. Women, such studies show, appear to be less corruptible that men.[15] Therefore, the underlying issue that Morehouse, the Catholic Church, and other organizations embroiled with cultures of rape and sexual abuse such as the Boy Scouts of America and the National Football League share is an institutional culture of uninterrupted and unchecked hypermasculinity.[16] Specifically at Morehouse, this results in specific *worst practices* where sexual assault allegations are handled as though Morehouse were and organization of cronies instead of an academic institution with federal compliance guidelines, oversight, and an accrediting body.

Morehouse's hypermasculine culture includes its board of trustees. The Association of Governing Boards, a consulting firm hired by the college, warned the college that its bloated body of forty members (college boards in the United States average around twelve members) grossly overrepresented "an insider group" of alumni who "are seemingly making the key decisions."[17] In January 2017, student leaders filed a restraining order against the trustees, and the following March the faculty issued a vote of no confidence against its then chairman.[18] Morehouse cannot change the echo chamber culture of its leadership if it cannot import trustees from across a spectrum of higher education and organizational leadership backgrounds. If it seems like Morehouse handles its sexual abuse problems like a fraternity, it is because its decisions are being made by a fraternity. An immediate practical step is to scale down the board to twelve or fewer members, to minimize alumni representation to an appropriate three to four members, and to insure that the outside voices of women and nonbinary trustees hold a balanced number of board seats.

From that radical change to its top brass, many of Morehouse's more alarming sexual misconduct mishandlings have a chance of permanently changing. An alarming turnover rate with the Title IX coordinator position must be immediately redressed for student legal protections. Past coordinators have included staffers who simultaneously held appointments in the public relations office, and thus the college ensured that its chief Title IX compliance officer would specialize in spinning bad press about college sex scandals. Most colleges and universities would find an obvious conflict of interest in dually holding these positions. While there is no legal requirement for Title IX officers to have legal training, Morehouse should overcorrect for past malfeasance by appointing an attorney to the position who has an extensive background in Title IX compliance and workplace sexual harassment training. From there, the Title IX officer must ensure that assault victims are not subjected to intimidation and humiliation by the college's disciplinary board, which, in the case of Spelman sophomore Victoria Hall, subjected her to inquiry before a panel made up of faculty, staff, and even male *students* who asked her what she was wearing on the night of her rape and why she would visit her attacker's house if she did not intend to have sex. I was appalled to learn that faculty and staff who had no training in law enforcement, sexual assault counseling, or any appropriate background for interrogating a victim also did not see the immediate gross impropriety of involving her peers in such a hearing.

There are numerous other infuriating instances of how sexual assault and harassment allegations are mishandled by the college, and a lawsuit filed against the college as recently as July 2020 by two students who were groped by a male staffer has shown how the college's efforts to hold perpetrators accountable are still insufficient. The best practical step, then, is not to address these problems individually, but for the college to ask itself why it has not learned from the best practices and policies of other institutions of higher education. For example, Morehouse's trans student policy, from the view of other single sex institutions' trans policies, punishes gender nonconforming students. Morehouse had the option of learning about trans admissions and protections from women's colleges, and yet administrators chose to create their own policy with no input from trans researchers, consultants, or activists. Throughout this book I've noted how Black male exceptionalism has distorted approaches to problems that affect Black male and female youth, but that Black male exceptionalism also holds an institutional meaning for the way that Morehouse operates. Too often administrators and trustees seem to believe that policies and practices that work for every other kind of college student are not suited to Black males. Thus, Morehouse is constantly out of step with higher education because administrators consistently treat Black male students as though they reside beyond the reaches of what researchers and consultants know works and does not work for colleges and universities. In order to turn the page on its corruption and assault mishandlings, Morehouse will have to abandon its religion of masculinity in favor of proven best practices in higher education.

As I conclude this book you, reader, should know that "the way forward" connotes an additional meaning for me, and that pertains to the men themselves. Entering someone's life through an intimate conversation about their innermost thoughts and about a place you both shared at such a seminal point in your lives forges a bond built on a commonality we already had. Several of the respondents have stayed in my life years after data collection concluded. They've been friends. I've watched them become fathers. We've bonded through times they battled serious illnesses. Twice now I've sobbed when their lives were cut short, and then have been reminded that with my hours of recordings I have one of the greatest memorials to their life anyone could ever give their families. The men who offered me a piece of themselves for this work have grown from their early thirties into their mid-forties now and have staked their places in the world. They're on your television screens and in your headlines now, reader, and working on behalf of our people.

My optimism for the structural changes the college can make for future cohorts of young Black men has to do with the growth and maturation I have witnessed from previous graduates. As human beings, Black men's lives move in chapters, volumes, where who one is as twenty-two is not the person one recognizes at forty-five. Even in their early thirties, many of them were already trying to reconcile the types of masculinity they learned in college with the kinds of masculinity that functioned in their lives. For the ones who were married to women, oftentimes their wives had "worked on" their perceptions of gender and expectations when functioning in modern egalitarian marriages. Fathering was, for many of them, an eye opening and emotionally filling experience where they prided themselves on being hands-on with their children and were learning brand new models of parenting for a new generation of Black men. Into their forties, many of these men came to rethink some of their previous views on sexuality, both for themselves and their closest classmates. I saw the seeds of this in their thirties, but into middle age many of the men seemed to understand the version of Morehouse they had helped keep in the closet, and how much life and happiness it was costing their friends to keep that part of their lives from them for decades.

I say all of this because the experience of "the brand" doesn't end at graduation, and not only does it incur a process of rethinking these learned race-gender ideologies, but also from what I can observe the life course of a Morehouse graduate requires *unlearning* parts of that institutional instruction. All of us unlearn components of our formative years, but Morehouse administrators must ask themselves if the cultural instruction their students are receiving is properly equipping them for their lives ahead in a world that seems to be evolving while the college clings to relic beliefs about "race men." In the second chapter of this book, I referenced scholarship that describes how HBCUs hold a social contract both with their membership and with the race that extends far beyond the goals of a conventional baccalaureate education.[19] Unlearning Morehouse, in my view, does not require graduates to jettison everything that has molded them through their college years, but it does require the college to revisit the terms of its social contract with students and to ask itself earnestly and critically, "is it working?"

I want to be clear that save for a few respondents, the men spoke very highly of the benefit of their college experience to their lives and were mostly very dedicated to defending the college's method of grooming students. While some like Davis, Roy, Ornette, and Percy were dyed-in-the-wool cheerleaders who have few significant critiques of the institution, the majority of the men measured the parts of the process that served their lives and the other ways that their professional and personal lives beyond college required adapting to cultures and situations in a world that Morehouse had presented to them as flat and unchanging, with cut-and-dried problems that would be solved by firm handshakes and impeccable manners.

My closing message, then, is to the men themselves. Your aggregated experiences provided me with a bird's-eye view for how to assess this institution and its influence on your lives. There are varying degrees to which you each credit the college (or do not) for its benefits to your lives, but in weaving each of your stories together and having been privileged to have known you throughout these pivotal years of your growth, my assessment is that the true value of this institution is not in the men it claims to make but in the men it brings together. Any number of institutions that would be equally dedicated to educating Black men in a Black space could have brought you together, and the myth of the Morehouse Mystique is that the college offers you more than you give to each other. You are each your greatest resource, as you have been resources to me. I've seen you each bring out the best in each other, challenging each other, raising the bar on growth and honesty and reflection as you carry forth as a cohort of men who share not only an experience but also a sense that you knew and were known by each other before the world knew who you would be and before you were men. There is no amount of script or necktie or business etiquette course that needs to polish up Black men when you are all testament to how growth arrives from acknowledging the human flaws that make our journey possible.

Acknowledgments

It takes a community to write a book worth reading. This book begins not on its first page, but half my life ago. It was born when I sat across the desks and in the classrooms of Professors Beverly Guy-Sheftall, Mona Taylor Phillips, M. Bahati Kuumba, Cynthia Neal Spence, and Bruce Wade—my intellectual parents at Spelman College. The community into which I was born is a fervent Black liberationist community that impassioned my politics. But Spelman College planted the seed of my intellectualism and completed my worldview by adding Black feminist groundings to it. It was the first place I learned that Black feminists had an intellectual history (that predated that of white women), and the first place I came to see myself as having a stake in that. I write, still, with making my Spelman faculty proud in mind. Spelman is also where I was pipelined into the Andrew W. Mellon Foundation and its Mellon Mays Undergraduate Fellowship (from which I graduated to doctoral and then faculty fellowships) that has flooded me with human and material resources on every step of my scholarly path.

It was that Spelman preparedness, and a gem of advice from my advisor, the late Dr. Bruce Wade, "You don't turn down the University of Michigan," that delivered me next to Ann Arbor, Michigan, which was a town exceedingly friendly and vastly lonely. I was isolated geographically, culturally, and racially, and I missed the tight-knit community of Spelman and Morehouse deeply. For all of the agony of those years, however, I found at Michigan the most significant friends I have yet made in this life. Doctors L'Heureux Lewis-McCoy, Maria Johnson, Courtney Cogburn, Flannery Stevens, and Lumas Helaire should be felt all throughout this book, both in their intellectual influence and in the extent to which I emotionally depended on their friendship to steer me through these years. One of the very best things that ever happened to the life of my mind is finding an advisor in Alford Young Jr., who was not impressed by anything short of intellectual rigor. Al so heavily guided and influenced my thinking on this book throughout all my dissertation stages that my original title was to be *Manhood within the Margins*—a nod to his book, *The Minds of Marginalized Black Men*. Other Michigan faculty who planted fertile seeds early in my mind include historian Hannah Rosen, sociologist Anthony Chen, and literary scholar Michael Awkward. Karyn Lacy served on my committee and was also exactly the faculty mentor I needed every time I needed her and a tremendous scholarly influence on my methodology and theoretical aims in this work.

There are also those at Michigan who intervened in ways that spared me an unwanted fate. As director of Graduate Studies for the Department of Women's Studies, Deborah Keller-Cohen saw me, a precandidate, crushed by withdrawal and checking out from all my coursework. She had the wherewithal to understand something else was awry with my transition to that space, and instead of putting me out of school, lit a gentle fire under me and devised a plan of cognate courses that resuscitated my mind and confidence as a thinker. She changed the way I see my role with my own struggling students.

As a joint PhD student, my funding was handled almost entirely through the Department of Sociology, which at the time had a draconian director of Graduate Studies who saw to it to "trim the fat" of the department and defund many of the students. That was the semester when I, at age twenty-nine, found a lump in my left breast but had no health insurance to do much about it. It progressed to Stage III breast cancer within a few months (a very cautious nurse practitioner put in the radiology order that saved my life). I thought for a moment that being sick would plunge my life into even more inescapable isolation, and yet everyone I needed—even when we hadn't been close before—appeared in my life as I needed them. My fellow Michigan Sociology graduate students were in the trenches with me. My world-class 811 Fifth Street neighbors immediately began caring for me (thank you Don and Ellen McGee). My friend Professor Sherie Randolph attended all my patient orientations with me as though I were her blood. Being sick was a financial burden for which my community back home in Kentucky, including my former Community Montessori School teachers, came to my aid because no matter where I go, I'm still their Saida. (Thank you, Mrs. Joanna Simpson, Ms. Peggy Somsel, and Mrs. Janet Ashby. And to the late Mrs. Elizabeth Farrar, the day you left us I sobbed as though you were my own mother.)

My last day of chemo and radiation was the first day I began seriously "dissertating." It was in the Minneapolis home of my aunt Professor Michelle Goodwin (mother of my surrogate baby sister, Sage), that I stuck to the most regimented writing schedule of my life. I got it done. I defended my thesis in July 2014 with my father choking back his tears as my committee announced "Congratulations, Dr. Grundy."

I have the great fortune of friends who are colleagues and colleagues who are friends, and they have been with me toiling on every paragraph of this book. At Boston University this included fellow faculty writing partners Professors Julie Klinger, Ashley Farmer, Catherine Connell, Jessica Simes, Hebatallah Gowayed, Ana Villareal, Robert Eschmann, Paula Austin, and Christopher Schmitt. Thank you to all the women colleagues who wrote this book with me at my dining room table. My colleagues in the Department of Sociology have consistently been a resource in this work, including helping secure my contract with the University of California Press. My colleagues in BU African American studies are like my Bundini Brown in this heavyweight title fight called tenure. My BU administrators, including Kenn Elmore, Louis Chude Sokei, Crystal Williams, Nazli Kibria, Nancy Ammerman, and Gina Sapiro, have always had my back. The Boston University Center for the Humanities should also be thanked for its support.

This work would also not be worth writing if I had not been counseled and befriended by beloved colleagues in the American Sociological Association, Association of Black Sociologists, the Du Bois Scholar Network, New England Workshop on Ethnicity and Race, Society for the Study of Social Problems, the Social Science Research Council, and the Institute for Citizens and Scholars (formerly Woodrow Wilson National Fellowship Foundation until reconsidering his staunch white supremacism). I am blessed with a constellation of friend-mentors ("friendtors") who have given me golden eggs of advice and inspiration for my work in this book and beyond. Insights from Professors Nicole Gonzalez Van Cleve, Laurence Ralph, Juan Battle, Marcus Hunter, Saher Selod, Freeden Blume Oeur, John Major Eason, Waverly Duck, Fred Wherry, and Steve D. Mobley have been invaluable. My Ace-Boons Professors Karida Brown (who workshopped dusty drafts of this book), Kellie Carter Jackson, Leah Wright Rigueur, Elizabeth Hinton, Ashley Farmer, Megan Francis, Sarah Jackson, Sherie Randolph, Orly Clerge, and Aisha Beliso-De Jesus have not only walked this life with me but are forever a garden of thought and Black feminist radicalism that holds me to the path.

My developmental editor Grey Osterud is worth her weight in gold. I met Grey in my second year of grad school when she edited a special issue journal that included my first article on Morehouse. She told me to come see her when I was ready for my book, and no other human being has seen this project from alpha to omega like Grey has. She made my work much easier to hand off to the team at the University of California Press (Naomi Schneider, Summer Farrah), who have been consummate professionals and believed in this work from day one.

My mind and spirit have been fed by thinkers and friends beyond academia. Tiffany Griffin and Dr. Rachel Westerfield have been there through it all. Dr. Amen Ra Mashariki was there for part of it and contributed an idea that became a chapter. Dr. Kimya Moyo is my second mother and a favorite friend. The Stroesser Family cheers me on by reading every word I write, as does Mrs. Wendy Batiste-Johnson. Damon Young, Dwayne Wright (also known by his sobriquet, Panama Jackson), Jenisha Watts, and Lauren Williams are writers who sharpen my sword and keep me reminded of what my ideas mean for those beyond the Ivory Tower.

I don't know what I did so well in the last life to be blessed with this family of mine in this one. I wish I could bottle them up and hand them out to everyone still yearning for an unconditional love where you know you are someone's best thing. On the eve of my job talk at Boston University, I was riddled with nervousness about how to convert this infant dissertation to a compelling lecture. "Everyone loves a good story," my sagacious mother hummed at me. "Tell them the story." This is that story, Mommy, and I'm singing it back to you, Aunt Carolyn, Uncle Luke, Uncle "Big Man," Uncle Isom, and Rev. and Mrs. Luke and Annie Maxie Beard. To my sister, Tulani—I don't know if anyone should attempt life without a big sister. Tulani is my bodyguard, my agent, the one who knows all the pieces of me. She was instrumental in helping locate respondents for this book and has treated this whole process with the excitement and anticipation of a book party that only Tulani would have. My brother (her husband) Othello is not your typical brother-in-law. We are thick as thieves and he is an intellectual sounding board, a counselor, and a coach in my life. Tulani and Othello gave me my two most prized possessions, my nephews Garvey and Gibran. I wrote this book for you because you are the future of Black manhood. When you both are grown men you will be two of my closest friends. To my extended cousins, aunts, and uncles in the families McKnight, Beard, Simms, and Grundy, I did this for our family name.

My father deserves his own paragraph. No one has read every word I've ever written in my life but him. His love is planetary with a gravitational pull toward the best version of myself. My father is not only my favorite kind of Black man—kind, nurturing, gentle, unwavering, and clever—but it was my father who I watched revel in all the best of Black people and find in being Black a thing of great beauty. Every day in our household we watched/heard/learned something extraordinary about Black people and what we create, from queer ballroom culture to sharecropping field hymns of the Delta. My father is a lifelong learner who can always hear new ideas and delights in my mind. As early as four years old I remember him ever so carefully turning the pages on the books he would read at the dining room table (my father always has a book or three on him). When he got to a passage that strung the chords of his mind, he would call me over from wherever I was playing, have me read the passage he selected, and then ask, "What do you think of that?" It's been that way for nearly forty years. In my father's love what I think always has a place to be heard.

Being an exceptional human being meant that my father also brought exceptional Black men into my life in the form of my surrogate uncles. Haki Madhubuti; my godfather the late great Morris FX Jeff; Frank X. Walker; David Hall and his son, Rahsaan Hall; and the indomitable immortal spirit of Leonard L. Brown who transitioned to the ancestral realm not long after I finished my first draft. My life has been covered by the very best of Black men, so much so that my standard for what Black men can be is far higher than any conventional standards for masculinity. In their seventies they are fiercely devoted to a vision of Black liberation that does not just serve half the race. To the men in my life anything short of that ain't really liberation at all.

Indeed, my challenge and my duty in writing about men at Morehouse is in having seen the long arc of evolution for the Black men who raised me. I, however, am the one to tell this story about Morehouse College and its men. It is the story I went to graduate school for, in order to master a scientific discipline just to get the story right, with the one clear objective that I had some truth on this institution that would benefit our people to know.

Respondent Demographics

	Low-resourced (n = 10)	Moderately resourced (n = 8)	Well-resourced (n = 14)
Father's Occupation[1]			
K–12 Education (1)	(0)	(0)	(1)
Professor/Researcher (2)	(0)	(0)	(2)
Attorney (2)	(0)	(0)	(2)
Physician (1)	(0)	(0)	(1)
Service Sector (1)	(1)	(0)	(0)
Civil Service (4)	(2)	(2)	(0)
Factory/Laborer (2)	(1)	(1)	(0)
Military (3)	(0)	(2)	(1)
Engineering (2)	(0)	(0)	(2)
Computing/IT (1)	(0)	(1)	(0)
Business/ Managerial (3)	(0)	(1)	(2)
Odd Jobs (2)	(1)	(1)	(0)
Unemployed (0)	(0)	(0)	(0)
Self-Employed (2)	(0)	(1)	(1)
Other (1)	(0)	(0)	(1)
Unknown (4)	(4)	(0)	(0)
Deceased (1)	(2)	(0)	(0)

	Low-resourced (n = 10)	Moderately resourced (n = 8)	Well-resourced (n = 14)
Father's Highest Level of Education[2]			
Some High School (3)	(2)	(1)	(0)
High School (10)	(4)	(6)	(0)
Some College (1)	(0)	(1)	(0)
Bachelor's Degree (5)	(1)	(2)	(2)
Professional (5)	(0)	(0)	(5)
Master's (5)	(0)	(0)	(5)
Doctorate (2)	(0)	(0)	(2)
Respondent's College Concentration			
Humanities (5)	(0)	(1)	(4)
Social Sciences (7)	(3)	(1)	(3)
Math, Natural/Phys. Sciences (5)	(0)	(0)	(5)
Business (11)	(5)	(3)	(3)
Education[5] (4)	(1)	(3)	(0)
Respondent's Post-Baccalaureate Education			
Law School (4)	(0)	(2)	(2)
Medical/Dental School (2)	(0)	(0)	(2)
Business School (8)	(2)	(3)	(3)
Graduate: PhD (5)	(2)	(0)	(3)
Graduate: MA (6)	(2)	(2)	(2)
None (6)	(2)	(1)	(3)
Respondent's Occupation			
Business/Managerial (9)	(3)	(2)	(4)
Public Health/Healthcare (1)	(0)	(1)	(0)
Accounting (1)	(0)	(1)	(0)
Attorney (3)	(0)	(1)	(2)
Physician/Dentist (2)	(0)	(0)	(2)
Higher Ed (admin/staff) (3)	(1)	(1)	(1)
Professor/Researcher (4)	(2)	(1)	(1)
K–12 Ed (1)	(1)	(0)	(0)

	Low-resourced (n = 10)	Moderately resourced (n = 8)	Well-resourced (n = 14)
Law Enforcement (2)	(0)	(1)	(1)
Government (2)	(2)	(0)	(0)
Self-Employed (2)	(0)	(0)	(2)
Unemployed (0)	(0)	(0)	(0)
Other (2)	(0)	(1)	(1)
Respondent's Marital/Family Status			
Never Married w/No Children (9)	(3)	(2)	(4)
Never Married w/Children (1)	(0)	(0)	(1)
Married w/Children (12)	(2)	(5)	(5)
Married w/out Children (7)	(3)	(1)	(3)
Engaged (2)	(1)	(0)	(1)
Divorced w/Children (2)	(0)	(1)	(1)
Divorced w/out Children (0)	(0)	(0)	(0)

[1] Includes stepfathers if stepfather was residential parent for majority of respondent's formative years 0–18.

[2] See note 1.

[3] For majority of respondent's formative years 0–18.

[4] Most respondents funded their college education by using multiple combinations of these categories.

[5] The Early Childhood Education concentration is offered through cross-registration with Spelman College. It is not a concentration offered by Morehouse's curriculum.

Participant Screening Questionnaire

Name: _____ Date of Birth: ___/____/____

Age at time of this interview: _____

Years enrolled at Morehouse: Fall/Spring _____ to Fall/Spring_____

Graduation Year (if applicable): _____

Reunioning Class (if different from graduating class): _____

Degree (BA/BS): _____

Concentration: _____

Other concentrations held while at Morehouse (or transfer institution if applicable): _____

Years enrolled at transfer institution (if applicable):

   Fall/Spring _____ to Fall/Spring _____

Graduation year from transfer institution (if applicable): _____

Dates not enrolled at any college (if applicable): ___/___/___ to ___/___/____

Highest level of education completed:

   ☐ some college
   ☐ AA
   ☐ BA or BS
   ☐ JD ☐ MD ☐ MBA ☐ DDS
   ☐ other professional degree [_____]
   ☐ MS [in_____]
   ☐ PhD [in _____]
   ☐ other graduate degree [_____]

Current occupation: _____

Your marital status:

☐ single   ☐ married
☐ engaged or living with partner   ☐ divorced or separated

How would you identify your race and national origin? _____

How would you identify your parents' race/races and national origins?

Mother: _____

Father: _____

High school graduation year: _____

What type of high school did you attend?

☐ Public
☐ Private/Parochial
☐ Other (please explain) [_____]

What, if any, is your religious affiliation? _____

How often do you attend religious services? _____

Parents marital status

☐ never married/single   ☐ divorced (if remarried,
☐ married   please check here ☐)
☐ separated   ☐ widowed

Parents/Guardians in your childhood household? (i.e., both biological parents, biological parent and stepparent, parent and their partner, custodial relative, primary caretaker, etc.): _____

To the best of your knowledge, what is the annual household income of your family of origin (parents or guardians)?

☐ Less than $24,999   ☐ $100,000–$149,999
☐ $25,000–$49,999   ☐ $150,000–$199,999
☐ $50,000–$74,999   ☐ $200,000–$299,999
☐ $75,000–$99,999   ☐ $300,000 and more

Parents/primary caretaker's occupations

Mother(s): _____

Father(s): _____

Primary Caretaker(s)_____

What is the highest level of education your parents/ primary caretakers obtained?

Mother(s) _____

Father(s) _____

Primary caretaker(s) _____

Informed Consent Contract

Title of Research Study: *Examinations of Black Men at Historically Black Colleges and Universities*

Principle Investigator: *Saida Grundy; Department of Sociology; University of Michigan, Ann Arbor, MI 48109. Email: grundy@umich.edu*

You are being asked to consent to participate in a study about experiences of Black men at your undergraduate college. Your participation is voluntary and it is completely your decision to participate or not to participate. In order to inform your decision, you will need to know the purpose of this study, as well as the possible risks, benefits, and advantages of being in this study. Typical interviews for this kind of study typically range from 30 minutes to an hour. You will not be paid or receive any form of compensation for participating in this study.

In addition to this written document, I will also be speaking with you about this study. Your decision does not need to be made now and you may take this form with you if you need time to decide if you are willing to participate. Feel free to share this form with family, teachers, or members of your community if you need help deciding. However, if you do not sign this document, you will not be able to participate in the study. Even after you have signed this form, you may at any time withdraw from participating in the study if you so choose. A copy of this form will be made available to you for your records and so that you may contact me for any questions or concerns in the future.

What is the purpose of this study?

The purpose of this study is to examine the experiences of Black men on historically black campuses. This study aims to learn more about these particular experiences and how these experiences are distinct from those of Black men at predominantly white colleges, and the experiences of Black men in the general population.

Why are you being asked to participate in this study?

Your experience as a Black male enrolled at any time at an historically Black college has qualified you for participation in this study. More specifically, as an individual you may represent experiences that are of particular interest to this study.

How long will you be in this study? How many other people will be in the study?

The duration of this study is approximately two years. The interview to which you are consenting will last approximately 30 minutes to an hour. Any follow-up contact with you will be made within a year of your initial interview. Your participation in these subsequent interviews is completely voluntary and you may decline participation at any time. Approximately 45 men will be interviewed in this study.

Where will this study take place?

It is up to your discretion, comfort, and convenience as to where your interview will be held. Typically, interviews are held in quiet, private places that are accessible by both the researcher and the participant.

What will you be asked to do?

You may opt to participate in this interview with or without it being audio recorded. All recordings are strictly confidential. You may choose to stop the interview at any time for any reason or skip any questions you do not want to answer. You will be asked to give information about your college experiences. This may include recalling detailed memories about events, people, and experiences.

What happens if I say no?

There is absolutely no penalty for declining participation in this study. This study is not connected to your college, and you will not be affected if you choose to say no. No record will be kept of your name or institution if you decline participation in the study and you will not be contacted again in the future regarding participation in this study.

What are the risks and benefits of joining the study?

This study covers many serious and sensitive issues that may be associated with social stigmas. However, your participation is completely confidential and I will not be using any identifying information about you (i.e., hometown, name of graduate institution, or names of organizations to which you belong). There are no direct benefits from participating in the study (i.e. compensation). The study aims to document the experiences men at historically Black colleges and universities and serves purely academic aims.

When is the study over? Can I leave the study before it ends?

This study will conclude in May 2010. After this initial interview, you may be asked to do a follow-up interview within the year. However, more than likely, this will be the only interview in which you will participate. Follow-up interviews are completely voluntary and you may withdraw your consent or change the conditions of your consent at any time.

How will confidentiality be maintained and protected?

If you have agreed that your identity nor any information that could be used to identify you should be disclosed in this study, then your participation in this study will remain completely confidential as is required by law. Informed consent is required by federal regulation. The University of Michigan adheres to these federal regulations in order to protect the human subjects participating in research. The Institutional Review Board (IRB) at the University of Michigan is responsible for protecting the rights and welfare of research volunteers like you. The IRB has access to study information. Any documents and audio recordings from this interview will be kept secured and locked under my possession. A professional transcriber and/or myself will transcribe all audio recordings. This transcriber is also required by law and the terms of the IRB of the University of Michigan to protect the confidentiality of all participants. These interviews will be used to produce a professional paper that may appear in scholarly journals with national distribution.

Will you have to pay for anything?

There are no costs associated with participating in the study.

Who do you contact if you have questions about your rights and welfare?

Should you have questions regarding your rights as a participant in research, please contact the Institutional Review Board, Behavioral Sciences, 540 E. Liberty #202, Ann Arbor, MI 48104, (734) 936-0933, email: irbhsbs@umich.edu.

Who do you contact if you have questions about the study?

If you have questions about the research study, please contact me: Saida Grundy; Department of Sociology; University of Michigan, Ann Arbor, MI 48109-1382; email: grundy@umich.edu

You must sign the consent form indicating your willingness to participate in the research project. You will receive a copy of this consent document. Please sign each of the relevant sections that follow.

Agreement to Participate in the Study

Do you agree to participate in the study? If so, please sign and date here.

Signature _____   Date: _____

Agreement to Tape Record the Interview

Do you agree to let me tape record the interview? If so, please sign and date here.

Signature _____   Date: _____

Permission to be re-contacted

If you agree to be re-contacted for a follow-up interview within one year of your initial interview please sign and date here.

Signature _____   Date: _____

Interview Number: _____   Date: _____

Notes

Introduction

1. In this book I capitalize the "B" in Black in keeping with political recognition that "Black" designates peoples of African descent, not simply an observable physical attribute in the way a wall may be painted black. Style guides for the *Chicago Manual of Style*, the *New York Times*, and the Brookings Institute comply with this punctuation, but almost a century ago W. E. B. Du Bois launched a letter-writing campaign to major news outlets insisting for the capitalization of the "N" in Negro as he found "the use of a small letter for the name of twelve million Americans and two hundred million human beings a personal insult." In contemporary versions of this insult, Black has often been rendered to lowercase "black" spellings because of claims that it cannot be capitalized without the accompanying capitalization of the "W" in "white." I do not and will not capitalize "white," as the term does not name a group of people who have had any proper nouns derived from them. "Irish," "Scottish," "Lithuanian," "Russian." "Jewish" and myriad other European ethnicities all enjoy proper nouns that any white person could have retained when the historical choice came to either forego or engorge themselves with the unearned advantages of whiteness in America. As Anne Price, president of the Insight Center for Community Economic Development, succinctly stated in a 2019 statement, "Spell It with a Capital 'B'," "We strongly believe that leaving white in lowercase represents a righting of a long-standing wrong and a demand for dignity and racial equity." https://insightcced .medium.com/spell-it-with-a-capital-b-9eab112d759a.

2. "Morehouse Student Found Guilty of Antigay Beating," *Advocate*, June 13,

2003, www.advocate.com/news/2003/06/13/morehouse-student-found-guilty
-antigay-beating-8949.

3. Price's legal team argued a "gay panic defense" to rationalize the assault as a crime of passion. The strategy backfired and incensed Judge Jerry Baxter. He later reduced the sentence to seven years in acknowledgment of his reaction to the defense. https://rodonline.typepad.com/rodonline/2006/05/morehouse _attac.html; www.advocate.com/news/2002/11/23/morehouse-attack-labeled -hate-crime-7031.

4. H. F. Fradella and J. M. Sumner, eds., *Sex, Sexuality, Law, and (In)justice* (New York: Routledge, 2016), 453–56.

5. See also Yoji Cole, "Morehouse College's Homosexuality Survey Called Culturally Incompetent," DiversityInc.com, May 12, 2003, www.nytimes.com /2019/04/14/us/morehouse-college-transgender.html.

6. Jill C. Morrison, "Redefining the 'Morehouse Man': Sexual Orientation and Gender Identity at Morehouse College in the Wake of Spelman's Decision to Accept Transwomen," *Journal of Gender, Race, and Justice* 22, no. 1 (2019): 79.

7. "Black Gay Men and Lesbians Make Strides in Atlanta," *Advocate*, August 16, 2005, www.advocate.com/news/2005/08/16/atlanta-new-mecca-black-gays.

8. Aliya S. King, "The Mean Girls of Morehouse," *Vibe*, October 11, 2010, www.vibe.com/features/editorial/mean-girls-morehouse-40456. The group cheekily called themselves "The Plastics" in homage to the movie *Mean Girls*, thus the title.

9. Anita Badejo, "What Happens When Women at Historically Black Colleges Report Their Assaults," *BuzzFeed News*, January 21, 2016, www.buzzfeednews .com/article/anitabadejo/where-is-that-narrative.

10. Michael Harriot, "The War at Morehouse," *The Root*, March 30, 2017, www.theroot.com/the-war-at-morehouse-1793541413.

11. Caitlin Dickerson and Stephanie Saul, "Two Colleges Bound by History Are Roiled by the #MeToo Moment," *New York Times*, December 2, 2017, www .nytimes.com/2017/12/02/us/colleges-sexual-harassment.html; Sarah Mervosh, "Morehouse College Investigates Sexual Misconduct after Students' Videos," *New York Times*, July 19, 2019, www.nytimes.com/2019/07/19/us/morehouse -sexual-harassment.html.

12. Grace Elletson, "How a 'Defunct' Title IX Office and a Culture of Hyper-masculinity Fueled a Sexual-Misconduct Problem at Morehouse College," *Chronicle of Higher Education*, September 6, 2019, www.chronicle.com/article/how -a-defunct-title-ix-office-and-a-culture-of-hypermasculinity-fueled-a-sexual -misconduct-problem-at-morehouse-college.

13. Historians have pointed out that while both Black and white political leadership called for reforms on crime and policing in Black communities, white congressional officials and President Clinton practiced a form of "selective hearing" that disregarded calls for community-based policing in lieu of harsher law enforcement tactics. Elizabeth Hinton, Julilly Kohler-Hausmann, and Vesla M. Weaver, "Did Blacks Really Endorse the 1994 Crime Bill?," *New York Times*, April 13, 2016, www.nytimes.com/2016/04/13/opinion/did-blacks-really-endorse-the -1994-crime-bill.html.

14. N. Akbar, *Visions for Black Men* (Nashville: Winston-Derek, 1991); Haki R. Madhubuti, *Black Men: Obsolete, Single, Dangerous? Afrikan American Families in Transition: Essays in Discovery, Solution, and Hope* (Chicago: Third World Press, 1990); P. A. Noguera, "The Trouble with Black Boys: The Role and Influence of Environmental and Cultural Factors on the Academic Performance of African American Males," *Urban Education* 38, no. 4 (2003): 431–59.

15. Meredith Blake, "How Bill Cosby's 'Pound Cake' Speech Backfired on the Comedian," *Los Angeles Times*, July 8, 2015, www.latimes.com/entertainment/tv /showtracker/la-et-st-bill-cosby-pound-cake-speech-20150708-story.html.

16. Keisha Lindsay, *In a Classroom of Their Own: The Intersection of Race and Feminist Politics in All-Black Male Schools* (Urbana: University of Illinois Press, 2018).

17. A. Lemelle, *Black Male Deviance* (Westport, CT: Praeger, 1995); R. Majors and J. M. Billson, *Cool Pose: The Dilemmas of Black Manhood in America* (New York: Touchstone, 1992).

18. Evelyn Brooks Higginbotham, *Righteous Discontent: The Women's Movement in the Black Baptist Church, 1880-1920* (Cambridge, MA: Harvard University Press, 1993).

19. Shamus R. Khan, *Privilege: The Making of an Adolescent Elite at St. Paul's School* (Princeton, NJ: Princeton University Press, 2011).

20. Ann Arnett Ferguson, *Bad Boys: Public Schools in the Making of Black Masculinity* (Ann Arbor: University of Michigan Press, 2000).

21. This information on the college is for the years 2009–13. Enrollment has declined by 16 percent since 2007. The enrollment in 1998–2002, the period during which the men in this study were enrolled, was approximately 2,800.

22. While Black male high school graduation rates have improved, the gap between Black and white males has widened, according to *Black Lives Matter: The Schott 50 State Report on Public Education and Black Males* (Schott Foundation for Public Education, 2012). Given the proven correlation between college preparedness and the rigor of high school math and science courses, the US De-

partment of Education assesses high school graduates' college preparedness on that basis. US Department of Education, Office of Civil Rights, "Civil Rights Data Collection Data Snapshot: College and Career Readiness," 2014, retrieved from https://www2.ed.gov/about/offices/list/ocr/docs/crdc-college-and-career -readiness-snapshot.pdf. According to Rhonda Bryant at the Center for Law and Social Policy, "An analysis of course enrollment data in the nation's 50 largest school districts reveals that African American males are underrepresented in all higher-level mathematics and science courses." Rhonda Bryant, *Uneven Ground: Examining Systemic Inequities That Block College Preparation for African American Boys*, CLASP, 2013, www.clasp.org/sites/default/files/publications/2017/04 /Uneven-Ground_FNL_Web.pdf.

23. See Schott Foundation 50 State Report on Public Education and Black Males, 2012.

24. Caren A. Arbeit and Laura Horn, "A Profile of the Enrollment Patterns and Demographic Characteristics of Undergraduates at For-Profit Institutions," Report for the National Center for Education Statistics, February 28, 2017, https://nces.ed.gov/pubsearch/pubsinfo.asp?pubid=2017416.

25. Eric Kelderman, "Morehouse College's Leader Seeks to Reverse De-cline," *Chronicle of Higher Education*, April 15, 2013, www.chronicle.com/article /morehouse-colleges-leader-seeks-to-reverse-decline.

26. See Morehouse College website, www.Morehouse.edu/about, retrieved January 19, 2020.

27. See Megan Matteucci, "Morehouse Student on Trial for Murder," *Atlanta Journal-Constitution*, October 15, 2009, www.ajc.com/news/local/morehouse -student-trial-for-murder/X24YaEtBohcCob6fi3Vl7M.

28. King, "Mean Girls of Morehouse."

29. David Love, "Morehouse Dress Code Is More about Homophobia Than Decorum," *The Grio*, October 19, 2009, https://thegrio.com/2009/10/19 /morehouse-college-that-legendary-institution; "Morehouse Takes a Page Out of *GQ*," *The Root*, October 13, 2009, www.theroot.com/morehouse-takes-a-page -out-of-gq-1790870419.

30. Imara Jones, "While Morehouse College's Decision to Admit Trans Men Is Significant, It's Completely at the Expense of Trans Women," *The Grio*, April 16, 2019, https://thegrio.com/2019/04/16/morehouse-college-decision-trans -men-significant-at-the-expense-of-trans-women.

31. Derrick Brooms, *Being Black, Being Male on Campus: Understanding and Confronting Black Male Collegiate Experiences* (Albany: State University of New York Press, 2017).

32. Michael Omi and Howard Winant, *Racial Formation in the United States: From the 1960s to the 1990s*, 2nd ed. (New York: Routledge, 1994), 82.

33. Michael L. Walker, "Race Making in a Penal Institution," *American Journal of Sociology* 121, no. 4 (2016): 1051–78, quotation on 1053.

34. US Department of Education, "White House Initiative on Historically Black Colleges and Universities," https://sites.ed.gov/whhbcu/one-hundred-and-five-historically-black-colleges-and-universities.

35. Victor Ray, "A Theory of Racialized Organizations," *American Sociological Review* 84, no. 1 (2019): 26–53.

36. Marcus Anthony Hunter and Zandria Robinson, *Chocolate Cities: The Black Map of American Life* (Oakland: University of California Press, 2018); K. R. Lacy, *Blue-Chip Black: Race, Class, and Status in the New Black Middle Class* (Berkeley: University of California Press, 2007); Orly Clergé, *The New Noir: Race, Identity, and Diaspora in Black Suburbia* (Oakland: University of California Press, 2019).

37. Michael C. Dawson, *Behind the Mule: Race and Class in African-American Politics* (Princeton, NJ: Princeton University Press, 1994).

38. Cathy J. Cohen, *The Boundaries of Blackness: AIDS and the Breakdown of Black Politics* (Chicago: University of Chicago Press, 1999).

39. As W. E. B. Du Bois put it, "The history of the American Negro is the history of this strife—this longing to attain self-conscious manhood, to merge his double self into a better and truer self." W. E. B. Du Bois, *The Souls of Black Folk* (1903; repr., New York: Dover, 1994).

40. Charles Lemert, "A Classic from the Other Side of the Veil: Du Bois's Souls of Black Folk," *Sociological Quarterly* 35, no. 3 (1994): 383–96; W. E. B. Du Bois, *The Souls of Black Folk* (1903; London: Longmans, Green, 1965); J. Itzigsohn and K. Brown, "Sociology and the Theory of Double Consciousness: W. E. B. Du Bois's Phenomenology of Racialized Subjectivity," *Du Bois Review: Social Science Research on Race* 12, no. 2 (2015): 231–48.

41. W. E. B. Du Bois, *Dusk of Dawn* (1940; New Brunswick, NJ: Transaction Publishers, 2012), 135–36.

42. Du Bois, *Souls of Black Folk* (Longmans 1965 ed.).

43. Only eleven of the 2,043 people on the 2018 Forbes list of the World's Billionaires are Black. Only three (Oprah Winfrey, Michael Jordan, and former Goldman Sachs executive Robert Smith) are Americans.

44. For the wealthiest Blacks—those in the 95th percentile of Black households—wealth barely crosses the quarter-million-dollar mark, while household wealth for the 95th percentile of whites approaches and exceeds $2,500,000.

See *Survey of Consumer Finances* (2013), in Matt Bruenig, "Wealth Inequality by Race," retrieved August 15, 2018, www.peoplespolicyproject.org/2020/09/29/wealth-inequality-across-race-and-class-in-2019/, retrieved October 22, 2021.

45. Sherry Ortner, *New Jersey Dreaming: Capital, Culture, and the Class of '58* (Durham, NC: Duke University Press, 2003).

46. All respondents in this work have been given pseudonyms that are the names of legendary bebop era jazz musicians, as a nod to my father, the jazz purist.

47. C. Williams and E. Heikes, "The Importance of Researcher's Gender in the In-Depth Interview: Evidence from Two Case Studies of Male Nurses," *Gender and Society* 7, no. 2 (1993): 280–91.

48. Norman M. Bradburn and Seymour Sudman, *Polls and Surveys: Understanding What They Tell Us* (San Francisco: Jossey-Bass, 1989).

49. Williams and Heikes, "Importance of Researcher's Gender in the In-Depth Interview."

50. For more on the completion rates of queer and trans students at HBCUs, see S. D. Mobley and L. Hall, "(Re)Defining Queer and Trans* Student Retention and 'Success' at Historically Black Colleges and Universities," *Journal of College Student Retention: Research, Theory and Practice* 21, no. 4 (2020): 497–519.

51. Ortner, *New Jersey Dreaming*, further notes that the problem of accuracy in memory-based interviews is not a concern of the method itself. The more pressing concern of accuracy involves how the memories presented and analyzed are ultimately interpreted by the reader, who can always interpret the text to say more (or less) than it does about recollections, patterns, and people.

52. Constance de Saint-Laurent, "Personal Trajectories, Collective Memories: Remembering and the Life-Course," *Culture and Psychology* 23 (2017): 263–79.

53. Craig Stark, "Truth, Lies, and False Memories: Neuroscience in the Courtroom," Report on Progress for the Dana Foundation, October 15, 2014, www.dana.org/article/truth-lies-and-false-memories-neuroscience-in-the-courtroom.

54. Shirley Hill, "Teaching and Doing Gender in African American Families," *Sex Roles* 47, no. 11 (2002): 493–506.

55. R. S. Weiss, *Learning from Strangers: The Art and Method of Qualitative Interview Studies* (New York: Free Press, 1994).

56. James W. Messerschmidt, "Adolescent Boys, Embodied Heteromasculinities, and Sexual Violence," *Center for Educational Policy Studies Journal* 7, no. 2 (2017): 113–26, quotation on 115.

57. The two colleges are so socially intertwined and so commingled within their alumni communities, homecoming celebrations, and extracurricular activities that this portmanteau term is regularly used instead of referring to them separately.

58. In the lore of campus and alumni life. Miss Maroon and White serves as the conventionally feminine figurehead of school spirit, a homecoming queen who reigns for an entire year. She is not only featured at sporting events, but she is also paraded (literally) by the college as a goodwill ambassador of the student body at major ceremonies, public events, and fundraisers, and even holds a designated seat in the Student Government Association. Because the bearer of the title is selected by the student body during a pageant (typically all contestants are Spelman students), former students usually feel a sense of tender proprietorship over "their queen." Most Morehouse alumni would not expect a former Miss Maroon and White to write a feminist critique of the college.

59. While I was conducting my graduate research, I was even contacted by a representative of Morehouse's administration who let me know of the then president's national fundraising efforts and asked, as a courtesy, that I keep the president's office abreast of any parts of my work that might be of concern to the college's public image.

60. Sample demographics are accurate for the dates between April 20 and September 30, 2011. Demographic status for many of the men changed in the years shortly following their interview, including marital and parental status as well as postgraduate education.

61. These degrees are not mutually exclusive, as some of the men had multiple degrees.

62. D. Squire and S. D. Mobley Jr., "Negotiating Race and Sexual Orientation in the College Choice Process of Black Gay Males," *Urban Review* 47, no. 3 (2015): 466–91, https://doi.org/10.1007/s11256-014-0316-3.

63. Margaret L. Andersen, "Studying across Difference: Race, Class, and Gender in Qualitative Research," in *Race, Ethnicity, and Research Methods*, ed. John Stanfield II and Rutledge M. Dennis (Newbury Park, CA: Sage Publishers, 1993); Maxine Baca Zinn, "Field Research in Minority Communities," *Social Problems* 27 (1979): 209–19; Marjorie DeVault, "Ethnicity and Expertise: Racial Ethnic Knowledge in Sociological Research," *Gender and Society* 9 (1995): 612–31; Robert Merton, "Insiders and Outsiders: A Chapter in the Sociology of Knowledge," *American Journal of Sociology* 78 (1972): 9–47; Nancy A. Naples, "A Feminist Revisiting of the Insider/Outsider Debate: The 'Outsider Phenomenon' in Rural Iowa," *Qualitative Sociology* 19 (1996): 83–106.

64. Alford A. Young, "Coming Out from Under the Ethnographic Interview," unpublished paper, 2010.

65. Other ethnographies have problematized the ideologies and actions behaviors that research subjects espouse and regard as solutions within their worldview. Consider, for example, an ethnography of Minutemen militia groups along the Texas border: H. Shapira, *Waiting for José: The Minutemen's Pursuit of America* (Princeton, NJ: Princeton University Press, 2013).

66. Sandra Harding, "Rethinking Standpoint Epistemology: What Is 'Strong Objectivity'?" in *Feminist Theory: A Philosophical Anthology*, ed. Ann E. Cudd and Robin O. Andreasen (Oxford: Blackwell Publishing, 2005).

67. Brenda J. Allen, "Feminist Standpoint Theory: A Black Woman's (Re)View of Organizational Socialization," *Communication Studies* 47, no. 4 (1996): 257–71.

Chapter 1. The Masculine Arc of Uplift

1. Barack Obama, "Barack Obama at Morehouse: Commencement Address Transcript," *Time*, June 2, 2016, https://time.com/4341712/obama-commencement-speech-transcript-morehouse-college.

2. Melvin L. Oliver and Thomas M. Shapiro, *Black Wealth/White Wealth: A New Perspective on Racial Inequality* (New York: Routledge, 1995).

3. Sarah Burd-Sharps and Rebecca Rasch, "Impact of the US Housing Crisis on the Racial Wealth Gap across Generations," Social Science Research Council, Report Commissioned by the American Civil Liberties Union, June 2015, www.aclu.org/sites/default/files/field_document/discrimlend_final.pdf.

4. Eric H. Holder, "Attorney General Eric Holder Delivers Remarks at the My Brother's Keeper Summit Closing Session, Memphis, TN, Tuesday, December 9, 2014," US Department of Justice, updated August 18, 2015, www.justice.gov/opa/speech/attorney-general-eric-holder-delivers-remarks-my-brothers-keeper-summit-closing-session. Holder attempted to appeal to those who want to get "tough on crime" and to support the "brave" boys in blue as well as those who object to racially biased policing and the consequent lack of trust between communities of color and law enforcement. Similar to the tone of Obama's commencement speech, saying what "must" be done because of "who were are" evades the question of who or what is responsible for creating the current situation and who will do what to change it.

5. See Martin Summers, *Manliness and Its Discontents: The Black Middle Class and the Transformation of Masculinity, 1900–1930* (Chapel Hill: University of North Carolina Press, 2004).

6. The organizing of the Brotherhood of Sleeping Car Porters by A. Philip Randolph is a prime example of the latter. See L. E. Williams, "A. Philip Randolph, Dean of Black Civil Rights Leaders," in *Servants of the People* (New York: Palgrave Macmillan, 1996).

7. This is the dominant form of decline that deindustrialization took, but the expanding sectors of the economy that offered stable, decently paid jobs tended to be in suburban locations and required a formal education beyond high school. New jobs in center cities were mainly in the service sector, which were low paid, insecure, and strongly associated with women. As many jobs traditionally done by Black women were eradicated by automation, Black men and women were left with few stable options for employment within urban centers.

8. Janet Roitman, *Anti-Crisis* (Durham, NC: Duke University Press, 2013). Roitman's "crisis narrative" pertains to the historical, philosophical, and cultural production of financial crises.

9. W. E. B. Du Bois, *The Negro American Family* (Atlanta: Atlanta University Center, 1908; repr., Cambridge, MA: MIT Press, 2000), 38.

10. Some historians argue that at times of intense collective struggle, for example during Reconstruction, World War I and World War II, and the civil rights movement, these cultural concerns tend to recede as political strategies come to the fore instead. They regain prominence in periods when cross-class Black movements have been defeated or at least contained.

11. Kevin Gaines, *Uplifting the Race: Black Leadership, Politics, and Culture in the Twentieth Century* (Chapel Hill: University of North Carolina Press, 1996).

12. Enslaved Africans did not necessarily share bourgeois Europeans' norms regarding the gender division of labor. These views have been revised by a long line of Black feminist historians, starting with Deborah Gray White. Enslaved women sometimes worked in all-female groups (as they had done in West Africa) and valued physical strength and agricultural skills. At the same time, Black men had privileged access to the most highly valued skilled trades on plantations. See Deborah Gray White, *Ar'n't I a Woman? Female Slaves in the Plantation South* (New York: Norton, 1987).

13. In the antebellum North, middle-class Black men propagated conventional gender ideals in newspapers, organizations, and pulpits as a means of establishing and validating Black society.

14. J. Horton, "Freedom's Yoke: Gender Conventions among Antebellum Free Blacks," *Feminist Studies* 12, no. 1 (1986): 51–76, quotation on 55.

15. Freed people were equally eager to legalize and secure their long-term partnerships and legitimate their children; many actively sought to formalize

their marriages, which could be done by federal agents as well as by clergymen. Their main concern at the time was preventing the forcible separation of husbands, wives, and children as well as sexual assaults on women and girls by white men. Having a recognized male protector was not sufficient, of course, but many women thought it would help. The experiences and perspectives of Black women during this period are documented by historian Brandi Clay Brimmer in *Claiming Union Widowhood: Race, Respectability, and Poverty in the Post-Emancipation South* (Durham, NC: Duke University Press, 2020), which compares the mores and practices of poor and middle-class Black women, showing that they shared many familial values but that their differing economic and social circumstances meant that they also had divergent expectations about sexual relations.

16. Michele Mitchell, *Righteous Propagation: African Americans and the Politics of Racial Destiny after Reconstruction* (Chapel Hill: University of North Carolina Press, 2004), 79.

17. Gaines, *Uplifting the Race*, 6. As he explained, "At worst this misplaced equation of racial progress with the status of the family blamed black men and women for 'failing' to measure up to dominant society's bourgeois gender morality, and seemed to forget that it was the state and the constant threat of violence, not some innate racial trait, that prevented the realization of black homes and families."

18. Mitchell, *Righteous Propagation*, 79.

19. Horton, "Freedom's Yoke."

20. Passive citizens were presumed to be represented in the polity by the adult males who headed the households in which they lived. Some feminist theorists prefer T. H. Marshall's terms, which differentiate among specific types of rights, as women of all races were denied some civil, economic, and social rights as well as political rights. While the gradual disenfranchisement of Black men mattered, it did not reduce them to the same position relative to the state as women.

21. James D. Anderson, *The Education of Blacks in the South, 1860-1935* (Chapel Hill: University of North Carolina Press, 1988).

22. M. Christopher Brown II and James Earl Davis, "The Historically Black College as Social Contract, Social Capital, and Social Equalizer," *Peabody Journal of Education* 76, no. 1 (2001): 31-49.

23. Brown and Davis, "Historically Black College," see p. 32.

24. The college relocated to Atlanta, Georgia, in 1879.

25. Edward A. Jones, *A Candle in the Dark: A History of Morehouse College* (Val-

ley Forge, PA: Judson Press, 1967); M. Warner, "Community Building: The History of Atlanta University Neighborhoods," City of Atlanta, 1978.

26. Jones, *Candle in the Dark*; Warner, "Community Building."

27. Anderson, *Education of Blacks in the South*.

28. During Reconstruction, this unofficial racial boundary was a racetrack located near present-day Interstate 20. Cornelia Cooper, "History of West End, 1830-1910," *Atlanta Historical Bulletin* 8, no. 30 (October 1945): 65-94.

29. The former Gammon Theological Seminary exists today as the Interdenominational Theological Center.

30. Du Bois served on Atlanta University's faculty of the History and Economics Department from 1897 to 1910 and was a founder of the university's School of Social Work.

31. David Levering Lewis, *W. E. B. Du Bois: A Biography, 1968-1963* (New York: Henry Holt, 2009), 213; Clifford M. Kuhn, Harlon E. Joye, and E. Bernard West, *Living Atlanta: An Oral History of the City, 1914-1946* (Athens: University of Georgia Press, 1990), 156-58.

32. Kevin Kruse, *White Flight: Atlanta and the Making of Modern Conservatism* (Princeton, NJ: Princeton University Press, 2005).

33. Carol Anderson, *White Rage: The Unspoken Truth of Our Racial Divide* (New York: Bloomsbury USA, 2016).

34. Many historians and sociologists differentiate between the Black bourgeoisie, which owned substantial amounts of property, and the Black middle class, which practiced the professions in Black communities but, given its lack of wealth, could not always pass on its standing to the next generation.

35. Summers, *Manliness and Its Discontents*.

36. Morehouse (then known as Atlanta Baptist Seminary) had an indirect link to US imperialist efforts on the continent. In 1909, President Taft appointed Sale and two other commissioners to go to Liberia on the west coast of Africa to assess matters there. Liberia had requested assistance in maintaining its independence. Liberia was originally founded as a colony by the United States in 1847 as a settlement for free Negroes. The commissioners spent two months there and presented a report to President Taft on their return. www.morehouse.edu/about/bio-gsale.html.

37. Jones, *Candle in the Dark*, 12.

38. For a scathing critique of Booker T. Washington's uplift model, which was palatable to white elite's beliefs of Black inferiority, and an analysis of the alternative view articulated by W. E. B. Du Bois, see Aldon Morris, *The Scholar De-*

nied: W. E. B. Du Bois and the Birth of Modern Sociology (Oakland: University of California Press, 2015).

39. Morehouse, however, did not pioneer the liberal arts education for Black men's colleges and, to the contrary, did not adapt a liberal arts education until decades after its seminarian founding. Lincoln University, founded in 1854 outside of Philadelphia, was nicknamed "the Black Princeton" in its early years and taught a rigorous curriculum of the classics. Lincoln went coeducational in 1953, but throughout the first half of the twentieth century it was considered the premier institution for Black men with nationally and internationally prominent alumni like Thurgood Marshall, Langston Hughes, poet Melvin Tolson, Nnamdi Azikiwe (the first president of Nigeria), and Kwame Nkrumah (the first president of Ghana). Morehouse's claims to be "the premier college" for Black men emerge only later in the twentieth century, and its clerical education prior to that point was not considered as intellectually rigorous as the premier liberal arts HBCUs of the day.

40. W. E. B. Du Bois and Conference for the Study of the Negro Problems, *The College-Bred Negro: Report of a Social Study Made under the Direction of Atlanta University in 1900*, 2nd abridged ed., Atlanta University Publications No. 5 (Atlanta University Press, 1902), 111.

41. Du Bois and Conference for the Study of the Negro Problems, *College-Bred Negro*, 114.

42. Evelyn Brooks Higginbotham, *Righteous Discontent: The Women's Movement in the Black Baptist Church, 1880-1920* (Cambridge, MA: Harvard University Press, 1993), 55.

43. Glenn Sisk, "Morehouse College." *Journal of Negro Education* 27, no. 2 (1958): 201-8.

44. Mitchell, *Righteous Propagation*.

45. See Thomas Aiello, *The Battle for the Souls of Black Folk: W. E. B. Du Bois, Booker T. Washington, and the Debate That Shaped the Course of Civil Rights* (Santa Barbara, CA: Praeger, 2016).

46. W. E. B. Du Bois, "The Development of a People (1904)," in *The Problem of the Color Line at the Turn of the Twentieth Century* (New York: Fordham University Press, 2020), 243-70, quotation on page 257.

47. W. E. B. Du Bois, *The Souls of Black Folk* (1903; New York: Dover, 1994), 58.

48. This statement appeared in the November 1915 call published in the *Daily Chronicle* titled "Active Members Wanted for the Universal Negro Improvement Association of Jamaica." For more on Marcus Garvey's political interest

in Black elites, see also Ula Yvette Taylor, *The Veiled Garvey: The Life and Times of Amy Jacques Garvey* (Chapel Hill: University of North Carolina Press, 2002).

49. Summers, *Manliness and Its Discontents*.

50. Summers, *Manliness and Its Discontents*.

51. Morehouse posts a list on its website. "Morehouse College: Prominent Alumni," https://morehousecollegealumni.org/prominent-alumni/, retrieved January 31, 2010.

52. St. Clair Drake and Horace R. Cayton, *Black Metropolis: A Study of Negro Life in a Northern City*, rev. ed. (New York: Harper and Row, 1962), 394.

53. Hazel Carby, *Race Men*, W. E. B. Du Bois Lectures, 1993 (Cambridge, MA: Harvard University Press, 1998), 4.

54. W. E. B. Du Bois, "The Talented Tenth," in *The Negro Problem: A Series of Articles by Representative American Negroes of To-Day* (New York: James Potts, 1903), 31–75, quotation on 33 (a digitized copy of the 1903 edition is available online at www.google.com/books/edition/The_Negro_Problem_A_Series_of _Articles_b/z08rAQAAIAAJ?hl=en&gbpv=1).

55. Du Bois, "Talented Tenth," 5.

56. Gaines, *Uplifting the Race*, 3.

57. M. Dawson, *Behind the Mule: Race and Class in African-American Politics* (Princeton, NJ: Princeton University Press, 1994).

58. Gaines, *Uplifting the Race*.

59. Hollie I. West, "A Gentleman Scholar," *Washington Post*, January 30, 1978, www.washingtonpost.com/archive/lifestyle/1978/01/30/a-gentleman-scholar /9f1d49c6-fb1c-4270-afbe-56ba9fe4ee72.

60. According to Carby, "In 1898 Maritcha B. Lyons was asked to present a paper" at the American Negro Academy. "It was read by E. D. Barrier, as Lyons could not attend. In 1908, at [a] panel discussion on education, a woman asked her opinion. These were the only two occasions in which women were asked to participate." Carby, *Race Men*, 5. See Alfred A. Moss, *The American Negro Academy: Voice of the Talented Tenth* (Baton Rouge: Louisiana State University Press, 1981), 78, 134. See also Shirley Moody-Turner and Anna J. Cooper, "'Dear Doctor Du Bois': Anna Julia Cooper, W. E. B. Du Bois, and the Gender Politics of Black Publishing," *Melus* 40, no. 3 (2015): 47–68; Joy James, *Transcending the Talented Tenth: Black Leaders and American Intellectuals* (New York: Routledge, 1997).

61. Thomas Curry, *The Man-Not: Race, Class, Genre, and the Dilemmas of Black Manhood* (Philadelphia: Temple University Press, 2017).

62. G. Gilmore, *Gender and Jim Crow: Women and the Politics of White Su-*

premacy in North Carolina, 1896–1920 (Chapel Hill: University of North Carolina Press, 1996), 44.

63. Quoted in Tommy J. Curry, *The Man-Not: Race, Class, Genre, and the Dilemmas of Black Manhood* (Philadelphia: Temple University Press, 2017), 64. It is impossible to ignore that Thomas Curry interprets Cooper's use of this adage in a way that contradicts the Black feminist consensus. For Curry, Cooper was arguing that Black male heads of household were the source from which Black women were the stream. Curry appears to be the only scholar who interprets Cooper this way.

64. Gaines, *Uplifting the Race*, 113.

65. Carby, *Race Men*.

66. W. E. B. Du Bois, *The Souls of Black Folk* (1903; repr., New York: New American Library, 1982).

67. W. E. B. Du Bois, *The Souls of Black Folk* (1953; New York: Modern Library, 1996).

68. The feud between Du Bois and Washington cemented the standard for positing masculinity and patriarchy as validation for racial leadership and indicting a lack of masculinity as detrimental to racial leadership. For example, Du Bois voiced a character in his romantic novel *Dark Princess* (1928) to belt out: "Won't we ever get any leaders?" A *Chicago Defender* columnist (March 29, 1930) begged: "We need men and we need them badly. We need men who have the capabilities to lead—men who can command the respect of those who must follow."

69. On the concept of Black "sartorial dandyism," see Monica L. Miller, "W. E. B. Du Bois and the Dandy as Diasporic Race Man," *Callaloo* 26, no. 3 (2003): 738–65, quotation at 739.

70. Carby, *Race Men*, 21.

71. W. E. B. Du Bois, *Dark Princess* (1928; Jackson: University Press of Mississippi, 1995), 200.

72. Gaines, *Uplifting the Race*, 101, 113.

73. A. Farmer, *Remaking Black Power: How Black Women Transformed an Era* (Chapel Hill: University of North Carolina Press, 2017).

74. The US Organization was founded in Los Angeles in 1965, under the primary leadership of Maulana Karenga, the creator of the Kwanzaa holiday. Its goal was to bring about revolution through cultural education and political coalition building. The organization envisioned itself as the movement successor of Malcolm X.

75. E. Frances White, "Africa on the Mind: Gender, Counter-Discourse, and African-American Nationalism," *Journal of Women's History* 2, no. 1 (1990): 73–97.

76. Daniel Patrick Moynihan, former Secretary of Labor under Lyndon B. Johnson, who went on to become a US senator, argued in "The Negro Family: The Case for National Action" (1965) (more commonly known as the Moynihan Report) that while Black families suffered greatly from racism and their origins in slavery, the root cause of widespread poverty was both their matriarchal structure and the pathological culture of poverty, which kept successive generations in despair. The report has been relentlessly criticized by successive generations of Black scholars, particularly Black feminists.

77. Farmer, *Remaking Black Power*, 97; Scot Brown, *Fighting for US* (New York: New York University Press, 2003).

78. Farmer, introduction to *Remaking Black Power*, 1–19.

79. See Sharon Hays, *Flat Broke with Children: Women in the Age of Welfare Reform* (New York: Oxford University Press, 2003).

80. Elizabeth Hinton, *From the War on Poverty to the War on Crime: The Making of Mass Incarceration in America* (Cambridge, MA: Harvard University Press, 2017).

81. Hinton, *From the War on Poverty to the War on Crime*.

82. This cover art referred to the discrimination that middle-class Black men reported facing throughout the 1980s and 1990s in major cities like New York, when taxicab drivers would refuse to pick them up.

83. Lerone Bennett, "Benjamin Elijah Mays: The Last of the Great Schoolmasters," *Ebony*, December 1977, 73–80.

84. Lerone Bennett Jr., "Introduction," *Ebony*, August 1983, 34–36.

85. Bennett, "Introduction," 36.

86. Bennett, "Introduction."

87. Bennett, "Introduction," 38.

88. Nathan J. Robinson, *Superpredator: Bill Clinton's Use and Abuse of Black America* (Somerville, MA: Current Affairs Publishing, 2016).

89. C. Franklin, *Men and Society* (Chicago: Nelson-Hall, 1988); J. T. Gibbs, *Young, Black, and Male in America* (New York: Auburn House Publishing, 1988); Willie Legette, "The Crisis of the Black Male: A New Ideology in Black Politics," in *Without Justice/or All: The New Liberalism and Our Retreat from Racial Equality*, ed. Adolph Reed Jr. (Boulder, CO: Westview Press, 1999); A. Lemelle, *Black Male Deviance* (Westport, CT: Praeger, 1995); J. MacLeod, *Ain't No Makin It: Aspirations and Attainment in a Low-Income Neighborhood*, 2nd ed. (Boulder, CO: Westview Press, 1995); Marc Mauer, *The Crisis of the Young African American Male and the Criminal Justice System* (Washington, DC: U.S. Commission on Civil Rights, 1999); Robert Staples, *Black Masculinity: The Black Man's Role in American Society*

(San Francisco: Black Scholars Press, 1982); Alford Young, *The Minds of Marginalized Black Men: Making Sense of Mobility, Opportunity, and Future Life Chances* (Princeton, NJ: Princeton University Press, 2004).

90. According to higher-education researcher Ivory Toldson, there were 600,000 more Black men in college than behind bars as of 2014: "The best research evidence suggests that the line was never true to begin with." See "9 Biggest Lies about Black Males and Academic Success," *The Root*, March 31, 2014, www.theroot.com/9-biggest-lies-about-black-males-and-academic-success -1790875135.

91. This erroneous statistic even appears in the Oscar-nominated documentary *13th*.

92. Thomas P. Bonczar and Allen J. Beck, "Lifetime Likelihood of Going to State or Federal Prison," *Bureau of Justice Statistics Special Report*, US Department of Justice, Office of Justice Programs, NCJ-160092, March 1997, https://bjs.ojp .gov/content/pub/pdf/Llgsfp.pdf. Jason Ziedenberg and Vincent Schiraldi, *Cellblocks or Classrooms?* Justice Policy Institute, a project of the Tides Center, www .justicepolicy.org, www.justicepolicy.org/uploads/justicepolicy/documents/02 -09_rep_cellblocksclassrooms_bb-ac.pdf.

93. M. Desmond and R. Kimbro, "Eviction's Fallout: Housing, Hardship, and Health," *Social Forces* 94, no. 1 (2015): 295; M. Desmond and T. Shollenberger, "Forced Displacement from Rental Housing: Prevalence and Neighborhood Consequences," *Demography* 52, no. 5 (2015): 1751–72; Rhonda Williams, *The Politics of Public Housing: Black Women's Struggles against Urban Inequality* (New York: Oxford University Press, 2004).

94. Bennett, "Introduction," 36.

95. P. Butler, "Black Male Exceptionalism? The Problems and Potential of Black Male-Focused Interventions," *Du Bois Review: Social Science Research on Race* 10, no. 2 (2013): 485–511.

96. Butler, "Black Male Exceptionalism?," 489.

97. See Robert Staples, "The Myth of Black Macho: A Response to Angry Black Feminists," *Black Scholar* 10, no. 6/7 (1979): 24–33, www.jstor.org/stable /41163829; Robert Staples, *Black Masculinity: The Black Male's Role in American Society* (San Francisco: Black Scholar Press, 1982). Quotations that follow are on pp. 8 and 7.

98. Staples, *Black Masculinity*, 9. Staples also pointed out that Black men's marriageability is tied to their income: "As incomes rise so do the numbers of black men who marry" (15), which counters Bennet's claim that there simply are

not enough straight Black men to marry Black women. Further, he remarked that Black men tend to hold egalitarian attitudes toward marriage.

99. See also Kimberlé Crenshaw's work on the lesser known but prevalent physical and sexual victimization of Black women by police. http://aapf.org /sayhername report.

100. Freeden Blume Oeur, *Black Boys Apart: Racial Uplift and Respectability in All-Male Public Schools* (Minneapolis: University of Minnesota Press, 2018).

101. In eleven states, according to the Schott 50 State Report, Latino males had the lowest graduation rate. "The Schott 50 State Report on Public Education and Black Males," 2012, www.opensocietyfoundations.org/publications/urgency -now-schott-50-state-report-public-education-and-black-males.

102. Shaun R. Harper, "Enhancing African American Male Student Outcomes through Leadership and Active Involvement," in *African American Men in College*, ed. Michael Cuyjet and associates (San Francisco: Jossey Bass, 2006), 1, 174–88.

103. Walter R. Allen, Edgar G. Epps, and Nesha Z. Haniff, *College in Black and White: African American Students in Predominantly White and in Historically Black Public Universities* (Albany: State University of New York Press, 1991); Cuyjet, *African American Men in College*; J. E. Davis, "College in Black and White: Campus Environment and Academic Achievement of African American Males," *Journal of Negro Education* 63, no. 4 (1994): 620–33.

104. Davis, "College in Black and White"; Frank Harris III, "College Men's Meanings of Masculinities and Contextual Influences: Toward a Conceptual Model," *Journal of College Student Development* 51 no. 3 (2010): 297–318. Project MUSE, doi:10.1353/csd.0.0132.

105. "Black Women Students Far Outnumber Black Men at the Nation's Highest-Ranked Universities," *Journal of Blacks in Higher Education*, 2006, www .jbhe.com/news_views/51_gendergap_universities.html.

106. "Black Women Students Far Outnumber Black Men at the Nation's Highest-Ranked Universities." Black women earn 70 percent of all master's degrees and more than 60 percent of all doctorates among African Americans. Black women also form a majority of all African Americans enrolled in law, medical, and dental schools.

107. Deborah J. Vagins, "The Simple Truth about the Gender Pay Gap," AAUW, accessed December 1, 2019, www.aauw.org/research/the-simple-truth -about-the-gender-pay-gap/.

108. Derrick R. Brooms, "'We Didn't Let the Neighborhood Win': Black Male Students' Experiences in Negotiating and Navigating an Urban Neighborhood,"

Journal of Negro Education 84, no. 3 (2015): 269–81; M. C. Brown and J. E. Davis, "The Historically Black College as Social Contract, Social Capital, and Social Equalizer," *Peabody Journal of Education* 76 (2001): 31–49; J. E. Davis, *African American Men in College* (San Francisco: Jossey-Bass, 1994); Michael J. Cuyjet, "African American Men on College Campuses: Their Needs and Their Perceptions," *New Directions for Student Services* 80, no. 5 (1997): 5–16; Ryan J. Davis, "African American Men in College," *Journal of Higher Education* 79, no. 3 (2008): 360–63; J. E. *Davis*, "What Does Gender Have to Do with the Experiences of *African American* College *Men?*," in *African American Males in School and Society*, ed. V. C. *Polite* and J. E. *Davis* (New York: Teachers College Press, *1999*), 134-48.

109. Derrick Brooms, *Being Black, Being Male on Campus: Understanding and Confronting Black Male Collegiate Experiences* (Albany: State University of New York Press, 2017).

110. See also Tressie McMillan Cottom, *Lower Ed: The Troubling Rise of For-Profit Colleges in the New Economy* (New York: New Press, 2017). Tolani Britton, "College or Bust…or Both: The Effects of the Great Recession on College Enrollment for Black and Latino Students" (PhD diss., Harvard University, 2017).

111. Eric Kelderman, "Morehouse College's Leader Seeks to Reverse Decline," *Chronicle of Higher Education*, April 15, 2013, www.chronicle.com/article/morehouse-colleges-leader-seeks-to-reverse-decline.

112. See the Morehouse College website, www.Morehouse.edu.

Chapter 2. Branding the Man

1. *Queer* is an umbrella term for people who do not identify as heterosexual and/or do not identify their gender on conventional terms in that their gender expression is the same as their biological sex. This includes people who consider themselves nonbinary, meaning that they identify neither as men nor women.

2. Eric Stirgus, "Transgender Groups Applaud Morehouse's Policy but Say It Needs Work," *Atlanta Journal Constitution*, April 15, 2019, www.ajc.com/news/local-education/transgender-groups-applaud-morehouse-policy-but-say-needs-work/YhiyrYjOjpzkdWEvoHg6II.

3. www.morehouse.edu/admissions/apply/requirements/gender-identity-policy/.

4. Morehouse "strongly encourages" any applicants whose gender identity "conflicts" with their sex assigned at birth to contact the admissions office "for a discussion around the desire to attend a single gender men's college and how they self-identify in terms of gender." The trans applicants the policy claims to include

are encouraged to out themselves to the admissions staff, with no assurance of fair consideration thereafter. www.morehouse.edu/media/genderidentity /Gender-Identity-Admissions-Matriculation-Policy-EA-100.2.pdf. https://www .morehouse.edu/admissions/apply/requirements/gender-identity-policy/.

5. In speaking to *Vibe* magazine, gender nonconforming students maintained that the two targets of the policy were not enforced equally by staff and administrators who were far more lenient and inconsistent in policing streetwear while they consistently harassed those carrying purses, or wearing makeup and heels. Aliya S. King, "The Mean Girls of Morehouse," *Vibe*, October 11, 2010, www.vibe .com/features/editorial/mean-girls-morehouse-40456. Sociologist Dawn Dow has shown that anxieties about the "thug" stereotype are so pervasive in the schooling of Black males that they are even a central concern for their parents. Dawn Marie Dow, "The Deadly Challenges of Raising African American Boys: Navigating the Controlling Image of the 'Thug,'" *Gender and Society* 30, no. 2 (2016): 161–88. See also S. D. Mobley Jr. and J. M. Johnson, "'No Pumps Allowed': The 'Problem' with Gender Expression and the Morehouse College 'Appropriate Attire Policy,'" *Journal of Homosexuality* 66, no. 7 (2019): 867–95.

6. Jafari Sinclaire Allen, "Truth/Reconciliation: Morehouse on My Mind," November 22, 2009, www.newblackmaninexile.net/2009/11/morehouse-on -his-mind.html.

7. Lesbian, Gay, Bisexual, Transgender, Queer (or Questioning), Intersex, and Asexual.

8. Danielle Ivanov, "Last Chance: Florida Considers Clemency Pleas by Felons for Last Time Ahead of Election," WUFT, September 24, 2020, www.wuft .org/news/2020/09/24/last-chance-florida-considers-clemency-pleas-by-felons -for-last-time-ahead-of-election.

9. Hannah Giorgis, "What Happens When You Don't Want to Be a Man at an All-Male HBCU," *BuzzFeed News*, November 7, 2015, www.buzzfeednews.com /article/hannahgiorgis/there-is-a-complexity-to-struggle.

10. Most famously, James Weldon Johnson penned the lyrics to "Lift Every Voice and Sing," also known colloquially as the Black National Anthem.

11. Kevin M. Kruse, *White Flight: Atlanta and the Making of Modern Conservatism* (Princeton, NJ: Princeton University Press, 2005), 31.

12. Pierre Bourdieu, *Distinction: A Social Critique of the Judgement of Taste*, trans. Richard Nice (Cambridge, MA: Harvard University Press, 1984).

13. See Annie S. Barnes, *The Black Middle Class Family: A Study of Black Subsociety, Neighborhood, and Home in Interaction* (Bristol, IN: Wyndham Hall, 1985); Dawn Marie Dow, "Negotiating 'The Welfare Queen' and 'The Strong Black

Woman': African American Middle-Class Mothers' Work and Family Perspectives," *Sociological Perspectives* 58, no. 1 (2015): 36–55; Cherise A. Harris, *The Cosby Cohort* (Lanham, MD: Rowman and Littlefield, 2013); Karyn R. Lacy, *Blue-Chip Black Race, Class, and Status in the New Black Middle Class* (Berkeley: University of California Press, 2007); Bart Landry, *The New Black Middle Class* (Berkeley: University of California Press, 1987); Vershawn Ashanti Young and Bridget Harris Tsemo, *From Bourgeois to Boojie: Black Middle-Class Performances* (Detroit: Wayne State University Press, 2011); Patrick Sharkey, "Spatial Segmentation and the Black Middle Class," *American Journal of Sociology* 119, no. 4 (2014): 903–54; Mary E. Pattillo, *Black Picket Fences: Privilege and Peril among the Black Middle Class* (Chicago: University of Chicago Press, 1999).

14. Lacy, *Blue-Chip Black Race, Class, and Status in the New Black Middle Class*; categorizes such college educated suburbanites as "Blue-Chip Blacks" and acknowledges the inseparable role college education plays in their notions of Black class aspiration.

15. This group included Blakey, Fitzgerald, Mort, Ornette, Philly, Roy, Milt, Monk, and Mingus. John Silvanus Wilson, former Morehouse president, places Black craftsmen and foremen in the blue collar Black middle class, but in the postindustrial era Pattillo, in *Black Picket Fences*, maintains that the blue-collar home-owning Black middle-class corresponds to the white working class.

16. This lowest resourced group included Percy, Dexter, Clifford, Bird, Horace, Ramsey, Lucky, Waller, and Dewey.

17. For more on Black Male Initiatives in higher education, see Derrick R. Brooms, "Exploring Black Male Initiative Programs: Potential and Possibilities for Supporting Black Male Success in College," *Journal of Negro Education* 87, no.1 (Winter 2018): 59–72.

18. Roger Caldwell, "Black Boys Need Rites of Passage Programs," *Philadelphia Tribune*, February 17, 2019, www.phillytrib.com/commentary/black-boys-need-rites-of-passage-programs/article_120001f9-9704-5a7f-ad7e-8e4dad016c56.html.

19. Michael S. Kimmel, *Guyland: The Perilous World Where Boys Become Men* (New York: Harper, 2008).

20. For a description and image of a mullet, see https://en.wikipedia.org/wiki/Mullet_(haircut).

21. P. W. Cookson and C. H. Persell, *Preparing for Power: America's Elite Boarding Schools* (New York: Basic Books, 1985).

22. Erving Goffman, *Asylums: Essays on the Social Situation of Mental Patients and Other Inmates* (Garden City, NY: Anchor Books), 11.

23. Such talk of branding hearkened my mind to the practice of slave branding, a common practice of marking enslaved Africans with hot irons (often on the chest or face) as property of their enslavers, or using such markings punitively, for example, marking runaways with an "R." Slave branding too focused on using the body to signify a process of transformation, in its case, from free African to property.

24. Ann Arnett Ferguson, *Bad Boys: Public Schools in the Making of Black Masculinity* (Ann Arbor: University of Michigan Press, 2000); Freeden Blume Oeur, "The Respectable Brotherhood: Young Black Men in an All-Boys Charter High School," *Sociological Perspectives* 60, no. 6 (2017): 1063–81; Freeden Blume Oeur, *Black Boys Apart: Racial Uplift and Respectability in All-Male Public Schools* (Minneapolis: University of Minnesota Press, 2018), https://doi.org/10.5749/j.ctv3znw69.

25. Joan Acker, "From Sex Roles to Gendered Institutions," *Contemporary Sociology* 21, no. 5 (1992): 565–69.

26. Julee Wilson, "Hampton University's Cornrows and Dreadlock Ban: Is It Right?," *HuffPost*, August 23, 2012, www.huffpost.com/entry/hampton-university-cornrows-dreadlock-ban_n_1826349.

27. Letter from W. E. B. Du Bois to Paul H. Hanus, June 19, 1916, W. E. B. Du Bois Papers, Special Collections and University Archives, University of Massachusetts Amherst Libraries, available online at Digital Commonwealth, www.digitalcommonwealth.org/search/commonwealth-oai:vm410004r.

28. M. J. Dumas, "My Brother as 'Problem': Neoliberal Governmentality and Interventions for Black Young Men and Boys," *Educational Policy* 30, no. 1 (2016): 94–113.

29. Mobley and Johnson, "No Pumps Allowed."

30. King, "Mean Girls of Morehouse."

31. The current Appropriate Attire Policy does not mention men wearing women's clothing: www.insidehighered.com/news/2009/10/19/what-more-house-man-wears. Was this prohibition removed in response to protests? See, for example, Lateef Mungin, "All-Male College Cracks Down on Cross-Dressing," CNN, October 17, 2009, www.cnn.com/2009/US/10/17/college.dress.code/.

32. C. J. Pascoe, *Dude, You're a Fag: Masculinity and Sexuality in High School* (Berkeley: University of California Press, 2007).

33. Elliot Liebow, *Tally's Corner: A Study of Negro Streetcorner Men* (Boston: Little, Brown, 1967).

34. A. Young, *The Minds of Marginalized Black Men: Making Sense of Mobility,*

Opportunity, and Future Life Chances (Princeton, NJ: Princeton University Press, 2004).

35. The lack of digitized records makes it difficult to ascertain the attrition rates for each graduating class for the men I interviewed, but data for 2014 show a 55 percent graduation rate for Morehouse. At the time it had the fourth highest attrition rate among HBCUs, which all struggle with retaining a drastically under-resourced population. "Tracking Black Student Graduation Rates at HBCUs," *Journal of Blacks in Higher Education*, November 24, 2014, www.jbhe .com/2014/11/tracking-black-student-graduation-rates-at-hbcus. This graduation rate has, on average, held steady for the past ten years.

36. "Spelman Graduation Rate and Retention Rates," n.d., www.college factual.com/colleges/spelman-college/academic-life/graduation-and-retention.

37. Only 52 percent of Black males graduate high school in four years, compared to 78 percent of white males. In thirty-eight of the fifty states and the District of Columbia, Black males have the lowest graduation rates of any group. See the Schott 50 State Report on Public Education and Black Males, 2012. www .opensocietyfoundations.org/publications/urgency-now-schott-50-state-report -public-education-and-black-males; https://www.fflic.org/1263/.

38. Blume Oeur, *Black Boys Apart*.

39. "Overview of Morehouse College," *US News and World Report*, www .usnews.com/best-colleges/morehouse-college-1582.

40. When men discussed academics as challenging, they overwhelmingly referred to structural, not intellectual challenges. A three-credit system requires students to take an unusually heavy course load to satisfy the eighteen credits required for full-time student status each semester.

41. This 2016–17 acceptance rate has not significantly fluctuated in the past decade.

42. "About," Morehouse College, retrieved January 31, 2010, www.morehouse .edu/about.

43. Noam Chomsky, "Academic Freedom and the Corporatization of Universities," lecture delivered at the University of Toronto, Scarborough, April 6, 2011. Partial transcript available at https://chomsky.info/20110406.

44. Andrea Mennicken, Christine Musselin, and Marion Fourcade, "Wendy Espeland and Michael Sauder, Engines of Anxiety: Academic Rankings, Reputation, and Accountability; New York, NY, Russell Sage Foundation, 2016," *Socio-Economic Review* 16, no. 1 (2018): 207–18.

45. Melissa Wooten, *In the Face of Inequality: How Black Colleges Adapt* (Albany: State University of New York Press, 2015).

46. Fifteen HBCUs have closed since 1997, and both public and private endowments at HBCUs taken together average 70 percent smaller than those at PWIs. According to the American Council on Education (2019), federal funding of HBCUs has declined 42 percent between 2003 and 2015. Data from the 2015 annual report of the Thurgood Marshall Foundation states that less than 9 percent of Black students enrolled in college were enrolled at HBCUs. Still, the same foundation's report notes that HBCUs account for 22 percent of Black college graduates. One hundred and one HBCUs produce one out of every five college-educated African Americans compared to some 2,400 bachelor's-degree-granting PWIs. While the proportion of HBCU attendance is declining for Black students, Black colleges can still be attributed for disproportionately educating African Americans. Thurgood Marshall College Fund 2015 Annual Report, www.tmcf.org/wp-content/uploads/TMCF-2015-Annual-Report-Web.pdf.

Chapter 3. Of Our Sexual Strivings

1. The title of this chapter is a reference to the W. E. B. Du Bois essay titled "Of Our Spiritual Strivings" in his 1903 masterpiece, *The Souls of Black Folk*.

2. Mark Anthony Neal, "Black Men Are Also Raping Black Women," *New Black Magazine*, retrieved January 29, 2020, www.thenewblackmagazine.com/view.aspx?index=661.

3. Robbie Brown, "Georgia: Four Morehouse College Students Face Sexual Assault Charges," *New York Times*, May 2, 2013, www.nytimes.com/2013/05/03/us/georgia-four-morehouse-college-students-face-sex-charges.html.

4. Anita Badejo, "What Happens When Women at Historically Black Colleges Report Their Assaults," *BuzzFeed News*, January 21, 2016, www.buzzfeednews.com/article/anitabadejo/where-is-that-narrative.

5. Badejo, "What Happens When Women at Historically Black Colleges Report Their Assaults."

6. Ellie Hall, "Ambassador Gordon Sondland Confirmed Trump Withheld US Support for Ukraine in Exchange for Investigations into His Political Rivals," *BuzzFeed News*, November 20, 2019, www.buzzfeednews.com/article/ellievhall/quid-pro-quo-ukraine-trump-giuliani-sondland-impeachment.

7. Caitlin Dickerson and Stephanie Saul, "Two Colleges Bound by History Are Roiled by the #MeTooMovement," *New York Times*, December 2, 2017, www.nytimes.com/2017/12/02/us/colleges-sexual-harassment.html.

8. Badejo, "What Happens When Women at Historically Black Colleges Report Their Assaults."

9. Grace Elletson, "How a 'Defunct' Title IX Office and a Culture of Hypermasculinity Fueled a Sexual-Misconduct Problem at Morehouse College," *Chronicle of Higher Education*, September 6, 2019, www.chronicle.com/article/how-a-defunct-title-ix-office-and-a-culture-of-hypermasculinity-fueled-a-sexual-misconduct-problem-at-morehouse-college.

10. Even with the chaotic reputation of its Title IX office, past coordinators have simultaneously served as the college's director of ethics and compliance—a position that helps the college to maintain its reputation, avoid scandals, and manage any media or legal blowback that may affect corporate partnerships and business operations.

11. These cases include a staff member, DeMarcus K. Crews, as well as a faculty member, Robert Peterson, who were separately accused of sexual misconduct and harassment of Morehouse students.

12. Previously, sexual misconduct allegations were brought before a student conduct/disciplinary hearing—a committee that included students' representatives who were privy to the intimate testimonies potentially made against their classmates, but which omitted any personnel trained in sexual misconduct proceedings. As a result of the investigation, the college has committed to working with outside counsel to review its misconduct policies, will hold Title IX hearings separate from student misconduct hearings, and will train faculty and staff to serve as hearing officers for a recently created Sexual Misconduct Panel. Significantly, the report showed that of the college's fifty-eight reported Title IX cases between 2016 and 2018, only thirty-seven had been closed, and twenty-six of those were closed without conclusive findings. Fewer than one out of five victims during those years received a decisive finding on their case. https://morehouse.edu/media/title-ix/TIX-Policy-0813-2020.pdf.

13. The most striking reactions include a statement issued by the Student Government Association condemning protests by Spelman students for disrupting their learning atmosphere, an offense for which they subsequently demanded an apology.

14. https://www.chronicle.com/article/how-a-defunct-title-ix-office-and-a-culture-of-hypermasculinity-fueled-a-sexual-misconduct-problem-at-morehouse-college/.

15. L. Musu-Gillette, A. Zhang, K. Wang, J. Zhang, and B. A. Oudekerk, *Indicators of School Crime and Safety: 2016*, NCES 2017-0 64/NCJ 250650 (Washington, DC: National Center for Education Statistics, US Department of Education, and US Department of Justice, Office of Justice Programs, 2017).

16. It is Tukes's handwriting on that protest sign that is displayed in the background on the cover of this book.

17. Badejo, "What Happens When Women at Historically Black Colleges Report Their Assaults."

18. Department of Justice, Office of Justice Programs, Bureau of Justice Statistics, National Crime Victimization Survey, 2013–2017, 2018, https://bjs.ojp.gov /content/pub/pdf/cv18.pdf.

19. L. E. Adams-Curtis and G. B. Forbes, "College Women's Experiences of Sexual Coercion: A Review of Cultural, Perpetrator, Victim, and Situational Variables," *Trauma, Violence, Abuse* 5, no. 2 (2004): 91–122; Karen Bachar and Mary P. Koss, "From Prevalence to Prevention: Closing the Gap between What We Know and What We Do," in *Sourcebook on Violence against Women*, ed. Claire M. Renzetti, Jeffrey L. Edleson, and Raquel K. Bergen (Thousand Oaks, CA: Sage Publications, 2001), 117–43.

20. Wendy Perkins and Jessica Warner, "Sexual Violence Response and Prevention: Studies of Campus Policies and Practices," *Journal of School Violence* 16, no. 3 (2017): 237–42; David Cantor, Bonnie Fisher, Susan Chibnall, Reanne Townsend, Hyunshik Lee, Carol Bruce, and Gail Thomas, *Report on the AAU Campus Climate Survey on Sexual Assault and Sexual Misconduct* (Washington, DC: Association of American Universities, 2015). Mary P. Koss, Kristine A. Gidycz, and Nadine Wizniewski, "The Scope of Rape: Incidence and Prevalence of Sexual Aggression and Victimization in a National Sample of Higher Education Students," *Journal of Consulting and Clinical Psychology* 55, no. 2 (1987): 162–70.

21. Kevin M. Swartout, Mary P. Koss, Jacquelyn W. White, Martin P. Thompson, Antonia Abbey, and Alexandra L. Bellis, "Trajectory Analysis of the Campus Serial Rapist Assumption," *JAMA Pediatrics* 169, no. 12 (2015): 1148–54.

22. Claire M. Rennison, "Rape and Sexual Assault: Reporting to Police and Medical Attention, 1992–2000," *Bureau of Justice Statistics Selected Findings* (US Department of Justice, Office of Justice Programs), NCJ194530, August 2002, https://bjs.ojp.gov/content/pub/pdf/cv18.pdf.

23. Department of Justice, Office of Justice Programs, Bureau of Justice Statistics, National Crime Victimization Survey, 2013–2017, 2018; Musu-Gillette et al., *Indicators of School Crime and Safety: 2016*.

24. K. Wang, Y. Chen, J. Zhang, and B. A. Oudekerk, *Indicators of School Crime and Safety: 2019*, NCES 2020-063/NCJ 254485 (Washington, DC: National Center for Education Statistics, US Department of Education, and US Department of Justice, Office of Justice Programs, 2020).

25. Susan Brownmiller, *Against Our Will: Men, Women, and Rape* (New York: Simon and Schuster, 1975); Emilie Buchwald, Pamela Fletcher, and Martha Roth, eds., *Transforming a Rape Culture* (1993; Minneapolis: Milkweed Editions, 2005); Diana E. H. Russell, *The Politics of Rape: The Victim's Perspective* (New York: Stein and Day, 1975); Martin D. Schwartz and Walter S. DeKeseredy, *Sexual Assault on the College Campus: The Role of Male Peer Support* (Thousand Oaks, CA: Sage Publications, 1997).

26. Elizabeth A. Armstrong, Laura Hamilton, and Brian Sweeney, "Sexual Assault on Campus: A Multilevel, Integrative Approach to Party Rape," *Social Problems* 53, no. 4 (2006): 483–99; Diane F. Herman, "The Rape Culture," in *Women: A Feminist Perspective*, ed. Jo Freeman (Mountain View, CA: Mayfield Publishing, 1989), 20–44; Chris O'Sullivan, "Fraternities and the Rape Culture," in *Transforming a Rape Culture*, ed. Emilie Buchwald, Pamela Fletcher, and Martha Roth (Minneapolis: Milkweed Editions, 1993), 23–30.

27. A. Ayres Boswell and Joan Z. Spade, "Fraternities and Collegiate Rape Culture: Why Are Some Fraternities More Dangerous Places for Women?," *Gender and Society* 10, no. 2 (1996): 133–47.

28. Candace West and Don Zimmerman, "Doing Gender," *Gender and Society* 1, no. 2 (1987): 125–51.

29. "A Rape Victim Speaks: The People v. Brock Allen Turner June 2, 2016," in *Encyclopedia of Rape and Sexual Violence, Vol. 2: S–Z*, ed. Merril D. Smith (Santa Barbara, CA: ABC-CLIO, 2018), 565–67; Alan Blinder, "Vanderbilt Rape Case Is Declared a Mistrial," *New York Times*, June 24, 2015, www.nytimes.com/2015/06/24/us/post-trial-disclosure-brings-mistrial-in-vanderbilt-rape-case.html.

30. Mo Barnes, "Morehouse College Student Circulates Contract for Sex in Dorm," *Rolling Out*, November 13, 2015.

31. A Morehouse dean swiftly condemned the Spelman student's response as an "alleged violation" and ordered her to "cease and desist."

32. Jose Itzigsohn and Karida Brown, "Sociology and the Theory of Double Consciousness: W. E. B. Du Bois's Phenomenology of Racialized Subjectivity," *Du Bois Review* 12, no. 2 (2015): 231–48.

33. W. E. B. Du Bois, *The Souls of Black Folk* (1903; repr., New York: Dover, 1994); Itzigsohn and Brown, "Sociology and the Theory of Double Consciousness"; Charles Lemert, "A Classic from the Other Side of the Veil: Du Bois's *Souls of Black Folk*," *Sociological Quarterly* 35, no. 3 (1994): 383–96.

34. Du Bois, *Souls of Black Folk*, 2.

35. W. J. T. Mitchell, *Seeing through Race* (Cambridge, MA: Harvard University Press, 2012).

36. K. Barrick, C. P. Krebs, and C. H. Lindquist, "Intimate Partner Violence Victimization among Undergraduate Women at Historically Black Colleges and Universities (HBCUs)," *Violence against Women 19, no. 8* (2013): 1014-33.

37. C. Shawn McGuffey. "Blacks and Racial Appraisals: Gender, Race, and Intraracial Rape," in *Black Sexualities*, ed. Juan Battle and Sandra Barnes (New Brunswick, NJ: Rutgers University Press, 2010), 273-98; C. Shawn McGuffey, "Rape and Racial Appraisals: Culture, Intersectionality, and Black Women's Accounts of Sexual Assault," *Du Bois Review: Social Science Research on Race 10, no. 1* (2013): 109-30, quotation on 110.

38. Ida B. Wells-Barnett, *A Red Record: Tabulated Statistics and Alleged Causes of Lynchings in the United States, 1892-1893-1894* (Chicago: Donohue and Henneberry, 1895).

39. Angela Y. Davis, *Women, Race, and Class* (New York: Vintage, 1983).

40. Derrick Brooms, *Being Black, Being Male on Campus: Understanding and Confronting Black Male Collegiate Experiences* (Albany: State University of New York Press, 2017); Kristie A. Ford, "Doing Fake Masculinity, Being Real Men: Present and Future Constructions of Self among Black College Men," *Symbolic Interaction 34, no. 1* (2011): 38-62; Shaun Harper, "The Measure of a Man: Conceptualizations of Masculinity among High-Achieving African American Male College Students," *Berkeley Journal of Sociology 48* (2004): 89-107; Brandon A. Jackson and Adia Harvey Wingfield, "Getting Angry to Get Ahead: Black College Men, Emotional Performance, and Encouraging Respectable Masculinity," *Symbolic Interaction 36, no. 3* (2013): 275-92; Dante L. Pelzer, "Creating a New Narrative: Reframing Black Masculinity for College Men," *Journal of Negro Education 85, no. 1* (2016):16-27.

41. W. E. B. Du Bois, *Dusk of Dawn: An Essay toward an Autobiography of a Race Concept* (1940; repr., New York: Oxford University Press, 2007), 186, 187.

42. William James, *The Principles of Psychology* (1890; Cambridge, MA: Harvard University Press, 1981), 293.

43. Mary P. Koss, Kristine A. Gidycz, and Nadine Wizniewski, "The Scope of Rape: Incidence and Prevalence of Sexual Aggression and Victimization in a National Sample of Higher Education Students," *Journal of Consulting and Clinical Psychology 55, no. 2* (1987): 162-70. See also Mary P. Koss, "Empirically Enhanced Reflections on 20 Years of Rape Research," *Journal of Interpersonal Violence 20, no. 1* (2005): 100-107; Mary P. Koss, "Detecting the Scope of Rape: A Review of Prevalence Research Methods," *Journal of Interpersonal Violence 8, no. 2* (1993): 198-222.

44. Perkins and Warner, "Sexual Violence Response and Prevention: Studies of Campus Policies and Practices."

45. Jane Liebschutz, Tracy Battaglia, Erin Finley, and Tali Averbuch, "Disclosing Intimate Partner Violence to Health Care Clinicians—What a Difference the Setting Makes: A Qualitative Study," *BMC Public Health* 8 (2008), https://doi.org/10.1186/1471-2458-8-229; Nancy Scheper-Hughes, *Death without Weeping: The Violence of Everyday Life in Brazil* (Berkeley: University of California Press, 1992).

46. *Strategic Plan*, US Naval Academy, retrieved January 29, 2020, www.usna.edu/StrategicPlan/attributes.php.

47. Melvin L. Oliver and Thomas M. Shapiro, *Black Wealth, White Wealth: A New Perspective on Racial Inequality* (New York: Routledge, 2006).

48. Josh Levs, *All In: How Our Work-First Culture Fails Dads, Families, and Businesses—and How We Can Fix It Together* (New York: HarperOne, 2015).

49. Christine H. Lindquist, Kelle Barrick, Christopher Krebs, Carmen M. Crosby, Allison J. Lockard, and Kathy Sanders-Phillips, "The Context and Consequences of Sexual Assault among Undergraduate Women at Historically Black Colleges and Universities (HBCUs)," *Journal of Interpersonal Violence* 28, no. 12 (2013): 2437–61; Christopher P. Krebs, Kelle Barrick, Christine H. Lindquist, Carmen M. Crosby, Chimi Boyd, and Yolanda Bogan, "The Sexual Assault of Undergraduate Women at Historically Black Colleges and Universities (HBCUs)," *Journal of Interpersonal Violence* 26, no. 18 (2011): 3640–66.

50. Farah Jasmine Griffin, "Black Feminists and Du Bois: Respectability, Protection, and Beyond," *Annals of the American Academy of Political and Social Science* 568 (2000): 28–40.

51. Ann Arnett Ferguson, *Bad Boys: Public Schools in the Making of Black Masculinity* (Ann Arbor: University of Michigan Press, 2000).

52. M. Brown and J. Davis, "The Historically Black College as Social Contract, Social Capital, and Social Equalizer," *Peabody Journal of Education* 76, no. 1 (2001): 31–49.

53. Lori S. Robinson, "The Rape of a Spelman Coed," *Emerge* magazine, May 1997, 355.

54. Beth A. Quinn, "Sexual Harassment and Masculinity: The Power and Meaning of 'Girl Watching,'" *Gender and Society* 16, no. 3 (2002): 386–402, quotation on 387.

55. Timothy Behrens, Timothy H. Muller, James C. R. Whittington, Shirley Mark, Alon B. Baram, Kimberly. L Stachenfeld, and Zeb Kurth-Nelson, "What Is a Cognitive Map? Organizing Knowledge for Flexible Behavior," *Neuron* 100, no.

2 (2018): 490–509; A. David Redish, *Beyond the Cognitive Map: From Place Cells to Episodic Memory* (Cambridge, MA: MIT Press, 1999).

56. Anthony S. Chen, "Lives at the Center of the Periphery, Lives at the Periphery of the Center: Chinese American Masculinities and Bargaining with Hegemony," *Gender and Society* 13, no. 5 (1999): 584–607; Raewyn Connell, *Gender and Power: Society, the Person, and Sexual Politics* (Stanford, CA: Stanford University Press, 1987); M. Donaldson, "What Is Hegemonic Masculinity?," *Theory and Society* 22 (1993): 643–57; Saida Grundy, "'An Air of Expectancy': Class, Crisis, and the Making of Manhood at a Historically Black College for Men," *Annals of the American Academy of Political and Social Science* 642, no. 1 (2012): 43–60; Michael S. Kimmel, ed., *The Sexual Self: The Construction of Sexual Scripts* (Nashville, TN: Vanderbilt University Press, 2006).

57. Michael S. Kimmel, *Guyland: The Perilous World Where Boys Become Men* (New York: Harper, 2008). Elsewhere, Kimmel extrapolates on this phenomenon. "We are under the constant careful scrutiny of other men. Other men watch us, rank us, grant us acceptance into the realm of manhood. Manhood is demonstrated for other men's approval. It is other men who evaluate the performance," 213–19. Michael S. Kimmel, "Masculinity as Homophobia: Fear, Shame and Silence in the Construction of Gender Identity," in *Toward a New Psychology of Gender*, ed. Mary M. Gergen and Sara N. Davis (New York: Routledge, 1997), 223–42, quotation on 214.

58. Tim Carrigan, Bob Connell, and John Lee, "Toward a New Sociology of Masculinity," *Renewal and Critique in Social Theory* 14, no. 5 (1985): 551–604.

59. Sharon R. Bird, "Welcome to the Men's Club: Homosociality and the Maintenance of Hegemonic Masculinity," *Gender and Society* 10, no. 2 (1996): 120–32; Harry Brod, *The Making of Masculinities: The New Men's Studies* (Boston: Allen and Unwin, 1987); Carrigan, Connell, and Lee, "Toward a New Sociology of Masculinity"; Chen, "Lives at the Center of the Periphery, Lives at the Periphery of the Center"; Cliff Cheng, "Marginalized Masculinities and Hegemonic Masculinity: An Introduction," *Journal of Men's Studies* 7, no. 3 (1999): 295–315.

60. Chen, "Lives at the Center of the Periphery, Lives at the Periphery of the Center"; Arlie R. Hochschild, with Anne Machung, *The Second Shift: Working Parents and the Revolution at Home* (New York: Viking Penguin, 1989); Deniz Kandiyoti, "Bargaining with Patriarchy," *Gender and Society* 2, no. 3 (1988): 274–90, quotation on 286.

61. Bird, "Welcome to the Men's Club"; Sharon R. Bird, "Sex Composition, Masculinity Stereotype Dissimilarity and the Quality of Men's Workplace Social Relations," *Gender, Work, and Organization* 10, no. 5 (2003): 579–604; C. J. Pas-

coe, *Dude, You're a Fag: Masculinity and Sexuality in High School* (Berkeley: University of California Press, 2007).

62. Laura Hamilton and Elizabeth A. Armstrong, "Gendered Sexuality in Young Adulthood: Double Binds and Flawed Options," *Gender and Society* 23, no. 5 (2009): 589–616; Lisa Wade, "What's So Cultural about Hookup Culture?" *Contexts* 16, no. 1 (2017): 66–68.

63. P. Butler, "Black Male Exceptionalism? The Problems and Potential of Black Male-Focused Interventions," *Du Bois Review* 10, no. 2 (2013): 485–511.

64. "Farrakhan Describes Cycle of Domestic Violence," *Washington Post*, June 27, 1994.

65. "Black Women Students Far Outnumber Black Men at the Nation's Highest-Ranked Universities," *Journal of Blacks in Higher Education* 51 (2006): 26–28.

66. See David R. Francis, "Why Do Women Outnumber Men in College?," *The Digest* (National Bureau of Economic Research), no. 1 (January 2007), www .nber.org/digest/jan07/w12139.html.

67. James Earl Davis, "College in Black and White: Campus Environment and Academic Achievement of African American Males," *Journal of Negro Education* 63, no. 4 (1994): 620–33.

68. Butler, "Black Male Exceptionalism?"

69. "Best Colleges: Ranking of Historically Black Colleges and Universities," *US News and World Report*, 2020, www.usnews.com/best-colleges/rankings /hbcu.

70. Howard University, Hampton University, and Clark Atlanta University are similarly well-known and well-attended HBCUs.

71. Richard Fauset, "Black College Faces Its Own Bias," *Los Angeles Times*, May 22, 2008, www.latimes.com/archives/la-xpm-2008-may-22-na -morehouse22-story.html.

72. In Fauset, "Black College Faces Its Own Bias."

73. Gordon Gekko is a fictional character from the 1987 film *Wall Street* who came to epitomize the machismo avarice and ruthlessness of that era's high-powered financial services sector.

74. While Davis harped on the inadequate support he felt the perpetrators received from Morehouse leadership, *Emerge* magazine reports from the incident aftermath include an account that a Morehouse chaplain decreed during a worship service that "women bring abuse upon themselves because of their attitudes and their dress." Robinson, "Rape of a Spelman Coed," 355.

75. Freaknik was originally founded in 1993 as a picnic by Spelman and Morehouse students and was ultimately shut down by Atlanta mayor Bill Camp-

bell in 2000 on mounting pressure by local businesses. An analysis of coverage of the event by media scholar Marian Meyers (see note 76 below) noted that news outlets cast Black women attendees as deserving of sexual violence while criminalizing Black men for property damage and *decriminalizing* them for assaults against Black women.

76. Marian Meyers, "African American Women and Violence: Gender, Race, and Class in the News," *Critical Studies in Media Communication* 21 (2004): 95–118.

77. That small group of Morehouse students later went on to found an organization called Men for the Eradication of Sexism. They issued a public manifesto denouncing sexual violence and accounting for their roles as Black men in maintaining patriarchy within the race.

78. Bird, "Welcome to the Men's Club"; Michael Kimmel, "'Bros before Hos': The Guy Code," in *Rereading America: Cultural Contexts for Critical Thinking and Writing*, 8th ed., ed. Gary Colombo, Robert Cullen, and Bonnie Lisle (Boston: Bedford/St. Martin's, 2014).

79. Molly Smith, Nicole Wilkes, and Leana A. Bouffard, "Rape Myth Adherence among Campus Law Enforcement Officers," *Criminal Justice and Behavior* 43, no. 4 (2016): 539–56.

80. It is an often-misunderstood fact that Title IX cases have a considerably different burden of proof than criminal cases. While Roy may be adamant in pointing out the fact that the accused men were not tried in criminal court (from which he falsely concludes their innocence), the burden of proof for colleges themselves is only 51 percent in sexual assault cases, that is, it need only be more likely than not that an incident occurred for a college to proceed accordingly with punishments for the perpetrators. Roy seems to be conflating criminal procedure with Title IX procedure.

81. Devon Carbado, "Black Male Racial Victimhood," *Callaloo* 21, no. 2 (1998): 337–61, quotation on 337.

82. bell hooks, *Yearning: Race, Gender, and Cultural Politics* (Boston: South End Press, 1990), 75.

83. Janet Halley, "Trading the Megaphone for the Gavel in Title IX Enforcement," *Harvard Law Review* 128 (2015): 103–17, quotation on 106.

84. In Robinson, "Rape of a Spelman Coed."

85. McGuffey, "Rape and Racial Appraisals."

86. Researchers have found that Black women are seldom seen as victims by the court system and are more likely to be viewed by juries as adults even when they are minors. See Rebecca Epstein, Jamilia Blake, and Thalia González,

Girlhood Interrupted: The Erasure of Black Girls' Childhood (Georgetown Law, Center on Poverty and Inequality, June 27, 2017), http://dx.doi.org/10.2139/ssrn .3000695.

Chapter 4. Who among You Will Lead?

1. See "Forbes 400 2019," *Forbes Magazine*, retrieved January 29, 2020, www .forbes.com/profile/robert-f-smith/#12ea0e752236.

2. Winfrey's foundation is also the largest benefactor for Morehouse student scholarships. Recent additions to the 2019 list of African American billionaires include IT CEO David Steward and entertainer Shawn Carter, a.k.a. rapper Jay-Z. *Forbes'* "billionaire declarations" can be unreliable, however, as its coverage can be bought or planted by publicists. Articles touting the rap artist's wealth were written by a *Forbes* senior editor who is promoting a book he authored on Carter's meteoric rise to fame and fortune.

3. Full transcript of Robert F. Smith commencement speech, *The Singju Post*, June 6, 2019, https://singjupost.com/robert-f-smiths-commencement-speech-at -morehouse-full-transcript/?singlepage=1.

4. See "Who Is Robert F. Smith? Learn More about the Billionaire Whose Generosity Shocked a Graduating Class," *Time* magazine, May 19, 2019, https:// time.com/5591629/robert-smith-billionaire-student-debt-gift. Smith has already pledged $50 million to Cornell University through personal and foundation gifts.

5. See "Forbes 400 2019."

6. P. Butler, "Black Male Exceptionalism? The Problems and Potential of Black Male-Focused Interventions," *Du Bois Review: Social Science Research on Race* 10, no. 2 (2013): 485–511.

7. The Leadership Center was founded in 1995 with a grant from the Coca-Cola Foundation and was the brainchild of President Walter Massey, who envisioned a "World House at Morehouse" that would cultivate "character, civility, and community as primary values in the development of leaders." www .morehouse.edu/bonner/internalpartners/leadershipcenter.html.

8. While both the Leadership Center and the Andrew Young Center for Global Leadership share many similar objectives, the latter seems to emphasize international diplomacy (Young is a former UN Ambassador) and "engaging complex global problems of marginalized groups, especially peoples of African descent." "About the Center," Morehouse College, retrieved January 29, 2020, www.morehouse.edu/aycgl/.

9. "Leadership Studies Program," Morehouse College, retrieved January 29, 2020, https://www.morehouse.edu/aycgl/leadershipstudiesprogram/.

10. "About the Center," Morehouse College.

11. "Mission & Vision," Morehouse College, retrieved January 31, 2020, www.morehouse.edu/aycgl/about/missionandvision.html.

12. Anthony S. Chen, "Lives at the Center of the Periphery, Lives at the Periphery of the Center: Chinese American Masculinities and Bargaining with Hegemony," *Gender and Society* 13, no. 5 (1999): 584–607.

13. See Leah Wright Rigueur, "Neoliberal Social Justice: From Ed Brooke to Barack Obama," May 30, 2017, submitted for the Social Science Research Council, retrieved January 29, 2020, https://items.ssrc.org/reading-racial-conflict/neoliberal-social-justice-from-ed-brooke-to-barack-obama.

14. Michael C. Dawson and Megan Ming Francis, "Black Politics and the Neoliberal Racial Order," *Public Culture* 28, no. 1 (78) (2016): 23–62. Significantly, Black neoliberalism has also guided much of the approach to social justice and aid for African peoples on the continent.

15. Lester K. Spence, *Knocking the Hustle: Against the Neoliberal Turn in Black Politics* (Brooklyn, NY: Punctum, 2015).

16. Keith L. Alexander, "How Robert F. Smith Helped Thousands of Minority-Owned Small Businesses Secure Urgent Aid in Washington," *Washington Post*, June 25, 2020.

17. Peter Whoriskey, Yeganeh Torbati, and Keith L. Alexander, "A Dodgy Deal Helped Make Him a Billionaire: It Worked, until Now," *Washington Post*, November 13, 2020.

18. R. Reich, *Just Giving* (Princeton, NJ: Princeton University Press, 2018).

19. Josh Mitchell and Andrea Fuller, "The Student Debt Crisis Hits Hardest at Historically Black Colleges," *Wall Street Journal*, April 17, 2019, www.wsj.com/articles/the-student-debt-crisis-hits-hardest-at-historically-black-colleges-11555511327.

20. Fred Hampton, "Power Anywhere Where There's People!," speech delivered at Olivet Presbyterian Church, Chicago, 1969.

21. Regarding antiracism and Black entrepreneurship, Marcia Chatelain explores the ties between Black McDonald's franchisees, the civil rights movement, and capitalism. Marcia Chatelain, *Franchise: The Golden Arches in Black America* (New York: Liveright, 2020).

22. See Rigueur, "Neoliberal Social Justice: From Ed Brooke to Barack Obama." See also Leah Wright Rigueur, *The Loneliness of the Black Republican:*

Pragmatic Politics and the Pursuit of Power (Princeton, NJ: Princeton University Press, 2016).

23. For example, see Robin D. G. Kelley's exploration of Black communists in rural Alabama, *Hammer and Hoe: Alabama Communists during the Great Depression* (Chapel Hill: University of North Carolina Press, 2015). Kelley's work was directly influenced by the seminal works on Black anticapitalist movements by Cedric Robinson. See Robinson's *Black Marxism: The Making of the Black Radical Tradition* (Chapel Hill: University of North Carolina Press, 2000).

24. Ashley D. Farmer, *Remaking Black Power: How Black Women Transformed an Era* (Chapel Hill: University of North Carolina Press, 2017).

25. See Andy Lewis, "Samuel L. Jackson: How I Became an Usher at Martin Luther King Jr.'s Funeral," *Hollywood Reporter*, April 3, 2018, www .hollywoodreporter.com/news/samuel-l-jackson-how-i-became-an-usher-at -martin-luther-king-jrs-funeral-guest-column-1099033.

26. On a related note, Yusuf left me with the impression that the Business Department was not particularly academically rigorous. He chose to major in economics when a faculty member stated bluntly that "Economics majors are the bosses of Business majors." The Business Department avoids this stigma about its lack of intellectual rigor ostensibly because it is strongly associated with hypercompetitive masculine professions, and, perhaps, because courses like Leadership and Professional Development (LPD) deem it *culturally* rigorous.

27. The website redirects those interested in these majors to Spelman's course listings. The short description of the drama major notes that "companies are also finding that applications for drama provide a 'contextual training model', that includes lifelike simulations for participants to practice managing complex human interactions in a safe and controlled learning environment." https://www .morehouse.edu/academics/drama/. In 2012 the college established a major in Cinema, Television, and Film studies.

28. Samuel L. Jackson recalled that his protests as a student in the late 1960s also revolved around the lack of a Black studies department at Morehouse and the large number of white trustees. At the time, not even this African American studies program existed.

29. Even as of this writing, the African-American Studies Program is not a department. It draws on affiliated faculty members for its core courses, and even its majors take most of their courses in other departments.

30. "Lifting as We Climb" was the motto of the National Association of Colored [later Negro] Women's Clubs. It is of note that Morehouse men were hear-

ing a mantra from the college that, while it was not acknowledged, originated with *women's* racial leadership.

31. See "30 Great Small College Business Degree Programs 2016," *Accounting Degree Review*, retrieved January 29, 2020, https://www.online-accounting -degrees.net/best/small-college-business-degree-programs.

32. As of 2018, 28 percent of declared majors were in the Business Department, making it by far the most popular major; the social sciences coming second, with 17 percent of declared majors. *US News and World Report*, www.usnews .com/best-colleges/morehouse-college-1582/academics.

33. Ornette seemed to imply that students who were otherwise unsure of their postgraduate plans gravitated toward the Business Department by default, perhaps because its many internship opportunities offer lucrative temporary placements for new graduates.

34. I was reminded of a scene from *Paris Is Burning*, the iconic 1990 cinema-verité-style documentary capturing the Black and Latinx underground queer ballroom culture of New York City. Corporate Executive Realness is a category of competition in these balls in which the suited gay man accomplishes "realness" by passing as butch, as assimilated, and as educated. The Business Department accomplishes similar "realness" by transforming the bodies of men who are not "supposed" to be in these settings.

35. For more on how Black ballroom culture both spoofs and mirrors many of the daily performances of dominant straight culture, see Marlon Bailey's *Butch Queens Up in Pumps: Gender, Performance, and Ballroom Culture in Detroit* (Ann Arbor: University of Michigan Press, 2013), an ethnography that emphasizes not only the gender and the racial spoofing but also the mutual aid among inner-city LGBTQ participants.

36. "Tight" is common slang for being impressive and in top shape, whether that be talent, aptitude, or even one's choice of outfit or luxury car.

37. While settings with white business elites may have been used as the context for LPD's career preparation emphasis, it seems fairly obvious that these instructions would be applicable to any times where men were on display to whites in general.

38. Shamus Rahman Khan, *Privilege: The Making of an Adolescent Elite at St. Paul's School* (Princeton, NJ: Princeton University Press, 2011), 62.

39. Khan, *Privilege*.

40. Freeden Blume Oeur and Saida Grundy, "Allyship in the Time of Aggrievement: The Case of Black Feminism and New Black Masculinities," in *Black*

Feminist Sociology: Perspectives and Praxis, ed. Zakiya Luna and Whitney Pirtle (New York: Routledge, 2022), 253–66.

41. Keisha Lindsay, *In a Classroom of Their Own: The Intersection of Race and Feminist Politics in All-Black Male Schools* (Urbana: University of Illinois Press, 2018).

42. Kimberlé Crenshaw and multiple authors (including Angela Y. Davis, Mary Francis Berry, Alice Walker, and Patricia Hill Collins among over 1,600 others), "Why We Can't Wait: Women of Color Urge Inclusion in 'My Brother's Keeper,'" June 17, 2014, retrieved from African American Policy Forum, January 30, 2020, http://aapf.org/recent/2014/06/woc-letter-mbk. For the full letter with signatories, see https://issuu.com/jusharpelevine/docs/whywecantwait _mbkletter.pdf_1_?e=0/15261424.

43. This public-private partnership worth $128 million "will connect young men to educational, employment, and mentoring opportunities across more than a dozen city agencies." "When we look at poverty rates, graduation rates, crime rates, and employment rates, one thing stands out: blacks and Latinos are not fully sharing in the promise of American freedom and far too many are trapped in circumstances that are difficult to escape," said Mayor Bloomberg. "Even though skin color in America no longer determines a child's fate—sadly, it tells us more about a child's future than it should. And so, this morning, we are confronting these facts head-on, not to lament them, but to change them, and to ensure that 'equal opportunity' is not an abstract notion but an everyday reality, for all New Yorkers." See "Young Men's Initiative to Aid Young Black and Latino Males," Bloomberg Philanthropies, August 4, 2011, retrieved January 30, 2020, www.bloomberg.org/press/releases/young-mens-initiative-to-aid-young -black-and-latino-males.

44. Barack Obama, "Remarks by the President on 'My Brother's Keeper' Initiative," February 27, 2014, https://obamawhitehouse.archives.gov/the-press -office/2014/02/27/remarks-president-my-brothers-keeper-initiative.

45. Michael Dumas, "My Brother as 'Problem': Neoliberal Governmentality and Interventions for Black Young Men and Boys," *Educational Policy* 30, no. 1 (2016): 94–113.

46. The May 30, 2014, "Letter of 200 Concerned Black Men Calling for the Inclusion of Women and Girls in 'My Brother's Keeper'" included Danny Glover; writer Kiese Laymon; civil rights icon James M. Lawson; and scholars such as Robin Kelley, James Turner, and Eduardo Bonilla Silva. It is available via the African American Policy Forum, retrieved January 30, 2020, https://aapf.org/recent /2014/05/an-open-letter-to-president-obama. For the full letter with signatories,

see https://issuu.com/jusharpelevine/docs/whywecantwait_mbkletter.pdf_1_?e =0/15261424.

47. According to the statement, the median wealth for both Black and Latina women is below that for men, the homicide rate for Black girls and women age ten to twenty-four is higher than for any other group of women, and Black girls have the highest rates of interpersonal victimization from assault and are the most likely to know their assailant compared to all other women. Black girls are three times more likely to be suspended from school than white girls, and Black women are three times more likely to be incarcerated than white women.

48. Nia Malika Henderson, "1,000 Women of Color Want Women and Girls Included in 'My Brother's Keeper,'" *Washington Post*, June 18, 2014.

49. Crenshaw and multiple authors, "Why We Can't Wait: Women of Color Urge Inclusion in "My Brother's Keeper." For the full letter with signatories, see https://issuu.com/jusharpelevine/docs/whywecantwait_mbkletter.pdf_1_?e=0 /15261424, retrieved January 30, 2020.

50. Elizabeth Hinton, *From the War on Poverty to the War on Crime: The Making of Mass Incarceration in America* (Cambridge, MA: Harvard University Press, 2016).

51. In 1996 O'Reilly joined Fox News but was fired in 2017 after a *New York Times* investigation revealed that he had sexually harassed and assaulted six women, whose lawsuits Fox had settled out of court for a total of $45 million. I make this point to note how even right-wing white men who commit serial sexual predation are offered opportunities to weigh in on the morality of Black families and Black youths.

52. Dumas, "My Brother as 'Problem.'"

53. Dumas, "My Brother as 'Problem.'"

54. Dumas, "My Brother as 'Problem,'" 94.

55. Lindsay, *In a Classroom of Their Own*.

56. Devon W. Carbado, ed., *Black Men on Race, Gender, and Sexuality* (New York: New York University Press, 1999).

57. The Walton family members are the descendants of Sam Walton, the founder of Walmart, and are regularly listed individually among the top wealthiest Americans with a combined fortune of approximately $191 billion as of August 2019. See www.bloomberg.com/features/richest-families-in-the-world.

58. See Kimberlé Williams Crenshaw, "The Girls Obama Forgot," *New York Times*, June 29, 2014, www.nytimes.com/2014/07/30/opinion/Kimberl-Williams -Crenshaw-My-Brothers-Keeper-Ignores-Young-Black-Women.html.

59. Dumas, "My Brother as 'Problem.'"

60. Founded in Chicago, Urban Prep Academies is a network of public Black male charter schools that began in 2002.

61. In an April 1989 article in *Education Week* titled "The Make-Believe World of 'Lean on Me'" (www.edweek.org/ew/articles/1989/04/26/08270016.h08 .html, retrieved January 31, 2010), school psychologist Irwin Hyman explained how Joe Clark, the real Eastside High principal who was portrayed in the film by Morgan Freeman, advanced the myth that test scores could be raised by extreme demands for obedience across students and faculty. His tactics played on the stereotype that Black teens were muggers, drug users, and deviants, which perfectly coalesced with conservative propaganda about rampant violence and drug use in urban public schools. Clark once famously said, "I'm a dictator and they love it," and was widely celebrated as a savior and model principal who was loved by students. In reality, only 24.1 percent of Eastside High students passed the basic skills test during his tenure. Nonetheless, this valorized image of disciplinarians bringing out the best in Black student achievement left an indelible mark on both policy and cultural approaches to Black student learning that has lingered for decades.

62. See Theodore Johnson and Leah Wright Rigueur, "The GOP's Long History with Black Colleges," *Politico*, February 27, 2017, retrieved February 2, 2020, www.politico.com/magazine/story/2017/02/trump-black-colleges-universities -hbcus-republicans-214834.

63. See Adam Harris, "HBCU Leader Says DeVos's 'School Choice' Comment Is Worrying on Multiple Levels," *Chronicle of Higher Education*, February 28, 2017, retrieved January 31, 2020, www.chronicle.com/article/hbcu-leader -says-devoss/239341.

64. See Kim Severson, "Chick-fil-A Thrust Back into Spotlight on Gay Rights," *New York Times*, July 25, 2012, www.nytimes.com/2012/07/26/us/gay -rights-uproar-over-chick-fil-a-widens.html.

65. Massey was formerly George H. W. Bush's appointed director to the National Science Foundation, and he had been chairman of the board of the Bank of America.

66. Afro-centrism espouses an approach to the world as African people and the continent as the source of history and humanity, in keeping with a growing body of scholarship and racial ideology from the 1960s that has been steadfastly critical of scholarly curriculums that place European contributions and disciplinary approaches at their intellectual center.

67. For classic examples of Black feminists calling for racial liberation to take on intersectional oppressions should it be effective, see (among many other ex-

amples) Audre Lorde, *Sister Outsider: Essays and Speeches* (Trumansburg, NY: Crossing Press, 1984); Toni Cade Bambara, *The Black Woman: An Anthology* (New York: New American Library, 1970); and Angela Y. Davis, *Women, Race, and Class* (New York: Random House, 1981).

68. For more discussion on Black nationalist cultural ideologies that promoted machismo and misappropriated claims of African gender roles, please refer back to chapter 2 herein.

69. K. Kruse, *White Flight: Atlanta and the Making of Modern Conservatism* (Princeton, NJ: Princeton University Press, 2005).

70. Conversation with Aimee Meredith Cox, October 2019, New Haven, CT.

71. National Research Council, *America Becoming: Racial Trends and Their Consequences*, vol. 1 (Washington, DC: National Academies Press, 2001).

Conclusion

1. Scott Jaschik, "What the Morehouse Man Wears," *Inside Higher Ed*, October 19, 2009, www.insidehighered.com/news/2009/10/19/what-morehouse -man-wears.

2. For the full policy, "Media: Student Conduct," Morehouse College, retrieved February 2, 2020, https://www.morehouse.edu/media/student-develop ment/Morehouse-College-Student-Handbook-2019-2020.pdf.

3. Historically, queer Black people have never been absent or low-profile in Black civil rights and liberation movements.

4. Laura Diamond, "Morehouse College Cuts Spending after Enrollment Drops," *Atlanta Journal-Constitution*, October 22, 2012, www.ajc.com/news /morehouse-college-cuts-spending-after-enrollment-drops/pi8mOuFtiIC2k TyIAhMc3J.

5. Mara Ostfeld and Michelle Garcia, "Black Men Shift Slightly towards Trump in Record Numbers, Polls Show," *NBC News*, November 4, 2020.

6. Keisha Lindsay, *In a Classroom of Their Own: The Intersection of Race and Feminist Politics in All-Black Male Schools* (Urbana: University of Illinois Press, 2018).

7. W. E. B. Du Bois, *The Souls of Black Folk* (1903; repr., New York: Dover, 1994); Jose Itzigsohn and Karida Brown, "Sociology and the Theory of Double Consciousness: W. E. B. Du Bois's Phenomenology of Racialized Subjectivity," *Du Bois Review* 12, no. 2 (2015): 231–48; Charles Lemert, "A Classic from the Other Side of the Veil: Du Bois's *Souls of Black Folk*," *Sociological Quarterly* 35, no. 3 (1994): 383–96.

8. Gracie Bonds Staples, "Morehouse College Betting on PrEP to Prevent HIV," *Atlanta Journal-Constitution*, November 23, 2018, www.ajc.com/lifestyles /morehouse-college-betting-prep-prevent-hiv/hwYfFfQPUcMrgrO41xWarM.

9. Dave Huddleston, "Atlanta's HIV 'Epidemic' Compared to Third World African Countries," WSB-TV, November 30, 2018, www.wsbtv.com /news/2-investigates/atlantas-hiv-epidemic-compared-to-third-world-african -countries/263337845.

10. Staples, "Morehouse College Betting on PrEP to prevent HIV."

11. S. D. Mobley Jr. and J. M. Johnson, "'No Pumps Allowed': The 'Problem' with Gender Expression and the Morehouse College 'Appropriate Attire Policy,'" *Journal of Homosexuality* 66, no.7 (2019): 867–95.

12. "Church Allowed Abuse by Priest for Years," *Boston Globe*, January 6, 2002, www.bostonglobe.com/news/special-reports/2002/01/06/church -allowed-abuse-priest-for-years/cSHfGkTIrAT25qKGvBuDNM/story.html.

13. Anita Badejo, "What Happens When Women at Historically Black Colleges Report Their Assaults," *BuzzFeed News*, January 21, 2016, www.buzzfeed news.com/article/anitabadejo/where-is-that-narrative.

14. Lori Robinson, "The Rape of a Spelman Coed," *Emerge* magazine, May 1997.

15. Julia Debski, Michael Jetter, Saskia Mösle, and David Stadelmann, "Gender and Corruption: The Neglected Role of Culture," CREMA Working Paper Series 2016-05, Center for Research in Economics, Management and the Arts (CREMA), 2016.

16. Eliana Dockterman, "These Men Say the Boy Scouts' Sex Abuse Problem Is Worse Than Anyone Knew," *Time*, June 1, 2019, https://time.com/longform /boy-scouts-sex-abuse; Dave Zirin, "An NFL Player Stands Up to Rape and Gives a Lesson in Consent," *The Nation*, May 3, 2016, www.thenation.com/article /archive/nfl-player-stands-up-to-rape-and-gives-a-lesson-in-consent.

17. Michael Harriot, "The War at Morehouse," *The Root*, March 30, 2017, https://www.theroot.com/the-war-at-morehouse-1793541413.

18. "Morehouse Student Trustee Temp Restraining Order," www.docdroid .net/txWZco7/morehouse-student-trusteetemp-restraining-order-pdf; Harriot, "War at Morehouse."

19. M. Christopher Brown and James Earl Davis, "The Historically Black College as Social Contract, Social Capital, and Social Equalizer," *Peabody Journal of Education* 76, no. 1 (2001): 31–49, www.jstor.org/stable/1493004.

Index

Figures are marked by "f" following page numbers.

accommodationism, 59–62, 71. *See also* Atlanta Compromise

achievement gap, Black–white, 221

Acker, Joan, 116

admissions policies. *See under* transgender students

African-American Studies Program, 204, 324nn28–29

AIDS. *See* HIV/AIDS crisis

Allen, Jafari Sinclaire, 89–90

Andrew Young Center for Global Leadership (Leadership Center), 191–92

Appropriate Attire Policy, 15, 123, 243–44

Archie, 111, 171–73

athletics, 237–38

Atlanta Baptist Seminary, 55, 56f, 59, 60f. *See also* Morehouse College

Atlanta Compromise, 118. *See also* accommodationism

Atlanta University Center (AUC), 57, 58, 93, 97, 234

attire. *See* Appropriate Attire Policy; dress

attrition rates: of HBCUs, 312n35, 313n46; "Look to your left, look to your right, one of you will be gone" (attrition), 126–28

Augusta Theological Institute, 55, 61

ballroom scene, 210

Beautillion, 99–101

Bennett, Lerone, Jr., 250; on Benjamin Elijah Mays, 69, 77; on Black male crisis and the plight of Black men, 69, 77–78, 80–82, 250; on exceptionalism, 81; on masculinity, 69, 77, 78, 81; Robert Staples and, 78, 81, 82

Biden, Joe: speech at Morehouse, 138, 139, 139f, 141, 142

Bird, 116, 126–27; dress and, 123; finances and, 25–26, 115; homophobia and, 123, 176; queerness and, 172, 173

"Black," capitalization of the term, 291n1

Black colleges. *See* Historically Black Colleges and Universities

Black cultural nationalism, 71–73

Black exceptionalism, 67, 199. *See also* Black male exceptionalism; exceptionalism

Black history: up from slavery through sexual and gender propriety, 50–63. *See also specific topics*

Black intellectual tradition. *See* intellectualism

Black male crisis. *See* crisis of the Black male/Black male crisis

Black male exceptionalism, 81, 257, 266; defined, 168–69, 189; Paul Butler on, 80–81; rhetoric of, 168–69. *See also* Black exceptionalism; exceptionalism

Black Male Initiative (BMI) programs, 109, 123, 218

Black male success. *See* success

Black Masculinity (Staples), 81. *See also* Staples, Robert

Black nationalism, 68, 71–73. *See also* Black cultural nationalism

Black Power movements, 75, 202

Blakey, 30, 192

Bourdieu, Pierre, 100

brand compliance, 104–14

branding, 253; the body, 122–26; New Student Orientation (NSO) and, 108–14, 209–10, 253. *See also* Morehouse brand

Brewer, Michael, 171

brother-sister matching ceremony, 161–62

Brown, M. Christopher, 54

Brown, Scot, 72–73

Burney, Myron Gerard, x

Business Department, 207–11, 213, 226

Cain, Herman, 64–65

capitalism: Morehouse brand and, 202–3; race and, 189, 190, 198, 201–3, 206, 207, 235, 237. *See also* neoliberalism; social justice capitalism

Carbado, Devon W., 182

Carby, Hazel, 65, 70, 71, 303n60

Carlos, Joseph, 240

catcalling, 161

Cayton, Horace R., 65

Chet, 106, 110–11

Clark, Joe, 328n61

Clark Atlanta University, 57, 168

class distinction, 100–102

Clifford, 107, 117, 178, 209–11, 230–34

clothing. *See* dress

Cohen, Cathy J., 19–20, 248

Cole, Johnetta, 177–78, 205–6

Coleman, 106, 122, 152, 155, 156

color line, 86

competition: as compensation, 165–71; Du Boisian theory and, 165, 168, 170; hegemonic masculinity and, 165–66, 170, 173

consent, sexual, 148, 156–59

Cooper, Anna Julia, 69, 70

corporatization, 209–10, 220, 227. *See also* Morehouse College: corporate business culture

COVID-19 pandemic, 200, 246

Cox, Aimee Meredith, 236

criminal justice system, 46. *See also* incarceration

"Crisis of the Black Male, The" (*Ebony* magazine special issue), 76

crisis of the Black male/Black male crisis, 21, 49, 75, 133, 169, 220; and Black women, 77–82, 250; crime, incarceration, and, 5, 80; "The Crisis of the Black Male: Challenges and Opportunity" (*Ebony* magazine), 76–77, 76f; efforts to solve, 82–86; history, 49; HIV/AIDS crisis and, 248, 249; ideologies and, 76, 82, 85; Lerone Bennett and, 69, 77–78, 80–82, 250; Morehouse and,

9, 10, 12, 16, 38, 50, 77, 85, 105, 129, 133, 248-49, 251; overview and nature of, 49-50; (moral) panic over, 5, 9, 16-17, 76-77, 80, 169; public and private institutions and, 82; reactive respectability and, 10, 249, 250; rhetoric of, 75-76, 78-80

Crown Forums, 121, 154, 208

cultural manhood, 133

Cunningham, Timothy ("Tim"), x-xi

Davis, 99-100, 150, 221; brand management and, 104; conformity and, 100, 104, 150; dress and, 104, 122, 124, 226; finance and, 128, 226; rape, rape accusations, and, 146, 177-84; success and, 99, 128, 150, 221, 222, 226, 227

Davis, Angela, 146

Davis, James Earl, 54

Dawson, Michael C., 18, 38, 67, 194, 198

Dewey, 36, 126-29, 153-54; "Look to your left, look to your right," 128

Dexter, 109, 211, 212

distinction, class, 100-102

diversity, 94-96

Dolphy, 32, 162, 193

dominance hierarchy. See hierarchies; pecking order/dominance hierarchy

double consciousness, 143-45, 149, 150, 159; Du Boisian veil and, 144, 165, 171; hegemonic masculinity and, 165-66, 184; overview and nature of, 144-45; racialization and, 144, 145, 165-66, 184-85; rape culture and, 143, 145, 149, 150, 159, 171, 184

Douglass, Frederick, 71

Drake, St. Clair, 65

dress, 71, 89, 210, 211, 242, 252; and branding the body, 122-26; Davis and, 104, 122, 124, 226

dress codes, 115, 123-24; banners and, 242-44, 262; gender-nonconforming students and, 3-4, 243; HBCUs and, 117, 123; Lucky and, 121; and the media, 123, 244. See also Appropriate Attire Policy

drugs, war on, 21, 79-80, 85, 232

Du Bois, W. E. B.: accommodationism and, 59-62, 71; Anna Julia Cooper and, 69, 70; Atlanta University and, 58; on Black exceptionalism, 67; Black liberation and, 61-63; vs. Booker T. Washington, 61-62, 70-71, 304n68; on capitalization of "Negro," 291n1; on color line, 86; on curricula, 59-60; on education, 60, 146; gentleman-scholars and, 71-73; Hampton Institute and, 117-18; Hazel Carby and, 70, 71; hegemonic masculinity and, 164-66, 170, 184; intellectualism and, 69-71, 118; manhood, masculinity, and, 20, 69-71, 73, 122, 165; *The Negro American Family*, 50-51; "Of Our Spiritual Strivings," 73; race man and, 69, 71, 122; on racialization, 20 (*see also* racialization: Du Boisian theory and); on sexual mores, 50-51; on Talented Tenth, 66, 67, 195-96; "The Talented Tenth," 66; women, feminists, and, 154

Du Boisian theory, 170; competition and, 165, 168, 170; hegemonic masculinity and, 165, 170; racialization and, 20, 22-23, 36-37, 145-47, 165, 184-85; rape culture and, 147, 184-85 (*see also under* rape culture). *See also* double consciousness

Du Boisian two-ness. *See* two-ness
Du Boisian veil, 20–21, 146–47, 155, 258; Cathy Cohen and, 20; on display, 226–28; double consciousness and, 144, 165, 171; gender and, 145, 154, 251, 254; homophobia and, 171, 254, 255; Morehouse's racial veil, 215, 227, 248, 251, 252; nature of, 248, 251; racialization and, 20, 36–37, 144, 248; rape culture and, 145, 165, 171, 254, 255; reactive respectability and, 250, 252; sexuality and, 154, 156; standpoint theory and, 36–37; visibility and, 252

Ebony magazine, 76, 76f, 77. *See also* Bennett, Lerone, Jr.
economic crisis, 47, 188, 200, 201, 208, 249, 250, 259. *See also* Great Recession
education, goal of, 60
Education Department, 204–5
elite Black athletes, 238
elite exceptionalism. *See* exceptionalism
elite schools, 115, 123
elite spaces, 228, 257, 258
elites, Black, 52–53; Du Bois on, 67 (*see also* Talented Tenth); Kevin Gaines on, 67, 70; leadership and, 70, 75, 82
elites, Black male, 14, 21–22, 37, 39, 75, 237, 249, 258; Black male crisis and, 21, 82, 220, 249, 251; business, corporations, and, 209–10, 220, 237, 251–52; at Morehouse, 11, 38–39, 260; race men and, 65–66, 68; social justice capitalism and, 201–2, 216, 251–52
elitism: Benjamin McLaurin and,

212–14; boarding schools and, 10; teaching, 211–13 (*see also* elite spaces). *See also* white elites
Elvin, 106–9, 119, 207
equal opportunity. *See* opportunity gaps
ethics. *See* morality
exceptionalism, 11, 14, 41, 136, 194, 195
Executive Realness, 210. *See also* realness

Farrakhan, Louis, 169
feminism, 69–70, 161, 247; and antifeminism, 81, 216, 240, 241, 247; Black, 246–47 (*see also* feminists, Black); Mort and, 159, 179
feminist critiques, 151, 247. *See also under* feminists, Black
feminist standpoint theorists, 36, 37
feminists, Black, 14, 33, 72, 240, 256; critiques, 70, 154, 232; model of partnership, 70; on My Brother's Keeper (MBK), 218, 219; on racial liberation, 328n67; rape and, 179, 256; Spelman College and, 271. *See also* feminism: Black
Fifteenth Amendment, 54, 58
financial crisis of 2007–2008, 45
Fitzgerald, 95–97, 152, 156, 167
Franklin, Robert M., 243–44
Freaknik, 179

Gaines, Kevin, 67, 70
Garvey, Marcus, 62–63
gay reputation of Morehouse, 176
gay students and gay men, 2, 15, 35, 89; HIV/AIDS and, 261. *See also* homophobia
gender conformity, 87–89

gender disparity in higher education, 169–70
gender-nonconforming students, 15, 308n4. *See also* queer students
gender propriety, 92. *See also under* Black history
gendered language, 88
gentleman-scholar, 68, 71–73, 150–51, 155, 245
Gilmore, Glenda, 70
"girl watching," 160–63; defined, 160–61
Goffman, Erving, 114, 210
Graves Hall, 56f
Great Recession, 45, 85, 208
"guy culture," 164, 165. *See also* masculine culture
Guy-Sheftall, Beverly, 69–70, 184
Guyland (Kimmel), 110, 168. *See also* Kimmel, Michael S.

hairstyles, 112–13, 117, 211
Hall, Victoria, 264–66
Halley, Janet, 184
Hampton, Fred, 201–2
Hampton Institute/Hampton University, 117–18
health care, 261
hegemonic masculinity, 170; competition and, 165–66, 170, 173; double consciousness and, 165–66, 184; Du Bois and, 164–66, 170, 184; nature of, 163–64; race and, 164–66, 170, 184; rape culture and, 163–64, 166, 184
hierarchies: of Blackness, 19–21, 38–39; dating, 168; racial (white-Black), 59, 61. *See also* pecking order/dominance hierarchy
Historically Black Colleges and Universities (HBCUs), 2–3, 132, 133, 146–47, 224f; attrition rates, 312n35, 313n46; codes of conduct, 117; conservatism, 225, 228, 231; criticisms of, 96, 132–33; curricula, 62; founding/creation, 54, 96–97; funding/finances, 201, 313n46; goals/purposes, 54–55; Morehouse contrasted with other, 13, 56–57, 85; in popular culture, 93–94; queer students at, 35, 262 (*see also* queer students); Republicans, politics and, 223–25, 229; sexual assault at, 145, 178, 179, 185; social contracts and, 54, 55; struggles with Black male student retention, 127; study of, 285–89
HIV/AIDS crisis, 19, 248, 249, 261
"hoe contract," 141–43, 142f, 260
Holder, Eric, 46
homophobia, 2, 89, 171, 254, 255, 262; among staff and administration, 123; Du Boisian veil and, 171, 254, 255; Mingus and, 174–77, 255; rape culture and, 171, 254, 255. *See also* transphobia
homophobic violence, 1–3, 14–15, 148, 262–64; the veiled threat, 171–77
hook-up culture, 153, 168, 254
hooks, bell, 182
Horace, 93–94, 96, 106, 163; "Morehouse was my first American experience," 96; sexual assault and, 157–59
Horton, James Oliver, 52
Hubbard, 106, 118–19
hypermarginalization, 248, 255, 261
hypermasculinity, cultures of, 4, 110, 137, 264

Ibrahim, 196–98, 211–15

imperialism, US, 60
incarceration, 178; mass, 5, 75; mass
  incarceration narrative, 79, 80;
  mass incarceration policies, 219;
  rates of, 79, 218, 249; sexual assault, rape culture, and, 179
individualism, 196, 202, 236; neoliberalism and, 190, 195
insider-outsider debate, 35
insider-outsider status, 33
institutionalization (Goffman), 114
intellectualism, 69–71, 118
invisibility. See under queer students

Jackson, Samuel L., 203
Jews, 23–24
Jheri curl, 113
Jim Crow laws, 58–59, 61, 63
Jones, Edward A., 61

Kimmel, Michael S., 110, 164, 168,
  319n57
King, Martin Luther, Jr., 63–65, 64f,
  122
Koss, Mary P., 148, 149, 158
Kuumba, M. Bahati, 137

Latinos, 13. See also My Brother's
  Keeper
leadership: assumed leadership and
  an imagined community, 190–203;
  Black elites and, 70, 75, 82; masculinism and, 55, 68, 70, 117, 257, 259;
  neoliberalism and, 190, 195, 201,
  235; Robert Smith and, 189–91; Roy
  on, 193–95, 257
Leadership and Professional Development (LPD), 211–12, 214–15
Leadership Center, 191–92
Lewis-McCoy, R. L'Heureux, 239

LGBTQIA counseling, lack of, 158,
  262
LGBTQIA students, 262. See also gay
  students and gay men; queer students; transgender students
Liebow, Elliot, 125
linked-fate theory, 18–19, 67, 149, 248
"Look to your left, look to your right,
  one of you will be gone" (attrition),
  126–28
Love, Gregory, 1, 3, 14–15
Lucky, 119–22, 129; "This is just what
  they did. It wasn't rules to them,"
  119

marginalization, social, 7–8, 14, 19,
  35, 131–32, 262
market-value assessment of alumni
  (career paths), implicit messages
  of, 203–6
masculine culture: rape culture and,
  163–64, 184, 254–55. See also "guy
  culture"
masculinism, 231, 232; Black nationalism and, 72; Du Bois and, 69–71;
  leadership and, 55, 68, 70, 117, 257,
  259; Morehouse and, 48, 49, 55, 68,
  73, 116–17, 159, 256–58; social justice capitalism and, 258–59
masculinist frames/masculinist
  frameworks, 49, 68
masculinist ideologies about race, 258
masculinist movements, 72–73
masculinist traits, 257, 258
masculinist uplift, 70
masculinity: and demasculinization,
  81–82; Du Bois and, 20, 69–71, 73,
  122, 164–66, 170, 184; Lerone Bennett on, 69, 77, 78, 81; Morehouse
  brand and, 92, 93, 106, 107, 176,

192, 197, 260; social justice capitalism and, 201–2, 216, 259. *See also* hegemonic masculinity; hypermasculinity; pecking order/dominance hierarchy

Massey, Walter, 177, 178, 228–29, 231, 322n7

Mays, Benjamin Elijah, 68–69, 72, 73, 77, 151

McCoy, 152–53, 156, 166–68, 193–95

McLaurin, Benjamin, 212–14

Milt, 94–95, 119, 192–93

Mingus, 25, 124, 210, 226, 227; homophobia and, 174–77, 255; queer students and, 175–77, 255, 260, 262; rape, rape accusations, and, 179–84, 263; student government and, 173, 176; success and, 173, 174, 208–10

Mitchell, Michelle, 9, 52

Monk, 94, 95, 173

morality: Du Bois on, 50–51. *See also* crisis of the Black male/Black male crisis: (moral) panic over

Morehouse, Henry, 60

Morehouse Board of Trustees, 4, 225, 226, 233, 264–65

Morehouse brand, 92, 192, 227; as built on "grit," 129; capitalism and, 202–3; corporate grooming and, 210; Davis on, 104 (*see also* Davis); masculinity and, 92, 93, 106, 107, 176, 192, 197, 260; Mingus and, 210, 227; nature of, 106, 107, 133; rape allegations and, 138. *See also* brand compliance; branding

Morehouse College: corporate business culture, 207–17 (*see also* corporatization); founded as seminary, 10–11, 55, 56; institutional para-

doxes, 10–17; and the way forward, 259–69

Morehouse Hymn, singing, 32f

Morehouse Mystique, 85, 111, 132, 269; nature of, 14, 85, 131

Mort, 25, 122, 173, 179, 192, 203–5, 227, 232; curriculum and, 203–5, 257–58; feminist awareness, 154, 159; race and, 229–33; on women, 154

Moynihan, Daniel Patrick, 305n76

Moynihan Report, 74

My Brother's Keeper (MBK), 236; critics of, 217–18; girls, women, and, 218, 236; neoliberalism and, 219, 220; Obama and, 44, 217–19; origin story, 44–46; overview and nature of, 44, 45, 217; and strange political bedfellows of Black male success, 217–21

Negro Family: The Case For National Action, The, 74

neoliberal ideologies, 195, 221. *See also* neoliberalism

neoliberal paternalism, 220

neoliberalism, 221; Black neoliberalism and neoliberal order, 198–99, 201, 251, 252; education and, 216, 217, 221; leadership and, 190, 195, 201, 235; Morehouse and, 190, 221, 251; My Brother's Keeper (MBK) and, 219, 220; "personal responsibility" and "no excuses" rhetoric, 6–7

New Student Orientation (NSO), 108–15, 209–11; brands, branding, and, 108–14, 209–10, 253; brother-sister matching ceremony, 161–62; leaders, 109, 111–13, 172; Spirit Night, 112–14 nonbinary students, 87, 89, 91, 123, 171. *See also* queer students

Obama, Barack: 2013 commencement address at Morehouse, 40–44, 44f, 190–91, 217; administration, 44–45, 47; on ideals for Black men, 41–44, 47, 190; My Brother's Keeper (MBK) and, 44, 217–19
Obama Foundation, 219–20
opportunity gaps, persistent, 44, 217
organizational sociology, 17–18
Ornette, 36, 203–4, 207; finances and, 97–98, 101; on gay students, 173; on leadership, 192; on Morehouse, 104, 168, 173, 192, 196, 207; on race, 167–68, 192, 196
Ortner, Sherry, 23–24
outsider intentionality, 36
outsiders. *See* sister-outsider

Pascoe, C. J., 124
pecking order/dominance hierarchy, masculine, 98, 163–64, 166–68. *See also* hierarchies
Percy, 31, 105, 129–31, 178
Platt, Matthew, 240
politically organized system, 17
poverty, war on, 74
predators, Black male, 53, 139, 146, 182. *See also* super-predators
"preponderance of the evidence" standard (Title IX), 182–83
Price, Aaron, 1, 3
prison. *See* incarceration
propriety: as prevention, 150–60; sexual, 51, 52, 92, 104, 144, 153–56, 159, 163, 235 (*see also under* Black history); undermining, 160–65

"queer," definition and scope of the term, 308n1
queer Black ballroom scene, 210
queer erasure, 89, 138–39, 261
queer people, 34–35
queer students: Bird and, 172, 173; clubs and advocacy groups, 173, 177, 260, 262; double consciousness and, 145, 171; HBCUs and, 35, 262; Mingus and, 175–77, 255, 260, 262; at Morehouse, 2–4, 35, 87, 89–91, 123, 171, 175, 177, 255, 260–62, 264; violence against, 145, 171, 264; (in)visibility, 35, 172, 173, 246, 255, 260, 262, 263

race man/race men, 63, 65–66, 103, 104, 154, 206, 268; defined, 48; Du Bois and, 69, 71, 122; gentleman-scholars and, 72; as men, 68–73; and the Morehouse Man, 107–8
Race Men (Carby), 70. *See also* Carby, Hazel
race ruiners, 73–86
race saviors, 63–67
racial uplift, 47, 51, 52, 67, 70; ideologies about, 17, 37, 61, 66, 70, 85; top-down vs. bottom-up, 196, 252 (*see also* trickle-down racial advancement)
racialization, 18, 19, 22, 96, 101, 250, 251; of Black colleges, 17; corporatization and, 227–28; definition and nature of, 17, 48; double consciousness and, 144, 145, 165–66, 184–85; Du Boisian theory and, 20, 22–23, 36–37, 145–47, 165, 184–85; Fitzgerald and, 96–97; gender and, 18, 49, 60, 68, 73, 92, 133, 164–66, 184–85; Leadership and Professional De-

velopment (LPD) and, 215; Morehouse and, 17, 18, 48–49, 73, 92; of
organizations, 17–18. *See also under*
sexual assault
racialized rape culture, 143, 145–47,
159, 165, 166, 179, 183–85, 251, 252,
254–56. *See also under* sexual assault
Ramsey, 108, 109, 111, 127, 161, 209,
211, 227
rape, 135; campus reactions to, 138,
260, 263, 265–66; consent and, 148,
156–59; definitions, 148, 158, 159;
epidemiology, 139–40; gang, 135
(*see also under* Spelman students);
gender and, 138–41, 256, 264; of
men, 138–40, 139f; men's discussions of, 148, 149, 156–58; Mingus
and, 179–84, 263; and Morehouse's
reputation, 138, 143, 260; trivializing, 140, 143, 159 (*see also* rape culture); of Victoria Hall, 264–66. *See
also* sexual assault
rape allegations, 181, 256; false, 146,
178, 184, 263; male solidarity in the
face of, 177–80; mishandling of, 4,
137, 141, 177–81, 263, 264, 266 (*see
also* Hall, Victoria); race and, 138,
146, 179–81, 184, 256. *See also* "hoe
contract"; sexual assault allegations
rape apologism, 256
rape culture, 264; defined, 140, 159;
double consciousness and, 143,
145, 149, 150, 159, 171, 184; Du Bois
and, 145, 147, 150, 184–85 (*see also*
double consciousness); Du Boisian
veil and, 145, 165, 171, 254, 255; gender, male dominance, and, 140–41,
147, 163–66, 179–80, 185, 251, 256;

hegemonic masculinity and, 163–
64, 166, 184; homophobia and, 171,
254, 255; masculine culture and,
163–64, 184, 254–55; Morehouse's,
141–43, 184–85, 251, 254–56, 264;
overview and nature of, 140–41,
184; racialized, 143, 145–47, 159,
165, 166, 179, 183–85, 251, 252, 254–
56 (*see also under* sexual assault);
rape myths and, 183–84; studying,
140, 148
rape myths, 183, 263; racialized, 183–
84
rape victims, maltreatment of, 142–
43, 264–66. *See also* Spelman students
reactive respectability (politics), 8–9,
250; Black leadership and, 9, 10,
249, 250; Du Boisian veil and, 250,
252; Morehouse and, 9, 10, 250–52,
260; and the politics of visibility,
260
realness, 210, 213, 325n34; defined,
210
Reconstruction era, 54, 55, 58, 146
recruitment: college, 13–14, 34, 35,
85, 130–31; professional/corporate,
208, 236–37
respectability. *See* reactive respectability
"riff raff," 129
Rigueur, Leah Wright, 198
Roy: family background, 102; on leadership, 193–95, 257; on race, 167,
180; on rape accusations, rape
myth, and 1996 gang-rape case,
178–84, 263

"scholar-gentleman," 68. *See also*
gentleman-scholar

segregation, racial, 57, 58, 223, 224
sex on campus, 162. *See also* propriety
sexual assault: Horace and, 157–59; racialization of survivors of, 145–46; racializing the repercussions of, 177–85; scope of the term, 148, 158, 159. *See also* rape; Spelman students
"Sexual Assault: What Every Morehouse College Student Should Know" (pamphlet), 157f, 158
sexual assault allegations, 157–58, 184. *See also* rape allegations
sexual consent, 148, 156–59
sexual propriety. *See* propriety: sexual
Shadow, 170, 215, 216, 229
sister-outsider, being a, 30–37
slave branding, 311n23
slavery, 50–52, 61, 299n12
Smart on Crime program, 46
Smith, Levar, 239, 245
Smith, Robert F., 14, 186–88, 199–201; background, 186–88; commencement speech, 186–88, 187f, 199; finances, 186, 190, 191, 200–201; leadership and, 189–91; overview, 186; philanthropy, 188–91, 199–201; public image, 188–91, 199–201; tax evasion scandal, 200–201; turning points of his early success, 189
social class. *See* class distinction
social contracts, 54, 55
social exclusion. *See* marginalization
social justice capitalism, 198–99, 201, 207, 216, 252, 256–57; Black male elites and, 201–2, 216, 251–52; individualism and, 236; masculinity and, 201–2, 216, 258–59. *See also* capitalism
sociology, organizational, 17–18
SpelHouse, 32, 33, 199

Spelman College, 168–71, 271–72; being a sister-outsider, 30–37; compared with Morehouse, 126, 130, 131; Grundy at, 2, 14; men taking courses at, 204, 258; Roy and, 181, 183; trans admissions policy, 87
Spelman-Morehouse network of alumni, 31, 90
Spelman students, sexual assaults of, 135–38, 143; 1996 gang rape of Spelman coed, 135, 136f, 177–81, 263
Spence, Lester K., 199
Spirit Night, 112–14
St. Paul's School (New Hampshire), 214, 215
Staples, Robert, 78, 81–82, 306n98
stereotypes, Black male, 81–83, 182, 189, 255
Stewart, Henry Allen, xi
success: Davis and, 99, 128, 150, 221, 222, 226, 227; Mingus and, 173, 174, 208–10; strange political bedfellows of Black male success, 217–21
suffrage, Black, 67. *See also* Fifteenth Amendment
Summers, Martin, 58, 59
super-predators, Black male, 5, 49, 78

Tadd, 106, 107, 109, 110, 162, 169, 207
Taft, William Howard, 301n36
Talented Tenth, 118, 172, 188–89, 193–95; Du Bois on, 66, 67, 195–96
talented tenth ideology, 66–67
Tally's Corner (Liebow), 125
time, mantras about, 125–26
"tissues of constraint" (Goffman), 114, 210
Title IX, 158, 182–83, 264, 265, 314n12, 321n80; Morehouse under investigation for violations of, 4, 14, 137, 182–83

Title IX coordinators, 137, 265
Title IX officers, 262, 265
Title VII of Civil Rights Act (equal
    employment opportunity), 237
transgender students, 3–4, 15, 91–92,
    127, 244, 266, 308n4; trans student
    admissions policy, 15, 87–91, 261,
    266
transphobia, 90, 262
trickle-down racial advancement,
    189, 196, 257. *See also* racial uplift
Trump, Donald, 224f
Tukes, Timothy, 138–39, 139f
two-ness, 30, 145, 146, 167

Universal Negro Improvement Asso-
    ciation (UNIA), 62, 63

veil. *See* Du Boisian veil
victimization, Black male, 182–84
Violent Crime Control and Law En-
    forcement Act (1994 Crime Bill),
    5, 24
visibility: politics of, 260. *See also*
    under queer students
voting patterns, Black, 18–19
voting rights. *See* suffrage
Voting Rights Act of 1965, 187

Walker, Michael L., 17
Waller, 99, 101, 115–16, 122, 127
Washington, Booker T., 61–62, 70–71,
    304n68
Watson, Devon, 123
wealth gaps, 84, 110, 189
welfare reform legislation, 79
Wes, 193, 203–5, 230–32; on African
    American studies, 203–4; on busi-
    ness, 207, 208; on the homeless in
    the surrounding community, 235
West End, Atlanta, 56, 57
White, 297n58
white elites, 60, 191, 215, 216, 228, 237
Wilson, John Silvanus, 139, 143, 263,
    310n15
women: degradation of, 153–54, 160,
    161 (*see also* "girl watching"); More-
    house students' relations with, 161–
    63 (*see also specific topics*); objectifi-
    cation of (*see* "girl watching"). *See
    also* "hoe contract"

Yusef, 111, 119, 167, 192, 205, 206,
    324n26

zero tolerance, 158, 159

Founded in 1893,
UNIVERSITY OF CALIFORNIA PRESS
publishes bold, progressive books and journals
on topics in the arts, humanities, social sciences,
and natural sciences—with a focus on social
justice issues—that inspire thought and action
among readers worldwide.

The UC PRESS FOUNDATION
raises funds to uphold the press's vital role
as an independent, nonprofit publisher, and
receives philanthropic support from a wide
range of individuals and institutions—and from
committed readers like you. To learn more, visit
ucpress.edu/supportus.

Printed in the USA
CPSIA information can be obtained
at www.ICGtesting.com
JSHW021019050324
58619JS00002B/13